WOMEN, WORK, AND HEALTH

Stress and Opportunities

The Plenum Series on Stress and Coping

Series Editor:

Donald Meichenbaum, *University of Waterloo, Waterloo, Ontario, Canada*

COPING WITH LIFE CRISES
An Integrated Approach
Edited by Rudolf H. Moos

COPING WITH NEGATIVE LIFE EVENTS
Clinical and Social Psychological Perspectives
Edited by C. R. Snyder and Carol E. Ford

DYNAMICS OF STRESS
Physiological, Psychological, and Social Perspectives
Edited by Mortimer H. Appley and Richard Trumbull

HUMAN ADAPTATION TO EXTREME STRESS
From the Holocaust to Vietnam
Edited by John P. Wilson, Zev Harel, and Boaz Kahana

INFERTILITY
Perspectives from Stress and Coping Research
Edited by Annette L. Stanton and Christine Dunkel-Schetter

INTERNATIONAL HANDBOOK OF TRAUMATIC STRESS SYNDROMES
Edited by John P. Wilson and Beverley Raphael

POST-TRAUMATIC STRESS DISORDER
A Clinician's Guide
Kirtland C. Peterson, Maurice F. Prout, and Robert A. Schwarz

THE SOCIAL CONTEXT OF COPING
Edited by John Eckenrode

STRESS BETWEEN WORK AND FAMILY
Edited by John Eckenrode and Susan Gore

WOMEN, WORK, AND HEALTH
Stress and Opportunities
Edited by Marianne Frankenhaeuser, Ulf Lundberg, and Margaret Chesney

WOMEN, WORK, AND HEALTH

Stress and Opportunities

Edited by

Marianne Frankenhaeuser

Karolinska Institute
Stockholm, Sweden

and

Ulf Lundberg

University of Stockholm
Stockholm, Sweden

and

Margaret Chesney

University of California, San Francisco
San Francisco, California

PLENUM PRESS • NEW YORK AND LONDON

Library of Congress Cataloging in Publication Data

Women, work, and health: stress and opportunities / edited by Marianne Frankenhaeuser and Ulf Lundberg and Margaret Chesney.
    p.   cm. — (The Plenum series on stress and coping)
    Includes bibliographical references and index.
    ISBN 0-306-43780-5
    1. Women — Health and hygiene. 2. Stress (Psychology) 3. Sex differences. 4. Job stress. I. Frankenhaeuser, Marianne. II. Lundberg, Ulf. III. Chesney, Margaret A. IV. Series.
RA564.85.W666 1991   91-17991
613'.04244 — dc20   CIP

ISBN 0-306-43780-5

© 1991 Plenum Press, New York
A Division of Plenum Publishing Corporation
233 Spring Street, New York, N.Y. 10013

Printed in the United States of America

Contributors

Rosalind C. Barnett, Center for Research on Women, Wellesley College, Wellesley, Massachusetts 02181

Monica Biernat, Department of Psychology, University of Florida, Gainesville, Florida 32611

Margaret A. Chesney, Prevention Sciences Group, School of Medicine, University of California, San Francisco, California 94105

Aila Collins, Psychology Division, Department of Psychiatry and Psychology, Karolinska Institute, S-104 01 Stockholm, Sweden

Cary L. Cooper, Manchester School of Management, University of Manchester, Institute of Science and Technology, Manchester M60 1QD, England

Marianne Frankenhaeuser, Department of Psychiatry and Psychology, Karolinska Institute, Stockholm University, S-106 91 Stockholm, Sweden

William Gerin, Cardiovascular Center, The New York Hospital, Cornell Medical Center, New York, New York 10021

Kerstin Hagenfeldt, Department of Obstetrics and Gynecology, Karolinska Hospital, S-104 01 Stockholm, Sweden

Suzanne G. Haynes, National Cancer Institute, Bethesda, Maryland 20892

Gary D. James, Cardiovascular Center, The New York Hospital, Cornell Medical Center, New York, New York 10021

Robert L. Kahn, Survey Research Center, Institute for Social Research, University of Michigan, Ann Arbor, Michigan 48106-1248

Robert A. Karasek, Institute of Psychology, University of Aarhus, Risskov DK 8240, Denmark

Eric Lang, American Institutes for Research, P.O. Box 1113, Palo Alto, California 94302

Ulf Lundberg, Department of Psychiatry and Psychology, Karolinska Institute, Stockholm University, S-106 91, Stockholm, Sweden

Eleanor E. Maccoby, Department of Psychology, Stanford University, California 94305-2130

Nancy L. Marshall, Center for Research for Women, Wellesley College, Wellesley, Massachusetts 02181

Thomas G. Pickering, Cardiovascular Center, The New York Hospital, Cornell Medical Center, New York, New York 10021

Carl F. Pieper, Cardiovascular Center, The New York Hospital, Cornell Medical Center, New York, New York 10021

Judith Rodin, Department of Psychology, Yale University, New Haven, Connecticut 06520-7447

Philip M. Sarrel, Obstetrics and Gynecology and Psychiatry, Yale University School of Medicine, New Haven, Connecticut 06510

Yvette R. Schlussel, Cardiovascular Center, The New York Hospital, Cornell Medical Center, New York, New York 10021

Peter L. Schnall, Cardiovascular Center, The New York Hospital, Cornell Medical Center, New York, New York 10021

Töres Theorell, National Swedish Institute of Psychosocial Factors and Health, S-104 01 Stockholm, Sweden

Ingrid Waldron, Department of Biology, University of Pennsylvania, Philadelphia, Pennsylvania 19104-6018

Camille Wortman, Department of Psychology, SUNY at Stony Brook, Stony Brook, New York 11794-8790

Foreword

Until recently, studies of women's health received scant research attention in the context of the overall magnitude of research conducted on health. Even for health issues that affect both men and women, most research has been limited to male subjects, leaving a large gap in our knowledge base concerning women's health. Finally, the decade of the 1990s is ushering in a shift in this inequity. In 1990 the U.S. National Institutes of Health issued a compelling report citing the lack of sufficient research on women's health as a major gap in our knowledge, and a mandate has been issued to add women as study subjects in research or to document why they have not been included. Such directives will undoubtedly lead to a much-needed burgeoning of research activities in the area of women's health as we approach the twenty-first century.

Despite limited research resources, however, there have been steady, scientifically rigorous voices in the wilderness for the last several years, and many of the best investigators are represented in this volume. These workers have led the vanguard in exploring psychosocial factors that are likely to differentially affect women's and men's health. For example, women and men engage in social roles that often differ, if not in quantity, then certainly in quality. Sex differences in role expectations, environmental qualities, role burdens related to the domains of work and family, and abilities to adapt to and cope with stressful situations may have a distinctive impact on health.

This volume emphasizes the intersection of women, work, and health as an especially critical area of research inquiry. Why has attention focussed on women's workforce participation and health in particular? Since World War II there has been a dramatic movement of women into the labor force. In 1986 two-thirds of all women aged 20 to 64 were in the labor force. This rate is expected to increase to over 80% by the year 2000.

vii

Sorensen and Verbrugge (1987) have suggested three theoretical paths by which workforce participation might relate to health outcomes.

The first model is the *health benefits model*, which emphasizes that there are direct advantages of employment—for example, financial remuneration, self-esteem, greater feelings of control, and social support—that may maintain and enhance women's health. LaCroix and Haynes (1987) have summarized the results of studies comparing risk factors for chronic diseases and health status indicators among employed and nonemployed women. In almost all studies conducted thus far, employed women do appear healthier than nonemployed women. In a longitudinal study of women, Waldron and Lye (1989) concluded that employment may increase social support and that job-related social support may have particularly beneficial effects on women's health.

The *job stress model* posits that the stress and strain of employment will ultimately harm women's health. Although the data so far do not support this alternative, it is theoretically possible that longer-term health-damaging effects may occur or that health effects other than cardiovascular disease may be important to consider. At the present time, the studies have largely focused on cardiovascular disease risk factors and outcomes. Certainly, it is also possible to assert that not only stress, but other factors in the work environment, may adversely affect workers' health, including environmental factors such as indoor air quality, work space, lighting, lead levels in water, and exposure to electromagnetic fields. The hazards of extended use of video display terminals (VDTs), for example, have recently received a great deal of public and professional attention. Because women often occupy the majority of secretarial, typist, and data entry positions, they are particularly prone to the adverse consequences of VDTs, including repetitive strain injury, for example, carpal tunnel syndrome, radioactive exposure, and eye and back strain. Wegman and Fine (1990) have recently reviewed this literature.

Finally, the *role expansion model* considers the indirect advantages of employment, suggesting that the work role enhances health through increased opportunities for reward and satisfaction. Furthermore, satisfaction in one role may provide protection against strain in another. There are data suggesting that involvement in multiple roles expands potential resources and rewards, including alternate sources of self-esteem, control, and social support. In turn, these benefits may enhance both mental and physical health (Sorensen & Verbrugge, 1987).

Continued research studies of women, work, and health are essential since many crucial questions remain unanswered. Undoubtedly, none of these models is singularly correct, and both health-promoting and health-damaging effects of workforce participation and increased role demands are likely. These analyses are urgently needed since we have recently shown (Rodin & Ickovics, 1990) that although women continue to hold an advantage in the mortality rate relative to men, this advantage has decreased in recent years, especially for persons aged 45 and over. We have proposed that these epidemiologic shifts are attributable in large part to the psychological and behavioral effects of new social trends, particularly changes that women and men have undergone during the past few decades in social structure and role, including changes in the types of roles they occupy in the workforce. To the extent that variations in health are related to variations in life-style, there should be corresponding shifts in the rates of disorder. These changes are evident (see Rodin & Ickovics, 1990, for a review).

Examination of the psychological and behavioral consequences of changing social trends, in interaction with relevant biological differences between men and women, must continue to be the focus of research attention. Indeed, the continuing existence of sex differences in morbidity and mortality supports the call for examining women's health independently of men's health. At the very least, it is likely that health results from studies of men may not be reliably extended to women. Moreover, research must include outcome measures differentially associated with women and men in order to clarify how sex differences may operate (Lennon, 1987). Finally, as this volume so impressively demonstrates, studying gender-related issues can also inform basic science questions about the etiology of disease—for instance, in asking what factors explain why relatively more men than women (particularly those at younger ages) have coronary disease, there must be some set of gender-related factors that could help explain these findings, thus better specifying potential risk and protective factors. These factors undoubtedly include not only biological differences, but also psychosocial and sociocultural determinants of health and illness. Further, as Russo (1987) has suggested, if we are to understand the role of gender not only in etiology, but also in diagnosis, treatment, and prevention, "research design and analysis must advance beyond the use of sex as a predictor variable in health surveys to conceptualizing gender as a dynamic construct that itself varies across ethnic groups and social classes and works in complex interactions with other physiological and social factors" (p. 54).

The chapters in this volume also highlight the important fact that women cannot be treated as a homogeneous group. Striking health differences exist on the basis of occupational role, socioeconomic status, race, and ethnicity. Differences also exist across the life cycle and are dramatically affected by historical moment. Changes between cohorts and within cohorts across time must be evaluated, because it is clear that when one studies work and health in particular, dramatic changes in women's working roles will make data collected on current cohorts of women perhaps nonapplicable or differentially applicable to future cohorts. Moreover, taking a life course perspective, one notes that there has been only minimal analysis of the health effects of multiple roles at various points in the family cycle. However, the demands of family and career fluctuate according to children's ages and women's stages of career development (Baruch, Biener, & Barnett, 1987). Ultimately, each phase of the individual and family life cycle will need to be analyzed separately to enhance our understanding of the link between roles and health and also so that appropriate service interventions and policies can be developed.

I am especially gratified to see this excellent volume reach fruition. As Chair of the John D. and Catherine T. MacArthur Foundation Network on Health and Behavior, I asked Marianne Frankenhaeuser and Karen Matthews to develop and lead a series of research and conference initiatives in the area of women's health. The MacArthur Foundation's mandate is to promote multidisciplinary dialogue and scholarship, with a focus on developing new or underaddressed areas of research. The Stockholm Symposium, on which this volume is based, was one of these projects. Frankenhaeuser invited leading investigators from around the world; under her guidance, the meeting provided an unsurpassed opportunity for the exchange of scientific information and ideas for future research in the important area of women, work, and health. My thanks go to Marianne Frankenhaeuser for bringing together the people and providing the momentum and intellectual leadership for this fine conference and book. Her own work stands as an example of one of the most imaginitive approaches to understanding how aspects of working life might impact on the health of both men and women, developing models for intensive laboratory and field studies of the same individuals in her groundbreaking analysis. As much as anything else, this volume is a tribute to her long and distinguished leadership in the field of women, work, and health and other fields relating to health and behavior.

Judith Rodin

Yale University

REFERENCES

Baruch, G. K., Biener, L., & Barnett, R. C. (1987). Women and gender in research on work and family stress. *American Psychologist, 42*, 130–136.

LaCroix, A. Z., & Haynes, S. G. (1987). Gender differences in the health effects of workplace roles. In R. C. Barnett, L. Biener, & G. K. Baruch (Eds.), *Gender and stress* (pp. 96–121). New York: Free Press.

Lennon, M. C. (1987). Sex differences in distress: The impact of gender and work roles. *Journal of Health and Social Behavior, 27,* 290-305.

Rodin, J., & Ickovics, J. R. (1990). Women's health: Review and research agenda as we approach the 21st Century. *American Psychologist, 45,* 1018-1034.

Russo, N. F. (Ed.). (1987). *Developing a national agenda to address women's mental health needs.* Washington D.C.: American Psychological Association, Women's Program Office.

Sorensen, G., & Verbrugge, L. M. (1987). Women, work and health. *American Review of Public Health, 8,* 235-251.

Waldron, I., & Lye, D. (1989). Employment, unemployment, occupation and smoking. *American Journal of Preventive Medicine, 5,* 142-149.

Wegman, D. H., & Fine, L. J. (1990). Occupational health in the 1990s. *Annual Review of Public Health, 11,* 89-103.

Preface

This book is based on an international symposium held at the Wenner-Gren Center in Stockholm on October 12–15, 1988, under the joint sponsorship of the Wenner-Gren Center Foundation and the John D. and Catherine T. MacArthur Foundation. The symposium represents one of several research initiatives in the women's health field taken within the frame of the MacArthur Foundation's Health and Behavior Network under the chairmanship of Judith Rodin. The special focus of this symposium was the future prospect for women in working life, viewed from the perspectives of the rapid changes now taking place in occupational and family patterns.

The symposium was prepared by an organizing committee with the following members: Margaret Chesney, professor of epidemiology and behavioral medicine; Aila Collins, assistant professor of psychology; Marianne Frankenhaeuser, professor of psychology; Gunn Johansson, professor of work psychology, and Ulf Lundberg, professor of human biological psychology.

The joint effort of a large group of people made the symposium, and thereby this volume, possible. We wish to take this opportunity to thank them all. Warm thanks are due to Ulla Falkenborg, Raija Lipasti, Anette Nylund, and Margareta Thorsell, who did much of the hard work behind the scenes. We also want to acknowledge David Ottoson, science secretary of the Wenner-Gren Center Foundation, and Gun Lennerstrand, administrative assistant, for providing valuable advice in planning the symposium. Special thanks are due to Peter Nathan of the MacArthur Foundation, who opened the symposium, and Lorraine Dennerstein, Carol Morse, Rita Liljeström, and Kerstin Uvnäs-Moberg for their interesting presentations during the scientific sessions. We are grateful to the Swedish Work Environment Fund and to Leif Wallin, Volvo's former Corporate Medical Director, for financial contributions.

The book is divided into four sections, each covering a specific aspect of the women, work, and health field: sex differences and social roles, work and family, work load and cardiovascular health, and interaction between women's work and reproductive issues.

The contributors have all made significant contributions to the understanding of the impact of women's changing roles on their health and well-being. There are two unique features of this book. First, it integrates research on women in the workforce with research on family as well as women's health issues. Second, it brings together research from the behavioral, biomedical, and social sciences.

Most of the symposium presentations are included in the volume, which also includes a foreword by Judith Rodin, who chaired one of the sessions, as well as a summary by Cary L. Cooper, who served as discussant during the symposium.

We expect the book to be of interest not only to university students and teachers in the behavioral, medical, and social sciences, but also to professionals in health policy, occupational health, and equal opportunity programs.

Marianne Frankenhaeuser
Ulf Lundberg
Margaret Chesney

Stockholm and San Francisco

Contents

PART IV. INTERACTION BETWEEN WOMEN'S WORK AND REPRODUCTIVE ISSUES

Chapter 11. Reproductive Technologies, Women's Health, and Career Choices

Kerstin Hagenfeldt

Philip M. Sarrel

Aila Collins

PART V. CONCLUSION

Cary L. Cooper

I

Sex Differences

Facts and Myths

1

Gender Segregation in the Workplace

Continuities and Discontinuities from Childhood to Adulthood

ELEANOR E. MACCOBY

When we consider women in their role as members of the work force outside the home, two major phenomena command our attention: (1) occupations are segregated by gender to a remarkable degree and (2) women are much more likely than men to interrupt their out-of-home work careers in order to care for children. The second topic is considered in some depth in other chapters in this volume; this chapter will focus primarily on the central fact that working women are clustered mainly in one set of occupations, men mainly in others.

Occupational segregation is a phenomenon that has proved to be relatively intractable. It prevails in a wide variety of cultures, from preliterate societies to modern industrialized cultures in which the two sexes have reasonably equal access to education, out-of-home jobs, and the rights of citizenship. A commonly used index of segregation is the proportion of people in the labor force who would have to change jobs if the ratio of men to women in all occupations were to match the proportion of the two sexes in the total labor force (Duncan & Duncan, 1955). In the United States in the early 80s, this index was declining, but was still over 60% (Reskin, 1984), and it is similarly high in Sweden (Statistics, Sweden, 1985) despite

ELEANOR E. MACCOBY • Department of Psychology, Stanford University, Stanford, California 94305-2130.

the long history of efforts to bring about equality of occupational opportunity in Scandinavian countries.

Clearly, we need to know more about the forces that are driving the sexual division of labor. Do men and women have different talents and different psychological dispositions that draw them into different occupations? If so, how could we identify what these different talents and dispositions are? A common approach to the study of sex differences has been to compare boys and girls, or men and women, with respect to the frequency with which they display specific behaviors or achieve certain levels of performance on standardized tests or measures (Maccoby & Jacklin, 1974). For example, one might compare the average scores of men and women on an IQ test or on a measure of motor coordination or self-esteem. When many studies of a given attribute or ability have been done using comparable measures, scholars have used meta-analyses to determine whether a consistent overall sex difference is found and to estimate the size and consistency of the gender effect. Two major conclusions can be drawn from research of this kind. For the psychological attributes studied so far: (1) the distributions of the two sexes overlap greatly and (2) the mean differences are small. That is, the individual's sex accounts for only a small portion of the variation in the attribute under study.

It seems unlikely that differences of the magnitude usually revealed in such studies could account for the very substantial influence of gender on the occupational niches individuals occupy. Furthermore, there appears to be little relationship between how segregated an occupation is and how much it calls for the particular talents and abilities that are presumed (or shown) to characterize one sex more commonly than the other (Strober, 1984). In particular, there are occupations that were once all-male and have become all-female (e.g., bank teller, secretary), and such shifts argue against the notion that any particular sex-linked ability or temperament is optimal for performance in these or (by inference) many other jobs. Clearly, there are many people of each sex who have the potential ability to do almost any given kind of work competently, enough so that nearly all occupations could be gender-integrated if initial abilities were the primary factor determining the occupations that people enter. I would like to argue, then, that sex-linked ability patterns are not a major factor causing occupations to become segregated.

My own impression is that the two sexes are very similar indeed when men and women or boys and girls are observed or tested individually in the absence of a social context. With respect to most intellectual functions assessed through tests administered to individuals—tests of reasoning, analytic abilities, understanding of written text—no consistent sex differences are found. Self-reported personality traits as assessed with standard personality inventories find few and modest sex differences. There clearly are some fairly large and recurring sex differences in activity preferences, which are reflected in the kinds of television programs the two sexes prefer to watch, the courses they elect to take in school and college, the leisure-time activities they choose, and so forth.

We do not know whether these different preferences are mainly the outcome of sex-typing pressure applied to boys and girls as they grow up or are more closely related to children's own self-socialization based on their growing understanding of the social roles of the two sexes. In either case, sex-typed preferences must reflect processes of social stereotyping to a considerable extent. The sex-differentiated activity preferences developed during childhood and adolescence no doubt influence the pre-job training individuals elect to receive and the entry-level occupational choices they make, thus leading men and women into different long-term career paths. But I believe there is an important factor in the analysis of sex differences that has been overlooked. While male and female persons perform at very similar levels and behave in very similar ways when tested or observed individually, some pronounced behavioral differences emerge in certain social contexts. I want to argue that a highly important aspect of social context, one that generates differences in the way male and female persons behave, is the gender of the other persons with whom the observed individual is interacting. I also believe that we can gain considerable understanding of adult interaction patterns by taking a developmental perspective.

When individuals enter a work setting, they bring with them a long personal history of interaction in social groups. Most people have had more experiences interacting with people of their own sex than they have had in cross-sex interactions. They develop habits, expectations, and ways of interpreting the behavior of others that differ according to the gender composition of the social group in which they find themselves. I would like to focus now on the interpersonal histories of boys and girls through the childhood and adolescent years on the assumption that these histories have a considerable bearing on how men and women interact in same-sex and mixed-sex situations in the workplace. My underlying assumption is that same-sex and cross-sex interaction patterns have a bearing on whether occupations are segregated.

THE PREVALENCE OF GENDER SEGREGATION
IN CHILDHOOD

Observations of children playing together in naturalistic situations have revealed a fairly high degree of gender segregation in the middle-childhood years. Of course, the extent of such segregation depends on the structure of the situations in which the children are involved. In societies that have coeducational schools, children spend a great deal of time in mixed-sex classrooms, but even in such classrooms the amount of inter-action between boys and girls is quite low (Lockheed & Klein, 1985). During unstructured time on school playgrounds or in lunchrooms, chil-dren congregate largely in same-sex groups (see Maccoby and Jacklin, 1987, and Maccoby, 1988, for reviews). The tendency toward gender segregation is observed in a wide variety of cultures. As Edwards and Whiting (1988) report on observations conducted in 12 communities in widely scattered parts of the world, "In sum, our findings . . . suggest that the emergence of same-sex preferences in childhood is a cross-culturally universal and robust phenomenon" (p. 81). In Western societies, the struc-tures set up by adults vary in whether they promote or run counter to the segregation of the sexes, but children appear to maintain segregation on their own initiative whether or not there is adult pressure to do so. Furthermore, adult efforts to break down children's preference for same-sex playmates have not been very successful (Serbin, Tonick, & Sternglanz, 1977; Lockheed & Harris, 1984).

At what age does same-sex preference first appear? The evidence is thin, but available studies indicate that the tendency begins to manifest itself at least by the third year of life (LaFreniere, Strayer, & Gauthier, 1984). Jacklin and Maccoby (1978) found that by 33 months children played more actively with a same-sex than an opposite-sex unfamiliar peer. Observational studies indicate that the degree of segregation in free play situations increases greatly from preschool to grade school years (Maccoby, 1988) and is especially marked from age 6 to about 11.

Within the normal range of sex-typing, an individual child's tendency to prefer same-sex playmates does not appear to depend on how masculine or feminine that child is. Quiet, studious boys who are not especially interested in masculine games usually do not gravitate to girls' play groups. And while a few tomboy girls do cross gender lines and play in boys' groups, these girls need not be unfeminine in other respects, and may be well integrated into girls' play groups as well (Thorne, 1986). In any case, the majority of boys and girls confine themselves mainly to same-sex com-panionship in situations where they have a choice.

CAUSAL FACTORS UNDERLYING GENDER SEGREGATION

What do we know about the reasons why gender segregation occurs in childhood? In reviewing existing studies, Maccoby (1988) has identified the following factors as probably pushing children toward same-sex pref-erence:

1. Boys and girls have somewhat different play styles. In particular, boys are considerably more interested in rough-and-tumble play. When another child signals an interest in initiating a bout of rough play, boys usually react with excited interest and girls with wariness. Boys thus build interest in one another as playmates and stop making overtures for rough play to girls.
2. Boys and girls have different modes of attempting to influence play partners. Boys are more directly demanding, and girls more given to indirect modes such as suggesting and questioning. Girls' influence styles work well with one another and with adults, but not with boys. A result is that in cross-sex encounters boys tend to dominate girls, a factor that probably leads girls to avoid interaction with boys.
3. Children interpret cross-sex friendships as evidence of romantic interest. They tease each other for "liking" or "loving" a child of the opposite sex, and contact between boys' groups and girls' groups on the playground often has sexual overtones. In the years from age 6 to 11 or 12, children take pains to avoid the appearance of romantic interest though they are intensely aware of the opposite sex as future romantic partners. Segregation appears to be partly based on an implicit taboo on sexuality.

We do not know precisely how biology and socialization interact to produce these phenomena. There is evidence that hormonal sensitization during the prenatal period contributes to the male pattern of rough-and-tumble play in both humans and subhuman primates (see Meany, Stewart, & Beatty, 1985). Ellis (1986) has assembled evidence for androgenic influences on male assertiveness in the sexual context, and on what he calls status-related aggression, that is, power assertion or dominance among males. We do not know to what extent the evolutionary history of our species may have selected for the patterns of cross-sex avoidance that we see in middle childhood. No doubt sociobiologists would suggest a scenario in which it is functional for humans to lose sexual interest in opposite-sex others with whom they have been raised in close contact. Such a tendency would protect the species against inbreeding. Avoidance of opposite-sex, unrelated peers during childhood, then, would help to maintain an outgroup of eligible sexual partners following puberty. All this is speculative.

The main point emerging from these considerations and from the work on hormonal sensitization is that there probably is some biological basis for the segregation of the sexes in childhood. Of course, any biologically preprogrammed tendencies of this sort that human beings have are quickly acted upon by the socialization pressures emanating from the culture in which a child is growing up. Cultural variations are wide, but the fact that children do gravitate toward same-sex playmates in all the cultures studied so far does suggest that cultures are probably acting upon preprogrammed human tendencies and are not free to arrange the lives of the two sexes without regard to these tendencies.

DISTINCTIVE CULTURES IN BOYS' AND GIRLS' GROUPS

The implication of gender segregation in childhood is that boys and girls grow up in somewhat different social milieus and develop different patterns of social behavior appropriate for an all-girl or all-boy group. How do boys' and girls' cultures differ? Traditionally, certain games have been played almost exclusively by one sex, although there are some games that are played by both. For example, in the United States, girls play jacks, jump rope, and hopscotch; boys play marbles, team ball games, and mumblety-peg (a knife-throwing game); both sexes play dodgeball. The recent emphasis on sports for women and girls has meant that more girls are participating in organized sports—basketball, soccer, tennis—but these activities take place largely in sex-segregated groupings. For the more informal games and out-of-school activities, groups of boys tend to play on streets and in other public places, while girls more often congregate in private homes or yards. On playgrounds, the boys' groups take up more space than the girls' groups, and boys' groups are somewhat larger. Girls tend to form intimate friendships with one or two other girls, and these friendships are marked by a sharing of confidences. Boys' friendships, on the other hand, are more often oriented around mutual interest in certain activities. The breakup of girls' friendships is usually attended by more intense emotional reactions than is the case for boys.

What are the interactions like in all-boy or all-girl groups? Among the boys in boys' groups there is more concern with dominance—with who is the strongest or the toughest—and activities are more hierarchically organized (Aries, 1976; Savin-Williams, 1979). There are reports from sociolinguists concerning the quality of verbal exchanges that occur among boys in their play groups and among girls in theirs. Summarizing the findings, Maltz and Borker (1983) note that boys in all-boy groups are more likely than girls in all-girl groups to do the following: interrupt one another; use commands, threats, or boasts of authority; refuse to comply with another child's demand; give information; heckle a speaker; tell jokes or suspenseful stories; top someone else's story; and call another child names. Girls in all-girl groups, on the other hand, are more likely than boys to do the following: express agreement with what another speaker has just said, pause to give another child a chance to speak, and acknowledge a point previously made by another speaker when starting a speaking turn. It appears that among boys speech serves largely egoistic functions; among girls, conversation is a more socially binding process.

Some recent work by Nancy Stein (as yet unpublished) points to similar processes. Stein set up situations in which children argued with same-sex partners concerning what they should do in a certain situation in which they would both be involved. Arguments between girls usually involved each asking about the other's reasons for wanting to take a given action and pointing out to each other what the consequences of a given action were likely to be. Boys more often took up a "win" strategy, trying to overpower an opponent verbally with *ad hominem* arguments and/or with direct accusations of "You're wrong!" Among boys, the style was more confrontational, while among girls it was more often oriented toward trying to persuade one another as to what would be the best course of action.

Studies of interactions in all-female or all-male groups of young adolescents or young adults indicate that the features noted in childhood are carried on fairly consistently to later ages. For example, Aries reports that in all-male groups of college students there is a good deal of dramatizing and telling of stories and anecdotes and that a sense of camaraderie is achieved through sharing of stories and laughter. In all-female groups, by contrast, there is more revealing of feelings and gaining of closeness through intimate self-revelations. The early work of Douvan and Adelson (1966) underscored this greater intimacy of female friendships.

GROUP MEMBERSHIP AND IN-GROUP LOYALTIES

Are boys' groups and girls' groups really groups in the psychological sense? That is, do boys and girls identify with their own sex and treat other same-sex children as an in-group and the other sex as an out-group? There is evidence that both boys and girls have a higher opinion of their own sex than of the other sex and entertain stereotypical views about the characteristics of the other sex. Under certain circumstances, children also give preferential treatment to members of their own sex, but this aspect of group membership is less well documented. Hogg and Turner (1987) point out that in situations where gender is made highly salient people become more conscious of their own gender identity and are more likely to stereotype themselves and others in sex-typed ways. They note, however, that this does not necessarily imply that their self-esteem as members of a preferred in-group will rise or that they will give preferential treatment to same-sex others. Thus, not all the in-group phenomena documented by Tajfel and followers (1982) operate for gender groupings. The Hogg and

Turner hypothesis is that the relationship between the sexes determines whether increasing the salience of gender results in stronger in-group pride and identification, and I believe they are right, although the evidence is just beginning to accumulate.

ADOLESCENCE AND CROSS-SEX ATTRACTION

We do not have good recent information concerning how and whether gender segregation continues into adolescence. Blyth, Hill, and Thiel (1982) report that same-sex peers are more frequently nominated by adolescents as close significant other persons in their lives than are opposite-sex peers, although, of course, the amount of cross-sex interaction is much greater in adolescence than in childhood. Dunphy (1963), in a classic study of Australian adolescents, reported that same-sex cliques are formed and that these cliques then develop loose associations with opposite-sex cliques. However, these larger mixed-sex groups dissipate as dating couples are formed. In other words, in Australia in the 60s, cross-sex interactions among adolescents were oriented toward the formation of couples. Traditionally, mixed-sex groups larger than pairs have probably been unstable, and in situations in which adolescents are not involved in attracting individual opposite-sex partners they have continued to spend much of their social life in same-sex groups just as they did in childhood. In some societies, this pattern continues into adulthood and after marriage, for example, among traditional working-class families in England where men congregate in pubs in the evening while their wives meet other women for tea or in parks while minding children. How rapidly these patterns of adult social segregation are breaking down is an open question.

Girls and boys emerge out of childhood and into adolescence with fairly distinct interaction styles and with relatively little experience interacting with one another in unstructured situations. At puberty comes not only the biological surge in sex drive but the social expectation that the time for cross-sex attraction and interaction has arrived. Adolescents, as we all know, become intensely preoccupied with being attractive to members of the opposite sex. Buss (1988) has recently studied the tactics the two sexes employ to make themselves attractive; both sexes emphasize such strategies as displaying a good sense of humor, being sympathetic toward the other person's troubles, being well groomed, and offering to help the other. There are some tactics that are more specific to one sex; for example, young men are more likely to display physical strength; indicate that they have prestige, money, or power; and express strong opinions. Young women rely more on enhancing their appearance with clothes, hairstyles, and makeup and on telling men what they want to hear. Adolescence and young adulthood is clearly a time when gender is highly salient, but, as noted earlier, this does not necessarily imply that ties to same-sex others are especially strong. On the contrary, as Buss (1988) notes, it is a time of within-sex rivalry and competition for desirable partners, processes that break down within-sex solidarity.

What are the quality and outcome of the cross-sex encounters that occur in adolescence and young adulthood? It is well documented that in mixed-sex groups women speak less than men and are less assertive in their styles of speech than they are when interacting in a group of women (e.g., see reviews in LaFrance & Mayo, 1978, and in Lockheed & Hall, 1976). Also, women interacting with men take up a stance of active listening, giving nonverbal signals of attentiveness (Duncan & Fiske, 1977), something Jesse Bernard (1967) has referred to as "silent applause." Men's voices are louder and are more listened to by both sexes than women's voices; men, in particular, are inclined to lose interest when listening to a taped woman's voice (Robinson & McArthur, 1982). In mixed groups, women focus their attention more on the men in the group and their responsiveness to the other women in the group drops, by comparison with their attentional patterns in all-female groups (Aries, 1976). Men, on the other hand, frequently direct their speech to the women in a mixed group and increase the frequency of feeling statements and self-disclosure. On the whole, a reasonable description of what occurs in many mixed-sex groups is that men dominate the interaction not only by talking more, but by taking a greater role in initiating activities; furthermore, they are more influential in that their viewpoints are more likely to prevail in problem-solving discussions (Lockheed & Hall, 1976).

During the process of becoming acquainted with members of the opposite sex, each sex draws upon the repertoire of interactive skills previously developed in single-sex groups, but also attempts to adapt to a new kind of partner and develop an interactive style that will be attractive and acceptable to the other sex. For men, the adaptation involves becoming less blunt, accepting intimacy, and showing more sensitivity to the concerns of a partner; however, a man can retain a central set of his all-male proclivities: forcefulness, dominance, taking the initiative. Women, I believe, have a more difficult time in adapting to male partners. As we saw with children, the influence techniques young women have used with one another are less effective with men. In dealing with men, women do not usually adopt a male style of counterdominance or joking, for example, and are more likely to play up to the male ego. Frequently, they find themselves at a disadvantage.

For women, encounters with men in the early stages of forming cross-sex relationships carry certain costs. In a study in which cross-sex encounters were set up experimentally, Hogg and Turner (1987) had two young men take one position in a debate and two young women take another. The participants were chosen so that all were initially committed to the positions they were taking; the outcomes were contrasted with situations in which young men and women were debating against same-sex opponents. After the cross-sex debate, the self-esteem of the young men rose and that of the young women declined. Furthermore, the men liked their women opponents better after debating with them, whereas the women liked the men less. In other words, the encounter was a pleasurable experience for the men but not for the women. In a similar vein, Davis (1978) set up get-acquainted sessions between pairs of young men and women. He found that the men took control of the interaction, dictating the pace at which intimacy increased, while the women adapted themselves to the pace the men set. The women reported later, however, that they had been uncomfortable about not being able to control the sequence of events, and they did not enjoy the encounter as much as the men did.

Of course, it is not easy to say who is dominant in couples who are becoming romantically involved. An exceptionally attractive young woman can dominate male suitors, who will go to great lengths to please her. The main point here, however, is that the early phases of courtship have their own routines, their own scripts, and involve at least a certain amount of ritual male display and female attentiveness and adaptation to male initiatives.

There is evidence that the degree of male dominance in cross-sex encounters depends on the duration and depth of the relationships between the persons involved. For example, Heiss (1962) compared casual daters, steady daters, and engaged couples and found that male dominance in the amount of talking decreased over the three groups, with talk time being divided nearly equally between engaged couples. Shaw and Sadler (1965) found that husbands and wives were equally active in their verbal encounters, whereas among previously unacquainted mixed dyads, men took the initiative in breaking silences twice as often as the women. Leik (1963) similarly reported that men and women took up traditional role relationships when unacquainted people were asked to simulate a family interaction, whereas in real families, the stereotypical role specialization (men "instrumental," women "expressive") did not occur.

An issue that has been studied in cross-sex interactions among couples is the management of conflict. Students of interaction consistently report that men are more likely than women to try to avoid conflict (Gottman & Levenson, in press; Kelley, Cunningham, Grisham, Lefebvre, Sink, & Yablon, 1978). This seems curious in view of the fact that there is evidence for men being the more aggressive sex. Gottman and Levenson cite evidence (drawing considerably on the work of Frankenhaeuser and colleagues, this volume) that under stressful conditions men's level of physiological arousal rises faster and further than that of women. When stress rises beyond a certain point, the male level of arousal is high enough to disrupt normal functioning. The implication is that men cannot function as well as women can when a conflict between them becomes intense. Within groups of males, conflict is avoided by joking relationships and by the establishment of clear dominance hierarchies in which there is consensus as to who has the right to exercise leadership. Within women's groups, there is less hierarchy and more open discussion even on conflicted issues, and positive ties between members are more likely to survive the expressive of negative affect (Ginsberg & Gottman, 1986). The Gottman–Levenson hypothesis is that when conflict is low, men will try to be conciliatory—they will do what they can to keep the conflict from escalating (see Rausch, Barry, Hertel, & Swain, 1974; Schaap, 1982). If conciliation does not work, however, they will break off the interaction to avoid the disruption of high conflict; they will leave the scene of the argument, hang up the phone, or become silent and refuse to continue a discussion (Komarovsky, 1976). It is a reasonable conjecture that women also must be at pains to try to keep the man's level of arousal from becoming too great, although this process has not been the focus of study. We may assume that women develop a repertoire of ways to placate or soothe men, for example, choosing a propitious moment for introducing a topic that may be arousing. At the same time, they experience considerable frustration over not being able to deal with issues frontally or to continue a discussion to a resolution.

What are the implications of all this for the relationships between women and men in the workplace? The history of women's lives is such that when they first take up out-of-home employment, they have already had experience interacting with males in two main contexts: their family of origin and the sexualized milieu of adolescent dating. In the family, the primary male figure is the father, with whom most young women have had a relationship of subordination and deference, however positive the relationship may have been on the whole. A woman will have had a chance of interaction on a more equal basis with brothers, if there were any in her family, but we know essentially nothing about the effect of being reared with brothers on a girl's future relationships with male coworkers. In adolescence, cross-sex interaction occurs primarily in the context of mate attraction and pairing off, and in this context women tend to play up to their male partners, at least early in the relationship. It is no surprise, then, that in the workplace men and women have slipped easily into the boss–

secretary or doctor–nurse relationship, where roles are congruent with what cross-sex relationships earlier in life have prepared each participant for.

What early experiences are relevant to adapting to the kind of equal-status mixed-sex groups that might be called for in a truly gender-integrated workplace? As well-integrated groups or teams are formed in the workplace, they do more than work together. Usually, they go out to lunch together, walk to the bus or parking lot together, and talk about their families, movie preferences, leisure-time activities. In short, they form nonsexualized friendships. This is what adult men and women have had little experience with earlier in their lives.

I believe that we are all ambivalent about how to handle cross-sex relationships in the workplace. Women generally do not want to abandon their femininity while working; usually, they take pains to dress attractively even while they are trying to behave in ways that do not invite either male dominance or sexual advances. Men, too, want to remain attractive to women even in the workplace. Discreet flirtation does go on, but anyone who does not want to be seen as romantically involved, or potentially involved, with a coworker will avoid lunch dates or too much casual conversation. In addition, the sex differences in interactive style and in modes of exerting influence on equal-status partners still exist, and on the average, people of each sex find it more comfortable to interact with people who have interactive styles to which they are already adapted. These forces, I believe, help to propel people toward same-sex congregation in the workplace, just as they did toward the formation of same-sex play groups in childhood.

Of course, these are not the only forces at work in producing occupational segregation by gender—probably not even the major forces. I merely want to suggest that they contribute and that we need to consider the interactive habits built up over the early portion of the life cycle if we want to understand—and perhaps change—the patterns of aggregation in the workplace. Strober (1984) has made a convincing case for the proposition that occupational segregation results largely from men having first choice of occupations, with women getting the jobs men find less desirable. One can see links between the childhood and adolescent cross-sex relationships described earlier and the ability of males in adulthood to dominate access to desirable occupations.

There may be changes currently going on in societies that will affect the strength of the forces producing segregation. There are experiments being conducted with school-age children in which work groups are organized in such a way as to reduce or eliminate male dominance and sex-role stereotyping. It is alleged that in coed college dormitories genuine cross-sex nonsexual friendships are formed and that mixed groups congregate comfortably without pairing off. Experience in such situations may provide a background that will permit people to work and form friendships in the workplace without regard to gender. My contention here is simply that anyone who wishes to modify existing patterns of gender segregation will not find it sufficient to try to change the workplace only. It will also be necessary to restructure some of the experiences young men and women have earlier in their lives if they are to have comfortable relationships with cross-sex coworkers as adults.

REFERENCES

Aries, E. (1976). Interaction patterns and themes of male, female, and mixed groups. *Small Group Behavior, 7,* 7–18.

Bernard, J. (1967). The second sex and the cichlid effect. *Journal of the National Association of Women Deans and Counselors, 31,* 8–17.

Blyth, D. A., Hill, J. P., & Thiel, K. S. (1982). Early adolescents' significant others: Grade and gender differences in perceived relationships with familial and non-familial adults and young people. *Journal of Youth and Adolescence, 11,* 425–450.

Buss, D. M. (1988). The evolution of human intrasexual competition: The tactics of mate attraction. *Journal of Personality & Social Psychology, 54,* 616–628.

Davis, J. D. (1978). When boy meets girl: Sex roles and the negotiation of intimacy in an acquaintance exercise. *Journal of Personality & Social Psychology, 36,* 684–692.

Douvan, E., & Adelson, J. (1966). *The adolescent experience.* New York: Wiley.

Duncan, G. D., & Duncan, B. (1955). A methodological analysis of segregation indexes. *American Sociology Review, 20,* 210–217.

Duncan, S. Jr., & Fiske, D. W. (1977). *Face-to-face interaction: Research, methods and theory.* Hillsdale, NJ: Erlbaum.

Dunphy, D. (1963). The social structure of early adolescent peer groups. *Sociometry, 26,* 230–246.

Edwards, C. P., & Whiting, B. B. (1988). *Children of different worlds.* Cambridge, MA: Harvard University Press.

Ellis, L. (1986). Evidence of a neuroandrogenic etiology of sex roles from a combined analysis of human, nonhuman primate and nonprimate mammalian studies. *Personality and Individual Differences, 7,* 519–552.

Ginsberg, D., & Gottman, J. (1987). The conversations of college roommates. In J. Gottman & J. Parker (Eds.), *Conversations of friends: Speculations on affective development.* New York: Cambridge University Press.

Gottman, J. M., & Levenson, R. W. (in press). The social psycho-physiology of marriage. In P. Noller & M. A. Fitzpatrick (Eds.), *Perspectives on Marital Interaction.* Multi-Lingual Matters Press.

Heiss, J. S. (1962). Degree of intimacy and male–female interaction. *Sociometry, 25,* 197–208.

Hogg, M. A., & Turner, J. C. (1987). Intergroup behavior, self stereotyping and the salience of social categories. *British Journal of Social Psychology, 26,* 325–340.

Jacklin, C. N., & Maccoby, E. E. (1978). Social behavior at 33 months in same-sex and mixed-sex dyads. *Child Development, 49,* 557–569.

Kelley, H. H., Cunningham, J. D., Grisham, J. A., Lefebvre, L. M., Sink, C. R., & Yablon, G. (1978). Sex differences in comments made during conflict in close relationships. *Sex Roles, 4,* 473–491.

Komarovsky, M. (1976). *Dilemmas of masculinity*. New York: Norton.

LaFrance, M., & Mayo, C. (1978). *Moving bodies: Nonverbal communication in social relationships*. Monterey: Brooks-Cole.

LaFreniere, P., Strayer, F. D., & Gauthier, R. (1984). The emergence of same-sex preferences among preschool peers: A developmental ethological perspectus. *Child Development, 55,* 1958–1965.

Leik, R. K. (1963). Instrumentality and emotionality in family interaction. *Sociometry, 26,* 131–145.

Lockheed, M. E., & Hall, K. P. (1976). Conceptualizing sex as a status characteristic: Applications to leadership training strategies. *Journal of Social Issues, 32,* 111–124.

Lockheed, M. E., & Harris, A. M. (1984). Cross-sex collaborative learning in elementary classrooms. *American Educational Research Journal, 21,* 275–294.

Lockheed, M. E., & Klein, S. S. (1985). Sex equity in classroom organization and climate. In S. Klein (Ed.), *Handbook for achieving sex-equity through education* (pp. 189–217). Baltimore, MD: Johns Hopkins University Press.

Maccoby, E. E. (1988). Gender as a social category. *Developmental Psychology, 24,* 755–765.

Maccoby, E. E., & Jacklin, C. N. (1974). *The psychology of sex differences*. Stanford, CA: Stanford University Press.

Maccoby, E. E., & Jacklin, C. N. (1987). Gender segregation in childhood. In H. W. Reese (Ed.), *Advances in child development and behavior* (Vol. 20, pp. 239–288). New York: Academic Press.

Maltz, D. N., & Borker, R. A. (1983). A cultural approach to male–female miscommunication. In J. A. Gumperz (Ed.), *Language and social identity* (pp. 195–216). New York: Cambridge University Press.

Meany, M. J., Stewart, J., & Beatty, W. W. (1985). Sex differences in social play: The socialization of sex roles. In (Ed.), *Advances in the study of behavior* (Vol. 15, pp. 1–58). New York: Academic Press.

Raush, H. L., Barry, W. A., Hertel, R. K., & Swain, M. E. (1974). *Communication, conflict and marriage*. San Francisco: Jossey-Bass.

Reskin, B. F. (Ed.). (1984). *Sex segregation in the workplace: Trends, explanations and remedies*. Washington, DC: National Academy Press.

Robinson, J., & McArthur, L. Z. (1982). Impact of salient vocal qualities on causal attribution for a speaker's behavior. *Journal of Personality and Social Psychology, 43,* 236–247.

Savin-Williams, R. C. (1979). Dominance hierarchies in groups of early adolescents. *Child Development, 50,* 923–935.

Schaap, C. (1982). *Communication and adjustment in marriage*. Lisse, The Netherlands: Swets & Leitlinger.

Serbin, L. A., Tonick, I. J., & Sternglanz, S. (1977). Shaping cooperative cross-sex play. *Child Development, 48,* 924–929.

Shaw, M. E., & Sadler, O. W. (1965). Interaction patterns in heterosexual dyads varying in degree of intimacy. *Journal of Social Psychology, 66,* 345–351.

Statistics, Sweden (1985). *Women and men in Sweden. Facts and figures*. Stockholm, Sweden.

Strober, M. (1984). Toward a general theory of occupational sex segregation. In B. F. Reskin (Ed.), *Sex segregation in the workplace: Trends, explanations, remedies* (pp. 144–156). Washington, DC: National Academy Press.

Tajfel, H. (1982). Social psychology of intergroup relations. *Annual Review of Psychology, 33,* 1–39.

Thorne, B. (1986). Girls and boys together, but mostly apart. In W. W. Hartup & D. Rubin (Eds.), *Relationships and development* (pp. 167–184). Hillsdale, NJ: Erlbaum.

2

Effects of Labor Force Participation on Sex Differences in Mortality and Morbidity

INGRID WALDRON

INTRODUCTION

This chapter analyzes the effects of men's and women's labor force participation on sex differences in mortality and morbidity. Labor force participation includes both employment and job seeking by the unemployed. Employment can have both harmful and beneficial effects on health (Palmore, Burchett, Fillenbaum, George, & Wallman, 1985; Repetti, Matthews, & Waldron, 1989; Sorensen & Verbrugge, 1987; Waldron, 1980). Employment can have harmful health effects due to exposures to physical and chemical occupational hazards and job stress. In addition, it has been hypothesized that strain or overload due to combined job and home responsibilities may have harmful effects on health, especially for employed women with children. Employment may also have beneficial effects on health due to increased income, social support from coworkers, and greater social status, self-esteem, and sense of accomplishment. Being an unemployed job seeker appears to have more harmful effects on health than being employed (Linn, Sandifer, & Stein, 1985; Moser, Fox, & Jones,

INGRID WALDRON • Department of Biology, University of Pennsylvania, Philadelphia, Pennsylvania 19104-6018.

1984). The relative importance of the specific harmful and beneficial health effects of labor force participation varies, depending on characteristics of the individual and his or her occupation. As a result, the overall effect of labor force participation on health varies, depending on individual characteristics and job characteristics (Repetti *et al.*, 1989).

There are substantial sex differences in labor force participation rates and occupations, as well as sex differences in characteristics that may modify the effects of labor force participation—for example, responsibility for child care and housework (Roos, 1985; Sorensen & Verbrugge, 1987). Given the multiple proved and postulated effects of labor force participation on health, it would be expected that the sex differences in labor force participation rates and occupations would influence sex differences in mortality and morbidity. This chapter summarizes several types of evidence related to this hypothesis.

The first section of the chapter provides a brief description of sex differences in mortality and morbidity. The next two sections present evidence concerning two hypotheses that link sex differences in mortality to specific effects of labor force participation. The first hypothesis proposes that men's greater exposure to occupational hazards contributes to men's higher mortality. The second hypothesis proposes that sex differences in labor force participation contribute to sex differences in health-related behavior such as smoking and that these sex differences in behavior contribute to sex differences in mortality.

The following two sections of the chapter review two different types of evidence concerning the overall effects of labor force participation on health. The first of these sections summarizes evidence from individual-level analyses of longitudinal data concerning the effects of labor force participation on men's and women's health. The other section summarizes evidence from ecological-level analyses concerning the relationship of labor force participation rates in different regions to male mortality, female mortality, and sex differences in mortality in these regions. The final section of this chapter presents tentative conclusions concerning the effects of labor force participation on sex differences in health, based on the varied types of evidence reviewed herein.

SEX DIFFERENCES IN MORTALITY AND MORBIDITY

In contemporary economically developed countries males have higher mortality than females at all ages and males have higher mortality for a broad range of causes of death (Lopez & Ruzicka, 1983; Preston, 1976; United Nations, 1982; Waldron, 1986a; Wingard, 1984). In the

United States male mortality is at least twice as high as female mortality for suicide, homicide, motor vehicle and other accidents, lung cancer and related cancers, emphysema and other chronic obstructive pulmonary diseases, ischemic heart disease, and chronic liver diseases, including cirrhosis of the liver (Table 1). Previous research has shown that males' higher mortality for these causes of death is due in large part to sex differences in behavior, including males' higher rates of cigarette smoking and heavy drinking (Waldron, 1986a, 1986b). Inherent sex differences in biology also contribute to males' higher mortality. This chapter discusses possible contributions of sex differences in labor force participation rates and occupations to men's higher mortality.

During the twentieth century in industrial countries there has been a general trend toward an increasing male mortality disadvantage (Lopez & Ruzicka, 1983; National Center for Health Statistics, 1987; United Nations, 1982; U. N. Secretariat, 1988; Waldron, 1986a; Wingard, 1984). For example, in the United States, the male disadvantage in life expectancy increased from 3.5 years in 1930 to 7.8 years in 1979. One important cause of men's increasing mortality disadvantage was the widespread adoption of cigarette smoking by men in the early twentieth century (Retherford, 1975; Waldron, 1986a). Very recently, the male mortality disadvantage has

Table 1. Sex Differences in Mortality by Cause of Death, United States, 1985

Cause of death	Male death rate	Female death rate	Sex difference in mortality	Sex mortality ratio
Suicide	18.8	4.9	13.9	3.8
Homicide	12.8	3.9	8.9	3.3
Other accidents	24.4	8.2	16.2	3.0
Malignant neoplasms of respiratory and intrathoracic organs (e.g., lung cancer)	60.0	22.4	37.6	2.7
Motor vehicle accidents	27.3	10.5	16.8	2.6
Chronic obstructive pulmonary diseases (e.g., emphysema)	27.9	12.5	15.4	2.2
Chronic liver disease and cirrhosis	13.6	6.1	7.5	2.2
Ischemic heart disease	177.9	84.2	93.7	2.1
All causes	716.8	409.4	307.4	1.8

Note. Death rates have been age-adjusted by the direct method with the total population in 1940 as the standard. Death rates are deaths per 100,000 people per year. A sex mortality ratio is the male death rate divided by the female death rate. This table lists the causes of death that were responsible for at least 1% of deaths and had a sex mortality ratio of at least 2.0. Data are from National Center for Health Statistics, 1987.

begun to decrease in some economically developed countries. For example, the male disadvantage in life expectancy has decreased in the United States recently, falling from 7.8 years in 1979 to 6.8 years by 1987 (National Center for Health Statistics, 1988). There has been some speculation that this decrease in the female longevity advantage may reflect harmful effects of women's increasing labor force participation. Evidence concerning the health effects of women's labor force participation in the contemporary United States is discussed in this chapter.

Earlier historical data for industrial countries and historical and contemporary data for economically developing countries indicate that females have had higher mortality than males in some cases. Although males generally have had higher mortality than females in infancy and for ages over 40, females have had higher mortality than males for ages between 1 and 40 in quite a few countries and time periods (Lopez & Ruzicka, 1983; Preston, 1976; U. N. Secretariat, 1988; Waldron, 1986a, 1987). Females' higher mortality appears to have been due in large part to higher infectious disease mortality for females and high maternal mortality. A major cause of females' higher infectious disease mortality appears to have been less adequate nutrition and health care for females. It has been hypothesized that this type of discrimination against females occurs more often in societies where females' economic contribution is smaller. To test this hypothesis researchers have analyzed the relationship between women's labor force participation rates and sex differences in mortality. The results of these analyses are summarized in this chapter.

Sex differences in morbidity vary, depending on the specific morbidity measure, the age group, and the particular culture considered (Verbrugge, 1985; Wingard, 1984). Contemporary evidence from the United States indicates that women generally report more symptoms, more acute conditions, more days of restricted activity due to illness, and more doctor visits than do men. Men are somewhat more likely than women to report activity limitations due to chronic conditions. Sex differences in the prevalence of diagnosed chronic conditions vary, depending on the specific condition considered. The morbidity data should be interpreted with caution, since many of these measures of morbidity are self-report measures or are based on actions taken in response to symptoms, for example, doctor visits or days of restricted activity. Thus, sex differences in these measures of morbidity may be influenced not only by sex differences in physical illness but also by sex differences in predispositions to notice symptoms, to report symptoms, or to take action in response to symptoms (Verbrugge, 1985; Wingard, 1984; Waldron, 1983). Evidence concerning the effects of labor force participation on morbidity is presented in this chapter.

CONTRIBUTIONS OF OCCUPATIONAL HAZARDS
TO SEX DIFFERENCES IN HEALTH

Exposure to physical and chemical occupational hazards is substantially greater for men than for women, at least in economically developed countries such as the United States (Leigh, 1988; Robinson, 1984; Roos, 1985; Waldron, 1980). Men are exposed more to occupational hazards because more men are employed, and among those who are employed more men than women work in hazardous occupations. The evidence summarized in the following paragraphs indicates that men's greater exposure to occupational hazards contributes to their higher mortality, although current estimates suggest that this effect may account for a relatively small proportion of total sex differences in mortality.

Recent data for the United States indicate that, due to sex differences in occupations held, employed men have about five times as high a risk of fatal work accidents as employed women (Leigh, 1988). Several studies suggest that approximately 95% of fatal work accidents involve men. On the basis of these data it appears that men's higher rates of fatal work accidents account for roughly a fifth of the sex difference in accident fatalities or about 2%–3% of the total sex difference in mortality in the United States (calculated from data in Kraus, 1985; Leigh, 1988; Stout-Wiegand, 1988; U.S. Department of Health and Human Services, 1985a, 1986).

Men are substantially more likely than women to be employed in occupations with exposures to known or suspected carcinogens (Waldron, 1980). Estimates for one region in England suggest that occupational exposures were responsible for 6% of male cancers but only 2% of female cancers (Higginson & Muir, 1979). One major occupational carcinogen is asbestos, which has been widely used in insulation and construction materials. Most of the jobs involving heavy asbestos exposure have been held by men. It has been estimated that in the United States occupational exposures to asbestos have been responsible for approximately one-tenth of men's lung cancer deaths, which is equivalent to about 15% of men's excess mortality due to lung cancer or 2% of males' excess mortality for all causes (Waldron, 1982).

In summary, on the basis of the effects of men's greater exposure to asbestos and other occupational carcinogens, men's greater risk of work accidents, and men's greater exposure to other chemical and physical occupational hazards, it seems likely that occupational exposures are responsible for roughly 5%–10% of excess male mortality in the United States.

Trends in exposures to occupational hazards to not appear to account for the increase in sex differences in mortality during the twentieth century. Indeed, working conditions may have been more hazardous in the early twentieth century, and occupational hazards may have made a greater contribution to men's higher mortality in this early period. Retherford (1975) has shown that males' higher mortality for accidents and other violence accounted for almost half of the total sex difference in mortality in the United States in 1910, and he suggests that accidents due to hazardous working conditions made a major contribution to males' higher accident mortality in this period. In subsequent decades, sex differences in mortality due to accidents and other violence decreased, probably due in part to improved working conditions resulting in decreased job accidents for men.

Men's greater exposure to occupational hazards would be expected to contribute to higher morbidity, as well as higher mortality, for men. Thus, sex differences in exposure to occupational hazards do not account for women's higher rates for many morbidity measures. However, for nonfatal accidents, males have higher rates than females, and men's higher rates of work accidents account for approximately half of this male excess for nonfatal work accidents (National Center for Health Statistics, 1986).

HEALTH-RELATED BEHAVIOR:
A POSSIBLE LINK BETWEEN LABOR FORCE
PARTICIPATION AND SEX DIFFERENCES IN HEALTH

Sex differences in health-related behavior make a major contribution to males' higher mortality (Retherford, 1975; Waldron, 1986a). It appears that cigarette smoking has been responsible for roughly half of the sex difference in adult mortality in the United States in recent decades (Waldron, 1986b). Males' higher rates of heavy alcohol consumption and males' greater risk taking in driving and recreation also contribute to males' higher mortality.

It has been argued that labor force participation increases smoking, drinking, and, possibly, other types of risky behavior among women. If it is assumed that labor force participation increases risky behavior among men as well as women, then this leads to the hypothesis that men's higher rates of labor force participation have contributed to men's higher rates of risky behavior, which in turn have been a major cause of men's higher mortality.

Contrary to these hypotheses, it appears that labor force participation does not have a significant influence on smoking in contemporary economically developed countries. Recent survey data for the United States show that women in the labor force are no more likely to be smokers than are full-time homemakers (Brackbill, Frazier, & Shilling, 1988; U. S. Department of Health and Human Services, 1985b; Waldron & Lye, 1989). Similarly, there appears to be no consistent relationship between labor force status and smoking for men. International data for contemporary economically developed countries indicate no relationship between women's labor force participation rates and either the prevalence of smoking among women or the magnitude of sex differences in the prevalence of smoking (Waldron, in press). In addition, current evidence indicates that neither employment in traditional male occupations nor employment in traditional female occupations influences smoking adoption or cessation for men or for women (Waldron & Lye, 1989). Thus, in contemporary economically developed countries it appears that employment does not have a significant influence on smoking for either women or men.

It should be noted that although contemporary evidence indicates little or no direct effect of sex differences in labor force participation on sex differences in smoking, historical evidence suggests that there may have been important indirect effects (Waldron, in press). In the early twentieth century relatively few women smoked, in large part due to strong social pressures against women's smoking. It appears that the social pressures against women's smoking were part of a general pattern of restrictions on women's behavior. These restrictions reflected men's greater social power and ability to regulate women's behavior, due in part to men's greater labor force participation and consequent greater economic power. As women's labor force participation and economic power increased during the mid-twentieth century, restrictions on women's behavior decreased, social acceptance of women's smoking increased, and sex differences in smoking decreased. Thus, the changing sex differences in labor force participation may have indirectly influenced the changing sex differences in smoking, and these in turn have had a major influence on the changing sex differences in mortality (Retherford, 1975; Waldron, 1986a, 1986b, in press). However, international data raise doubts concerning the importance of the hypothesized link between sex differences in labor force participation and sex differences in smoking. These data show that, for contemporary economically developed countries, there is no correlation between sex differences in labor force participation rates and sex differences in the prevalence of smoking (calculated from data in sources cited in Table 2, Waldron, in press).

It has also been hypothesized that employment increases women's alcohol consumption. Current evidence is inconsistent, but several studies suggest that, among younger women, employed women may be more likely than housewives to be problem drinkers or heavy drinkers (Waldron, 1988). If women's labor force participation does increase heavy drinking, it would be expected that the recent rapid increases in women's labor force participation rates would have resulted in increases in women's alcohol consumption. However, it appears that there have been only relatively minor increases in women's alcohol consumption in recent decades. Due to the conflicting evidence, it is unclear to what extent sex differences in employment have contributed to sex differences in drinking.

Other behavioral factors that contribute to men's higher mortality include males' greater use of guns, more frequent physical risk taking, and more hostile, competitive or Type A behavior pattern (Waldron, 1983, 1986a). Traditional differences in male and female roles have probably contributed to the cultural evolution of differences in the socialization of males and females, and the sex differences in socialization probably contribute to the sex differences in these risky behaviors.

EFFECTS OF LABOR FORCE PARTICIPATION ON WOMEN'S AND MEN'S HEALTH

This section summarizes evidence from analyses of individual-level longitudinal data concerning the effects of women's labor force participation on their health, the effects of men's labor force participation on their health, and the effects of women's labor force participation on their husbands' health.

In evaluating evidence concerning the effects of labor force participation on health, two major methodological problems must be considered. First, in order to assess the effects of labor force participation, it is necessary to have a comparison group of adults who are not in the labor force. For women, a natural comparison group is full-time homemakers. For men at prime working ages, it is difficult or impossible to obtain a satisfactory comparison group, since very few men at prime working ages are out of the labor force and those who are out of the labor force tend to be quite deviant in characteristics such as their health. Consequently, analyses of the effects of labor force participation on health have generally focused on women at prime working ages or on older men and women at retirement ages. The effects of labor force participation on health may be different at older ages than at prime working ages due to differences in physiology and, particularly for men, differences in social norms concerning the acceptability of being out of the labor force.

The second major methodological problem has been the difficulty of distinguishing between the effects of labor force participation on health and the effects of health on labor force participation. For example, the observation that women in the labor force have better health than women who are not in the labor force does not necessarily imply that labor force participation has beneficial effects on women's health (Repetti *et al.*, 1989; Waldron, 1980). Current evidence indicates that women in good health are more likely to join the labor force and less likely to leave the labor force, and this may be the primary reason why women in the labor force have better health (Repetti *et al.*, 1989; Waldron & Jacobs, 1988). Similarly, it appears that men in better health are less likely to retire, and this is one reason why older workers tend to be healthier than retirees (Palmore *et al.*, 1985; Minkler, 1981). One recent study found that retired men had a substantially higher risk of death due to coronary heart disease, but this apparent increase in risk was reduced to a marginally significant effect when a partial control was introduced for the presence of previous coronary heart disease that may have influenced retirement decisions (Casscells, Hennekens, Evans, Rosener, De Silva, Lown, Davies, & Jesse, 1980). Thus, it is essential to distinguish between the effects of health on labor force participation and the effects of labor force participation on health, and this is difficult or impossible to accomplish in analyses of cross-sectional data.

Similar ambiguities can arise in the interpretation of longitudinal data unless care is taken in the analyses (Minkler, 1981; Repetti *et al.*, 1989; Waldron & Jacobs, 1989). For example, several longitudinal studies have analyzed the relationship between retirement during the interval between an initial survey and a follow-up survey and change in health during the same follow-up interval (Ekerdt, Baden, Bosse, & Dibbs, 1983; Palmore *et al.*, 1985). The results of these analyses are ambiguous, since health trends during the early part of the follow-up interval would be expected to influence the probability of retirement during the interval and, consequently, the relationship between retirement and health trends over the entire follow-up interval reflects the effects of health trends on retirement as well as the effects of retirement on health trends.

Three major studies have analyzed longitudinal data concerning the relationships between women's initial labor force status or employment history and subsequent changes in health (Table 2). These studies analyzed data for general population samples of middle-aged and older women. The findings indicate that, on the average, labor force participation had no significant effect on coronary heart disease risk or mortality. The findings also suggest that for married white women labor force participation had no effect on general health, on average, whereas for married black women and unmarried women labor force participation had beneficial effects on general health. Social support from coworkers

Table 2. Effects of Labor Force Participation on Women's Health: Evidence from Longitudinal Studies

A. Description of Studies

Study	Sample	Labor force measure	Change in health measure	Controls
Framingham Heart (Haynes, Eaker, & Feinleib, 1984)	737 women, ages 45–64 at beginning of study interval, approx. 1966–1976, Framingham, Mass.	Worked outside home for over half adult years	Incidence of new cases of coronary heart disease	Study excluded women who had coronary heart disease initially.
General health (Waldron & Jacobs, 1988, 1989)	3,300 women, ages 40–54 at beginning of study interval, 1977–1982, U.S.	Employed or looking for work at time of initial survey	Increase in self-reported general health problems	The analyses controlled for race, marital status, age, education, and initial health.
Mortality (Kotler & Wingard, 1989)	1,457 women, ages 35–64 at beginning of study interval, 1965–1982, Alameda County	Employed full-time at least half adult years	Mortality	The analyses controlled for race, age, education, income, health behavior, social contacts, life satisfaction, and initial health.

B. Relationships between Initial Labor Force Status and Subsequent Change in Health

	Coronary heart disease incidence (%)		Increase in health problems				Mortality (%)	
			White women		Black women			
	Working women	House-wives	In the labor force	Not in labor force	In the labor force	Not in labor force	Working women	House-wives
All women	8.5	7.1	—	—	—	—	13.6	14.1
Married	8.9	6.2	0.42[a]	0.27	0.59	1.43[b]	—	—
Previously married	9.4	10.3	0.61	1.70	0.65	1.73	—	—
Never married	5.7	—					—	—
Married[c]								
No children	7.8	—	0.52	0.26	0.87	0.77	—	—
1–2 children	8.9	8.2	0.24	0.29	0.21	2.00	—	—
3+ children	11.0	5.7					—	—
Not married								
No children	—	—	0.63	1.56	0.55	0.93	—	—
1 or more children	—	—	0.59	1.79	0.79	2.41	—	—
Occupation[d]								
Managerial, professional, and technical	5.2	—	0.46	0.14	0.74	0.08	—	—
Clerical and sales	12.0	—	0.36	0.58	0.77	1.76	—	—
Blue collar	7.1	—					—	—

Note. Dashes indicate data were not available.

[a] This indicates that the average number of health problems reported by the married white women in the labor force increased by 0.42 (out of 22 possible) during the follow-up interval.

[b] For significant differences between women in the labor force and women not in the labor force ($p \le .06$), the underlined number indicates the labor force status group that experienced more increase in health problems. It appears that none of the differences in coronary heart disease incidence between housewives and working women was significant, due in part to the relatively small number of coronary heart disease cases.

[c] For coronary heart disease incidence, these data include previously married as well as currently married women.

[d] For increase in health problems, these data are restricted to married women. For women not in the labor force, occupation refers to most recent occupation.

may have particularly beneficial effects on health for unmarried women and married black women, since unmarried women lack the social support provided by a husband and available evidence suggests that black husbands may provide less social support for their wives than do white husbands (Waldron & Jacobs, 1988). Additional evidence suggests that the health effects of labor force participation may also vary, depending on occupation and whether a woman has children (Haynes, Eaker, & Feinleib, 1984; Kotler & Wingard, 1989; Waldron & Jacobs, 1988, 1989).

In summary, the effects of labor force participation on women's health appear to vary, depending on race and marital status. Considering women as a whole, these studies indicate that, on the average, labor force participation does not have harmful effects on the health of middle-aged and older women.

As discussed earlier, most of the available studies of the health effects of retirement suffer from major methodological problems (Minkler, 1981). Findings from one well-designed longitudinal study suggest that, on the average, retirement does not have significant effects on general health (Wan, 1982). Specifically, this study analyzed longitudinal data for older men and unmarried women who at the time of the initial survey were employed and reported no functional disabilities. The results showed that retirement during the initial 2-year follow-up interval was not significantly related to change in self-reported general health during either of two subsequent 2-year follow-up intervals. In conclusion, there is no clear evidence for either beneficial or harmful health effects of retirement.

There appears to be very little evidence available concerning the effects of women's labor force participation on their husbands' health. Data from the Framingham Heart Study indicate that the risk of coronary heart disease was similar for men married to working women and men married to housewives (Haynes, Eaker, & Feinleib, 1983).[1]

In summary, current evidence suggests that, on the average, women's or men's labor force participation does not have harmful effects on their health and that women's labor force participation does not significantly affect their husbands' coronary heart disease risk. These conclusions must be considered tentative because they are based on a small number of studies that have analyzed longitudinal data using adequate methodology. There appear to be no studies that have analyzed longitudinal data to assess the effects of labor force participation on sex differences in health in

---

[1] Another study also found that a husband's coronary heart disease risk was not related to his wife's employment status (Carmelli, Swan, & Rosenman, 1985). However, in this study it appears that the wives' employment status was assessed after their husbands developed heart disease, so the interpretation of this result is ambiguous.

general population samples.[2] Thus, on the basis of current evidence it is unclear what effect, if any, men's and women's labor force participation may have on sex differences in health.

LABOR FORCE PARTICIPATION RATES AND SEX DIFFERENCES IN MORTALITY–ECOLOGICAL ANALYSES

As discussed earlier, labor force participation rates may influence sex differences in mortality in several different ways. First, labor force partici-pation can affect the health of individual men and women in the labor force. Second, high labor force participation rates for women may result in changes in general attitudes toward women's behavior, including reduced restrictions on health-damaging behaviors such as cigarette smoking. The third proposed effect of labor force participation rates on sex differences in mortality is postulated to occur primarily in relatively poor areas where

[2] Two analyses of cross-sectional data have evaluated relationships between labor force partici-pation and sex differences in health (Haavio-Mannila, 1986; Passannate & Nathanson, 1987). Unfortunately, these cross-sectional data do not provide useful information concerning the effects of labor force participation on sex differences in health because the observed relationships are strongly influenced by the effects of health on labor force participation. For example, one study found that the mortality advantage for women relative to men was greater for those who were in the labor force than for the total population (Passanate & Nathanson, 1987). However, this observation does not imply that labor force participation increases sex differences in mortality. Rather, it appears that (1) women in the labor force had lower mortality than women in the total population because healthier women were more likely to join the labor force, (2) there was almost no difference in mortality between men in the labor force and men in the total population because almost all men were in the labor force, and (3) these differential selection effects were the primary reason why sex differences in mortality were greater for those who were in the labor force than for the total population.

Similarly, findings that sex differences in mortality are reduced within specific occupational groups may reflect selection effects rather than effects of occupation on mortality. For example, sex differences in mortality have been shown to be lower for Finnish and U.S. doctors than for general population samples and lower for high-level U.S. government workers than for general population samples (Asp, Hernberg, & Collan, 1979; Detre, Feinleib, Matthews, & Kerr, 1987; Goodman, 1975). The effects of health on labor force participation may influence sex differences in mortality within these occupations. In addition, selective recruitment of female smokers into administrative occupations appears to have contributed to smaller sex differences in smoking among administrative workers; recruitment of male nonsmokers into professional occupations appears to have contributed to smaller sex differences in smoking among professional workers; and the smaller sex differences in smoking in these occupations appears to be one reason for the smaller sex differences in mortality (U.S. Department of Health and Human Services, 1980, 1985b; Waldron & Lye, 1989). Because of these multiple reciprocal causal effects, it is difficult or impossible to use cross-sectional data to assess the effects of specific occupations on sex differences in health.

families have limited food and access to health care. This hypothesis proposes that if females generally are not involved in productive economic activity outside the home, then families may invest resources such as food and health care more in males than in females. As a result, females may receive inadequate nutrition and health care, and consequently females may have elevated mortality relative to males (Lopez & Ruzicka, 1983; Rosenzweig & Schultz, 1982; Waldron, 1986a).

A number of ecological analyses have assessed relationships between labor force participation rates in various regions and longevity in those regions (Table 3). The results of these analyses indicate that higher female labor force participation rates are generally associated with a greater female longevity advantage. For economically developed countries the data also indicate that higher male labor force participation rates are associated with a smaller female longevity advantage. In addition, one study has found that greater female relative to male labor force participation is associated with a greater female longevity advantage. Limited data suggest that these associations may be due to a positive association between female labor force participation rates and female longevity and a positive association between male labor force participation rates and male longevity.

A major problem with these studies is that most of the analyses failed to control for potentially important confounding variables. For example, it appears that high divorce rates may increase both women's labor force participation rates and males' mortality disadvantage (POLIWA, 1977; Waldron, 1986a). Thus, the effects of divorce could be responsible for the observed association between higher women's labor force participation rates and a greater female longevity advantage. Other characteristics that appear to be associated with larger sex differences in mortality and may be important confounding variables include urbanization, more foreigners or in-migrants in a community, and higher illegitimacy rates (POLIWA, 1977; Preston, 1976; Sauer & Donnell, 1970). The potential importance of these confounding effects is indicated by the finding that in one study the correlation between women's employment rates and men's death rates was reduced from $+.61$ to $+.38$ when controls were introduced for a single variable, the proportion with rural farm residence (calculated from data in Sauer & Donnell, 1970). Unfortunately, many of the ecological analyses included no control variables or only a control for income, and even those analyses which included multiple control variables lacked controls for a number of potentially important confounding variables (see Table 3). At an even more fundamental level, it should be noted that statistical analyses have shown that it may be impossible to adequately control for confounding factors in analyses of ecological data and an association observed in ecological analyses may differ substantially from the corresponding association observed in analyses of individual-level data (Greenland & Morgenstern, 1989; Piantadosi, Byar, & Green, 1988; Richardson, Stucker, & Hemon, 1987).[3]

Given the methodological problems, it is very difficult to draw conclusions concerning the effects of labor force participation rates on sex differences in mortality on the basis of ecological-level analyses. However, causal interpretations can be made with greater confidence if they are supported by the findings of both the ecological-level analyses and the previously discussed analyses of individual-level longitudinal data.

The findings of both types of study suggest that, for adults in economically developed countries, increases in women's labor force participation do not reduce women's longevity advantage. This conclusion is supported by the findings that (1) in ecological-level analyses, women's labor force participation rates appear to be positively, not inversely, related to the female longevity advantage and (2) in analyses of individual-level longitudinal data, labor force participation does not appear to have harmful effects on women's health, on the average, nor beneficial effects on their husbands' health. Less evidence is available concerning the effects of men's labor force participation on health, but the limited available evidence suggests the tentative conclusion that increases in men's labor force participation do not increase men's mortality disadvantage.

Data from economically developing countries are more limited, and findings from ecological analyses appear to be inconsistent with findings from analyses of individual-level data. One ecological analysis suggests that in India higher female labor force participation rates are associated with more favorable survival rates for girls relative to boys (see Table 3).[4]

[3]There is an additional problem that makes it difficult to draw conclusions about causal relationships on the basis of findings from these ecological analyses: any observed relationship between labor force participation rates and sex differences in mortality may reflect reciprocal causal effects. Not only may labor force participation rates affect sex differences in mortality, but also sex differences in mortality may affect female labor force participation rates. Specifically, it has been proposed that excess male mortality results in a lower proportion of males in the population, which decreases marriage rates for women, which in turn may lead to increases in women's labor force participation rates (South & Trent, 1988).

[4]An additional analysis, not listed in Table 3, used a two-stage least squares regression procedure to relate sex differences in child survival to predicted female and male employment, based on both individual- and ecological-level data for rural households in India (Rosenzweig & Schultz, 1982). This analysis indicated that higher employment rates for women were associated with a smaller female survival disadvantage for children.

One potentially important methodological problem in the ecological analyses for India has been suggested by Das Gupta (1987), who has argued that in some regions of India discrimination against females may contribute to underreporting of women's employment as well as to higher mortality for females. This methodological problem could result in a spurious inverse correlation between women's employment and girls' mortality.

INGRID WALDRON

Table 3. Ecological Analyses of the Relationships between Labor Force Participation and Longevity

A. Description of Studies

Study[a]	Sample	Labor force measure	Longevity or mortality measure	Controls
U.S. (I) (Ram, 1984)	50 states + Washington, D.C., 1970	Labor force participation rate	Life expectancy	Per capita income
U.S. (II) (Sauer & Donnell, 1970)	231 economic areas, 1959–1961	Employment rate	Death rate, whites, ages 65–74	None
Belgium (POLIWA, 1977)	43 districts, 1970	Employment rate	Life expectancy at age 1	None
Sweden (Starrin, Larsson, & Brenner, 1988)	91 local authority areas, 1979–1983	Employment rate	Ischemic heart disease death rate, ages 45–64	None[b]
International (I) (Ram, 1984)	118 countries, about 1970	Labor force participation rate	Life expectancy	Per capita gross domestic product, fertility rate, whether economically developed
Economically developed (I) (Ram, 1984)	17 countries, about 1970	Labor force participation rate	Life expectancy	Per capita gross domestic product
Economically developing (Ram, 1984)	101 countries, about 1970	Labor force participation rate	Life expectancy	Per capita gross domestic product
India (Rosenzweig & Schultz, 1982)	295 rural districts, 1961	Employment rate	Estimated child survival from about ages 2–7	Farm characteristics, % rural, education, religion, castes
International (II) (Preston, 1976)	40 countries, 1960–1964	Sex difference in nonagricultural labor force participation	Differences between observed sex differential in age-adjusted mortality and expected sex differential, given the mortality level	Multiple measures of education, health care, nutrition, housing, income, % rural
Economically developed (II) (Pampel & Zimmer, 1989)	18 countries, 1950–1980	% of labor force that is female	Difference between observed sex differential in life expectancy and expected sex differential, given the level of life expectancy	Per capita gross national product, MDs and cigarette consumption, % calories from animal sources, Gini coefficient of income inequality, sex difference tertiary school enrollment

B. Associations between Labor Force Participation Rates and Longevity[c]

	Study	Female labor force participation rate	Male labor force participation rate	Female relative to male labor force participation
Female longevity	Belgium	+	+	
	Sweden	0	0	
Male longevity	U.S. (II)[d]	−	+	
	Belgium	0	+	
	Sweden[d]	+	+	
Female relative to male longevity	U.S.(I)	+	−	
	Belgium	0 (almost significant +)	0 (almost significant −)	
	International (I)	+	0	
	Economically developed (I)	0	−	
	Economically developing	+	0	
	India[d]	+	0	
	International (II)			0
	Economically developed (II)			+

[a]Roman numerals identify different studies in the same geographical area.

[b]Although this study reports multiple regressions with controls, the results of these analyses are not considered here because it appears that they were subject to considerable statistical problems due to multicollinearity.

[c]A + indicates a positive association between the labor force measure and the longevity measure with $p \leq .05$; a − indicates an inverse association with $p \leq .05$; 0 indicates no significant association. One additional study suggests positive associations between women's employment and female and male longevity and between men's employment and female longevity, but this study is not included here because no tests of statistical significance are available for these analyses (Anson, 1988).

[d]For these studies, signs from the original analyses have been reversed, because the analysis used a measure of mortality rather than longevity (for Sweden and U.S.) [II] or because the analysis used a measure of male survival advantage rather than female survival advantage (for India).

However, analyses of individual-level data for each of 10 Asian countries have shown no significant relationship between mother's work history and sex differences in mortality for infants or young children (Weinberger & Heligman, 1987). One possible interpretation is that the effect of women's employment on sex differences in child survival is primarily an ecological-level phenomenon and not an individual-level phenomenon. It may be that, historically, women's economic roles have influenced cultural beliefs and practices concerning differential care of female and male children, and this ecological-level phenomenon may be more important than any immediate effect of maternal employment on differential care and survival of daughters and sons. Another possible interpretation is that methodological problems, such as confounding in ecological-level analyses, may be responsible for the apparent discrepancy between findings from individual-level and ecological analyses (Greenland & Morgenstern, 1989; Richardson *et al.*, 1987).

CONCLUSIONS

Labor force participation has a variety of harmful and beneficial effects on health. The balance between harmful and beneficial health effects varies for different occupations. Thus, the widespread sex differences in labor force participation rates and occupations would be expected to influence sex differences in mortality and morbidity. The evidence reviewed in this chapter supports several conclusions concerning the effects of sex differences in labor force participation and occupation on sex differences in health.

More men than women are employed in hazardous occupations, and men's greater exposure to work accidents, carcinogens, and other occupational hazards appears to be responsible for roughly 5%–10% of excess male mortality in the contemporary United States. There is little support for the hypothesis that sex differences in labor force participation contribute to sex differences in risky behaviors, such as smoking, that have been major causes of men's higher mortality. However, it may be that traditional sex differences in economic roles contributed to the cultural evolution of social pressures against smoking and drinking by women and thus sex differences in labor force participation may have contributed indirectly to sex differences in mortality.

Two types of analyses have attempted to assess the overall effects of labor force participation on women's health, men's health, and sex differences in health. Analyses of individual-level longitudinal data indicate that, on the average, labor force participation does not have harmful effects on health, at least for middle-aged or older women in contemporary economically developed countries. Indeed, it appears that for some subgroups, such as unmarried women, labor force participation may have beneficial effects on health.

Ecological-level analyses indicate that higher female labor force participation rates are generally correlated with a greater longevity advantage for females. Given the substantial methodological problems with ecological analyses, this finding cannot be interpreted as evidence that women's labor force participation increases their longevity advantage. However, the findings from the ecological-level analyses, taken together with the findings from the analyses of individual-level longitudinal data, support the conclusion that in contemporary economically developed countries increases in women's labor force participation rates do not reduce females' longevity advantage.

In conclusion, current evidence indicates that men's employment in more hazardous occupations makes a modest contribution to men's higher mortality. However, women's labor force participation does not appear to harm their health or reduce their longevity advantage. Due to methodological problems and limited evidence it is not possible at present to make a quantitative estimate of the overall effects of sex differences in labor force participation and occupation on sex differences in mortality and morbidity.

REFERENCES

Anson, J. (1988). Mortality and living conditions. *Social Science and Medicine, 27*, 901–910.

Asp, S., Hernberg, S., & Collan, Y. (1979). Mortality among Finnish doctors, 1953–1972. *Scandinavian Journal of Social Medicine, 7*, 55–62.

Brackbill, R., Frazier, T., & Shilling, S. (1988). Smoking characteristics of U.S. workers, 1978–1980. *American Journal of Industrial Medicine, 13*, 5–41.

Carmelli, D., Swan, G. E., & Rosenman, R. H. (1985). The relationship between wives' social and psychologic status and their husbands' coronary heart disease. *American Journal of Epidemiology, 122*, 90–100.

Casscells, W., Hennekens, C. H., Evans, D., Rosener, B., De Silva, R., Lown, B., Davies, J. E., & Jesse, M. J. (1980). Retirement and coronary mortality. *Lancet* (June 14), 1288–1289.

Das Gupta, M. (1987). Selective discrimination against female children in rural Punjab, India. *Population and Development Review, 13*, 77–100.

Detre, K., Feinleib, M., Matthews, K. A., & Kerr, B. W. (1987). The federal women's study. In E. D. Eaker, B. Packard, N. K. Wenger, T. B. Clarkson, & H. A. Tyroler (Eds.), *Coronary heart disease in women: Proceedings of an N. I. H. Workshop* (pp. 78–82). New York: Haymarket Doyma.

Ekerdt, D. J., Baden, L., Bosse, R., & Dibbs, E. (1983). The effect of retirement on physical health. *American Journal of Public Health, 73*, 779–783.

Goodman, L. J. (1975). The longevity and mortality of American physicians, 1969–1973. *Milbank Memorial Fund Quarterly, 53*, 353–375.

Greenland, S., & Morgenstern, H. (1989). Ecological bias, confounding, and effect modification. *International Journal of Epidemiology, 18*, 269–274.

Haavio-Mannila, E. (1986). Inequalities in health and gender. *Social Science and Medicine, 22*, 141–149.

Haynes, S. G., Eaker, E. D., & Feinleib, M. (1983). Spouse behavior and coronary heart disease in men: Prospective results from the Framingham Heart Study, Part I. Concordance of risk factors and the relationship of psychosocial status to coronary incidence. *American Journal of Epidemiology, 118*, 1–22.

Haynes, S. G., Eaker, E. D., & Feinleib, M. (1984). The effect of employment, family, and job stress on coronary heart disease patterns in women. In E. B. Gold (Ed.), *The changing risk of disease in women: An epidemiologic approach* (pp. 37–48). Lexington, MA: Heath.

Higginson, J., & Muir, C. S. (1979). Environmental carcinogenesis. *Journal of National Cancer Institute, 63*, 1291–1298.

Kotler, P., & Wingard, D. L. (1989). The effect of occupational, marital and parental roles on mortality: The Alameda County Study. *American Journal of Public Health, 79*, 607–612.

Kraus, J. F. (1985). Fatal and nonfatal injuries in occupational settings: A review. *Annual Review of Public Health, 6*, 403–418.

Leigh, J. P. (1988). Odds ratios of work-related deaths in United States workers. *British Journal of Industrial Medicine, 45*, 158–166.

Linn, M. W., Sandifer, R., & Stein, S. (1985). Effects of unemployment on mental and physical health. *American Journal of Public Health, 75*, 502–506.

Lopez, A. D., & Ruzicka, L. T. (Eds.). (1983). *Sex differentials in mortality.* Canberra: Australian National University, Demography Department.

Minkler, M. (1981). Research on the health effects of retirement: An uncertain legacy. *Journal of Health and Social Behavior, 22*, 117–130.

Moser, K. A., Fox, A. J., & Jones, D. R. (1984). Unemployment and mortality in the OPCS longitudinal study. *Lancet*, December 8, 1324–1329.

National Center for Health Statistics. (1986). Current estimates from the National Health Interview Survey, U. S., 1985. *Vital and Health Statistics*, Series 10, No. 160.

National Center for Health Statistics. (1987). Advance report of final mortality statistics, 1985. *Monthly Vital Statistics Report* 36, No. 5, Supplement.

National Center for Health Statistics. (1988). Annual summary of births, marriages, divorces and deaths; U. S., 1987. *Monthly Vital Statistics Report* 36, No. 13.

Palmore, E. B., Burchett, B. M., Fillenbaum, G. G., George, L. K., & Wallman, L. M. (1985). *Retirement—Causes and consequences.* New York: Springer.

Pampel, F. C., & Zimmer, C. (1989). Female labor force activity and the sex differential in mortality: Comparisons across developed nations, 1950-1980. *European Journal of Population, 5*, 281–304.

Passanante, M. R., & Nathanson, C. A. (1987). Women in the labor force: Are sex mortality differentials changing? *Journal of Occupational Medicine, 29*, 21–28.

Piantadosi, S., Byar, D. P., & Green, S. B. (1988). The ecological fallacy. *American Journal of Epidemiology, 127*, 893–904.

POLIWA. (1977). *Etat demographique de la Wallonie et elements pour une politique de population.* Rapport POLIWA. Universite Catholique de Louvain, Departement de Demographie.

Preston, S. H. (1976). *Mortality patterns in national populations.* New York: Academic Press.

Ram, R. (1984). Market opportunities, intrafamily resource allocation, and sex-specific survival rates: An intercountry extension. *American Economic Review, 74*, 1080–1086.

Repetti, R. L., Matthews, K. A., & Waldron, I. (1989). Effects of paid employment on women's mental and physical health. *American Psychologist, 44,* 1394–1401.

Retherford, R. D. (1975). *The changing sex differential in mortality: Studies in population and urban demography #1.* Westport, CT: Greenwood Press.

Richardson, S., Stucker, I., & Hemon, D. (1987). Comparison of relative risks obtained in ecological and individual studies: Some methodological considerations. *International Journal of Epidemiology, 16,* 111–120.

Robinson, J. C. (1984). Racial inequality and the probability of occupation-related injury or illness. *Milbank Memorial Fund Quarterly, 62,* 567–590.

Roos, P. A. (1985). *Gender and work: A comparative analysis of industrial societies.* Albany: State University of New York Press.

Rosenzweig, M. R., & Schultz, T. P. (1982). Market opportunities, genetic endowments, and intrafamily resource distribution: Child survival in rural India. *American Economic Review, 72,* 803–815.

Sauer, H. I., & Donnell, H. D. (1970). Age and geographic differences in death rates. *Journal of Gerontology, 25,* 83–86.

Sorensen, G., & Verbrugge, L. M. (1987). Women, work and health. *Annual Review of Public Health, 8,* 235–251.

South, S. J., & Trent, K. (1988). Sex ratios and women's roles: A cross-national analysis. *American Journal of Sociology, 93,* 1096–1115.

Starrin, B., Larsson, G., & Brenner, S. (1988). Regional variations in cardiovascular mortality in Sweden. *Social Science and Medicine, 27,* 911–917.

Stout-Wiegand, N. (1988). Fatal occupational injuries in US industries, 1984. *American Journal of Public Health, 78,* 1215–1217.

United Nations, Department of International Economic and Social Affairs. (1982). *Levels and trends of mortality since 1950.* New York: United Nations, Sales No. E.81.XII.3.

United Nations Secretariat. (1988). Sex differentials in survivorship in the developing world: Levels, regional patterns and demographic determinants. *Population Bulletin of the United Nations, 25,* 51–64.

U.S. Department of Health and Human Services. (1980). *The health consequences of smoking for women: A report of the Surgeon General.* Rockville, MD: U.S. Dept. HHS.

U.S. Department of Health and Human Services. (1985a). *Vital Statistics of the United States, 1980: Vol. II—Mortality.* Hyattsville, MD: U. S. Dept. HHS.

U.S. Department of Health and Human Services. (1985b). *The health consequences of smoking— Cancer and chronic lung disease in the workplace: A report of the Surgeon General.* Rockville, MD: U.S. Dept. HHS.

U.S. Department of Health and Human Services. (1986). Advance report of final mortality statistics, 1984. *NCHS Monthly Vital Statistics Report, 35* (No. 6, Supplement 2): 1–44.

Verbrugge, L. M. (1985). Gender and health: An update on hypotheses and evidence. *Journal of Health and Social Behavior, 26,* 156–182.

Waldron, I. (1980). Employment and women's health. *International Journal of Health Services, 10,* 435–454.

Waldron, I. (1982). An analysis of causes of sex differences in mortality and morbidity. *In* W. R. Gove & G. R. Carpenter (Eds.), *The fundamental connection between nature and nurture* (pp. 69–116). Lexington, MA: Lexington Books.

Waldron, I. (1983). Sex differences in illness incidence, prognosis and mortality: Issues and evidence. *Social Science and Medicine, 17,* 1107–1123.

Waldron, I. (1986a). What do we know about causes of sex differences in mortality? A review of the literature. *Population Bulletin of the United Nations,* No. 18-1985: 59–76.

Waldron, I. (1986b). The contribution of smoking to sex differences in mortality. *Public Health Reports, 101*, 163–173.

Waldron, I. (1987). Patterns and causes of excess female mortality among children in developing countries. *World Health Statistics Quarterly, 40*, 194–210.

Waldron, I. (1988). Gender and health-related behavior. In D. S. Gochman (Ed.), *Health behavior: Emerging research perspectives* (pp. 193–208). New York: Plenum.

Waldron, I. (in press). Patterns and causes of gender differences in smoking. *Social Science and Medicine.*

Waldron, I., & Jacobs, J. (1988). Effects of labor force participation on women's health: New evidence from a longitudinal study. *Journal of Occupational Medicine, 30*, 977–983.

Waldron, I., & Jacobs, J. (1989). Effects of multiple roles on women's health: Evidence from a national longitudinal study. *Women and Health, 15*, 3–19.

Waldron, I., & Lye, D. (1989). Employment, unemployment, occupation and smoking. *American Journal of Preventive Medicine, 5*, 142–149.

Wan, T. T. H. (1982). *Stressful life events, social-support networks and gerontological health.* Lexington, MA: Lexington Books.

Weinberger, M. B., & Heligman, L. (1987). Do social and economic variables differentially affect male and female child mortality? Paper presented at the 1987 Annual Meeting of the Population Association of America, Chicago.

Wingard, D. L. (1984). The sex differential in morbidity, mortality, and lifestyle. *Annual Review of Public Health, 5*, 433–458.

3

The Psychophysiology of Sex Differences as Related to Occupational Status

MARIANNE FRANKENHAEUSER

This chapter is based on research carried out in the author's laboratory during the past decades (see reviews by Frankenhaeuser 1979, 1983, 1986). The central theme of the chapter is the study of the mechanisms by which psychosocial factors influence the health and behavior of men and women. The approach is multidisciplinary, focusing on the dynamics of stressful person–environment interactions, viewed from social, psychological, and biomedical perspectives.

A BIOPSYCHOSOCIAL FRAMEWORK

Research on stress and coping has become a meeting place for several disciplines concerned with health and behavior. New avenues for research have been opened by advances in biomedical techniques that permit ambulatory recording of bodily responses under conditions of daily life. It is now possible to monitor people's reactions during work without interfering with their ordinary activities. (See Chapter 9, this volume.)

One of the notions underlying the use of biomedical recording techniques in working life is that the impact of specific factors in the

MARIANNE FRANKENHAEUSER • Karolinska Institute, Department of Psychiatry and Psychology, Stockholm University, S-106 91 Stockholm, Sweden.

environment can be determined by measuring the activity of the body's organ systems. Thus, functional assessments can be obtained of various organ systems that are controlled by the brain and reflect its level of activation.

The biopsychosocial model depicted in Figure 1 provides a strategy for identifying stress-inducing environmental factors and analyzing their influence on health, well-being, and efficiency at the individual level. A key concept in the model is cognitive assessment: when the individual is challenged by environmental demands, he or she appraises their nature and strength. This cognitive appraisal process involves weighing the importance and the severity of the demands against one's own coping abilities. Any stimulus or situation that is perceived as a threat to something one values or as a challenge requiring effort generates signals from the brain's cortex to the hypothalamus and, via the autonomic nervous system, to the adrenal medulla. This gland responds by putting out epinephrine and norepinephrine. These two catecholamines, often referred to as stress hormones, mobilize bodily "fight or flight" responses. Along another route the brain sends messages via the hypothalamus to the

A biopsychosocial model

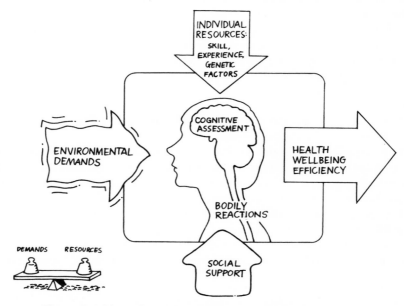

Figure 1. A biopsychosocial model for stress–health interactions.

adrenal cortex, which secretes corticosteroids, for example, cortisol, which plays an important part in the body's immune defense. This route involves the release of the adrenocorticotropic hormone (ACTH) from the pituitary gland.

New techniques for the determination of catecholamines and cortisol in blood and in urine have stimulated novel approaches to stress and health problems. These hormones serve important adaptive functions, but when secreted excessively they may be harmful, particularly in promoting cardiovascular pathology. Hence, their measurement plays a twofold role in stress research. First, measurements help to assess the impact of a particular environment on a person, pinpointing aversive as well as protective factors. Second, measurements of these hormones serve as early warnings of long-term health risks. For both these reasons the study of these biological mediators plays a key role in early intervention and prevention of health damage at the workplace.

The biopsychosocial model also provides a framework for the study of sex differences in stress and coping. Within this framework, sex differences in environmental exposure can be analyzed separately from sex differences in mediating and outcome variables. The mediating variables include genetic as well as learned individual characteristics such as values, attitudes, personality factors, and psychophysiological reactivity. They also include social support systems. The interaction of all these influences determines the outcome in terms of health, well-being, and efficiency.

CHANGING PATTERNS OF SEX DIFFERENCES IN REACTIVITY

The biopsychosocial model emphasizes the influence of a person's attitudes and values on bodily stress responses. This means that sex differences in values will be reflected on the physiological level and that *changes* in values will be manifested in physiological indicators of stress. When, for example, men and women become more alike in their judgments of what is important in life and worth fighting for, their physiological stress reactions will also become more similar. The fact that these reactions are similar is evident today as women enter traditionally male occupations. The changing patterns of women's stress responses will be illustrated in this chapter by comparing results from our early sex difference studies with more recent data.

The most striking and most consistent sex difference in stress response demonstrated in our laboratory during the 1970s was the finding that women were less prone than men to respond to achievement demands with increased epinephrine secretion. During rest and relaxation sex differences in catecholamine output were found to be slight (provided body weight was taken into account), but challenging performance situations elicited consistent differences, particularly in epinephrine secretion. (See reviews by Frankenhaeuser, 1988, 1983; Collins, 1985.)

Figure 2 summarizes data from different studies, each pair of bars showing the epinephrine output of male and female subjects in a stress situation, expressed as a percentage of the value obtained for each sex at the same time of day under similar baseline conditions, where sex differences were slight. In the studies represented in Figure 2 stress was induced by intelligence testing (Johansson & Post, 1974), a color–word conflict task, venous puncture (Frankenhaeuser, Dunne, & Lundberg, 1976), and an arithmetic task (Johansson, Frankenhaeuser, & Magnusson, 1973). The common characteristic of all these situations was the absence of an epinephrine increase during stress in the female subjects and, in contrast, the pronounced rise in the male subjects. The picture was similar for norepinephrine although the sex differences were much less marked and did not reach statistical significance. The age range of the subjects in these studies was 13 to 35 years.

It is important to note that the absolute amount of catecholamines excreted increases from infancy to adulthood whereas in relation to body surface area catecholamine excretion remains about the same over the life cycle (de Schaepdryver, Hooft, Delbeke, & van den Noortgaete, 1978). Results obtained on 3- to 6-year-old children studied during play activities at a day-care center and in their home setting (Lundberg, 1983) showed that epinephrine excretion was significantly higher in the boys under both conditions. Thus, sex differences in reactivity appear early in life. (See Maccoby's chapter, this volume, on sex differences in children's play styles.)

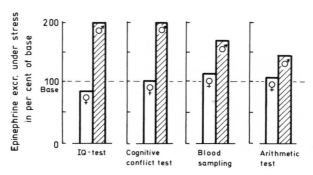

Figure 2. Epinephrine excretion (expressed as a percentage of baseline level) in male and female groups during various stress situations.

The situations depicted in Figure 2 represent a mild degree of stress. We wanted to find out how male and female subjects respond when exposed to more severe stress situations (Frankenhaeuser, Rauste-von Wright, Collins, von Wright, Sedvall, & Swahn, 1978). Results obtained in a study of students undergoing a challenging examination (Figure 3) showed that the sex difference in epinephrine excretion was much less pronounced than under the less severe stress conditions shown in Figure 2. Under intense achievement stress the females did increase their epinephrine excretion to a significant degree although the rise for the males was still significantly greater. The pattern was similar for cortisol.

In these experiments, catecholamines were determined fluorometrically in urine. The picture with regard to sex differences was the same when plasma catecholamines were determined by a radioenzymatic technique (Forsman & Lindblad, 1983).

It is important to note that the female subjects performed at least as well as the male subjects in all of the situations depicted in Figures 2 and 3; insofar as there were any sex differences in performance, they were in favor of the female subjects.

The fact that women are less reactive than men in terms of catecholamine secretion when faced with the pressure to achieve may mean that they have a more "economic" way of coping, so that their "cost" of adapting to achievement demands could, in fact, be lower. This leads to the speculation that the greater vulnerability of men to coronary heart disease could be related to their more intense and more frequent neuroendocrine stress responses (see Frankenhaeuser, 1983). This, in turn, prompts the

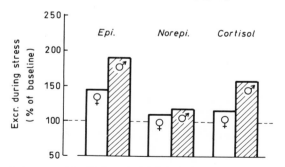

Figure 3. Epinephrine, norepinephrine, and cortisol excretion in male and female high school students during a matriculation examination, expressed as percentages of values obtained during a day of ordinary schoolwork. (Based on Frankenhaeuser *et al.*, 1978.)

question of to what extent sex differences are genetically determined and to what extent they are learned.

Insofar as genetic factors are involved, possible hypotheses are that estrogens inhibit or that androgens facilitate catecholamine secretion. This question was addressed in collaboration with gynecologists and endocrinologists. Results from a study of postmenopausal women exposed to the same performance demands before and after estrogen replacement therapy (Collins, Hanson, Eneroth, Hagenfeldt, Lundberg, & Frankenhaeuser, 1982) indicates that estrogens do not markedly modify the neuroendocrine stress responses. The same appears to hold for androgens, as shown in a study of stress responses of women with hirsutism and oligomenorrhea before and after anti-androgen therapy (Lundberg, Hanson, Eneroth, Frankenhaeuser, & Hagenfeldt, 1984). In other words, no support was obtained for the assumption that interactions between sex hormones and stress hormones account for the sex differences in reactivity.

Differences between the sexes in reactivity patterns that may be influenced by social factors are likely to be reduced as the social roles of men and women become more similar. We approached this problem by studying women who had entered traditional male occupations, the hypothesis being that these women would tend to exhibit the psychoendocrine stress responses typical of men. The results showed that, on the whole, these "nontraditional" women tended to respond to achievement demands by almost as sharp an increase in epinephrine secretion as that of men. This is illustrated (Figure 4) by a laboratory experiment in which male and female engineering students were exposed to a color-word conflict task (Collins & Frankenhaeuser, 1978). The students had been chosen from the most male-dominated study courses (e.g., metallurgy and

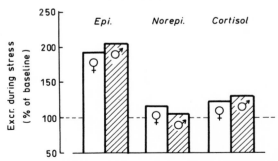

Figure 4. Epinephrine, norepinephrine, and cortisol excretion in male and female engineering students during a color–word conflict task. (Based on Collins & Frankenhaeuser, 1978.)

electromechanics). The results showed that epinephrine and cortisol secretion increased during stress exposure to nearly the same degree in the female and male students.

The same picture was seen in bus drivers and lawyers while they were engaged in their daily work (Rissler, 1985), the participants being selected so that the men and women in each occupation had work situations as similar as possible.

While these results highlight the influence of social factors on reactivity, they do not rule out genetic influences. The similarities between the sexes in the occupational groups studied might arise from these particular women being constitutionally like men in terms of responding to achievement demands; this may be why they have chosen a male work role. Alternatively, these women could have been "shaped" by their occupational role.

The next step in our analysis was to change the nature of the demand. All situations considered so far had challenged the traditional male field of competence, which emphasizes asserting oneself, achieving, and producing. We now wanted to test the hypothesis that women are more vulnerable than men when challenged in areas in which they, by tradition, are expected show more competence. The emphasis here is on social skills such as the ability to maintain harmonious relationships between people. We had the opportunity to perform a well-controlled study within the traditional female sphere of family and children (Lundberg, de Chateau, Winberg, & Frankenhaeuser, 1981), comparing mothers and fathers who took their 3-year-old child to a hospital for a medical checkup. In this demanding but noncompetitive situation the women secreted as much epinephrine, norepinephrine, and cortisol as the men (Figure 5). These results show that interpersonal confrontations are effective triggers of stress responses in women and support the hypothesis that psychosocial factors are powerful determinants of psychoendocrine stress responses.

STRESS ON AND OFF THE JOB
IN WHITE-COLLAR WORKERS AT VOLVO

The changing neuroendocrine reactivity patterns of women entering men's occupations combined with the fact that increasing professional involvement does not seem to reduce involvement in home and family raises important questions about the stress related to women's multiple roles and its possible health consequences. Will the stresses and strains from different roles add up? Or will the awards and satisfaction from one role modulate and reduce the stress from another? (See Chapter 6.)

ARRIVAL AT HOSPITAL (10 a.m.)

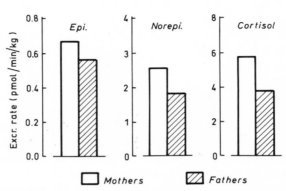

Figure 5. Epinephrine, norepinephrine, and cortisol excretion in mothers and fathers arriving at a hospital for a medical checkup of their 3-year-old child. (Based on Lundberg *et al.*, 1981.)

We decided to apply our biopsychosocial approach to studying men and women exposed to specific demands related to their occupational role. The study, part of which will be reviewed here, was carried out at Volvo in Gothenburg. (For a detailed account see Frankenhaeuser, Lundberg, Fredrikson, Melin, Tuomisto, Myrsten, Bergman-Losman, Hedman, & Wallin, 1989.)

Participants

Sixty white-collar employees, ages 30–50, volunteered as participants. There were four groups: 15 male and 15 female managers, 15 male and 15 female clerical workers. They all fulfilled the following criteria for inclusion in the study: full-time employment (40 hours/week) and feeling healthy and not suffering from any disease requiring treatment with beta-blockers or diuretics (which are known to affect the variables to be studied, namely, excretion of catecholamines and blood pressure). For the same reason, smokers were excluded as well as diabetics and pregnant women.

All but four of the participants were or had been married. The typical family had two children. Seven participants had no children; five of these were female managers.

All subjects had been employed in the company for at least 5 years. The managers' position was that of middle manager, in charge of a staff of 5 to 10. Male managers were primarily concerned with production and construction whereas female managers were involved in administration, finance, and personnel. In the nonmanagerial groups, most of the women worked as secretaries whereas the men held a variety of jobs commonly involving service and maintenance.

General Design

Each subject was examined individually for 12 consecutive hours under each of two conditions: (1) during a normal day at work (9 A.M.– 5 P.M.) and after work (6 P.M.–9 P.M.) and (2) for the same time period during work-free conditions at home. Measurements at home were performed one week after those at work to obtain physiological baseline values. Blood pressure and heart rate were recorded once every hour. Self-reports of mental state and urine samples for the determination of catecholamines and cortisol were obtained every second hour.

Measurements at work were made on a "normal" work day. The work-free day at home was at the company's expense and did not affect the employees' salaries. The participants were asked to spend the day relaxing, reading magazines, and listening to music. Four months later all participants took part in a laboratory stress experiment. They were also given a videotaped Type A interview, a medical checkup including blood lipid determination, a semistructured interview, and questionnaires covering the following areas:

- Causes and expressions of stress, ways of coping
- Autonomy and control, attitudes toward work and leadership, social support at work and outside work
- Total work load, including demands from the paid work as well as from family, household, and role conflicts
- Masculine and feminine personality traits

Results from the Interviews

The four groups had similar views about many aspects of stress and work, with positive attitudes predominating. Each group, however, had its specific characteristics, as illustrated in the following paragraphs.

Managers of both sexes reported heavy work load, time pressure, deadlines, and responsibility for others as stressful. They considered their work stimulating and independent but expressed a wish for more appreciation.

Women managers, more often than men, mentioned lack of communication at work as a source of stress. They reported finding it hard to convey their opinions to superiors. One-third stated that they have to perform better than their male colleagues to be judged as equals. Women managers emphasized "inner" values of their work such as an interesting job, good relationships, and so forth. They felt they were entitled to information concerning work (e.g., information about changes planned by management with regard to organization, new technology, personnel, etc.) and a better work organization.

"There are not enough hours in the day," "I neglect my friends," "Work intrudes on my time with my children," were common complaints of stress outside the workplace. Of the four groups the women managers reported experiencing the strongest conflict between work and family.

The male managers reported the heaviest work load as well as the highest work satisfaction. They tended to feel able to influence their work conditions and experienced little difficulty conveying opinions not shared by others. In contrast to other groups they felt that top management would listen to them. When under stress the male managers seemed to try harder than female managers to conceal their feelings, a sex difference noted in the nonmanagerial groups as well. While the male managers reported experiencing conflicts between work and home occasionally, it seemed a much smaller problem for them than for their female colleagues (see Chapter 5).

The clerical workers too experienced deadlines and heavy work load as sources of stress. In contrast to the managers, however, they mentioned lack of influence, too much routine, and too simple tasks as causes of stress. They regretted missing opportunities to develop new skills.

Like the female managers, the female clerical workers reported a feeling of having to perform better than the men to be considered as equals. But on the whole they enjoyed their jobs. A higher proportion than in any other group reported seeking support from a fellow worker or from their partner at home when under stress. They did not feel torn between work and home although, like the female managers, they felt they neglected their friends because of their heavy work load.

Male clerical workers too were largely positive towards their jobs, but according to the interviews their work satisfaction was relatively lower than that of the other groups. They viewed their superiors positively but expressed a wish for better relationships with top management. Only a few of the male clerical workers felt stressed by their duties at home, and they reported spending more time with their children than any other group.

Autonomy at Work

As expected, the male and female managers experienced more autonomy at work than the two clerical groups, as measured by seven self-report scales (Figure 6). The differences between managers and clerical workers were particularly marked on the subscales for "variety," "the chance to

AUTONOMY AT WORK

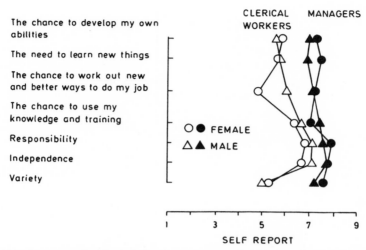

Figure 6. Self-reports of male and female managers and clerical workers on seven scales measuring autonomy at work. (Based on Frankenhaeuser *et al.*, 1989.)

work out better ways to do my job," "the need to learn new things," and "the chance to develop my own abilities." The sexes did not differ significantly in terms of the autonomy experienced at work.

Social Support

The results of self-reports of nine aspects of social support at the work place are shown in Figure 7. The larger the shaded area in each of the four diagrams, the stronger the support experienced at the workplace. With respect to social support the women clerical workers were far better off than any other group. The female managers did not have the support of a strong network. Had they lost the support of fellow workers on their way up the organization, and if so, how can this be restored? One of the chief complaints of the women managers was that nobody listens to them and that they have no means of communicating with higher level managers.

Total Work Load

The concept of total work load refers to the combined load of demands related to paid work and unpaid work (mostly family and

SOCIAL SUPPORT ON THE JOB

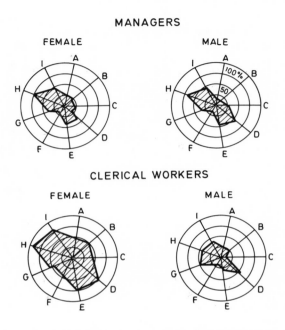

A. People cooperate very well within my own department

B. I have very much confidence in my immediate superiors.

C. A place of work where I feel people care about me as a person.

D. A job with good relations to my immediate superior.

E. A job that allows me to work with people I like.

F. A job where good work receives recognition.

G. Feel I can talk to my supervisor about difficulties at work.

H. People really care about me at work.

I. Not treated badly in any way.

Figure 7. Self-reports of social support at work. Scores represent the percentage of male and female managers and clerical workers agreeing to each statement. The dark area in each diagram depicts the total amount of social support reported by the group. (Based on Frankenhaeuser *et al.*, 1989.)

household). In a questionnaire (revised version of an instrument constructed in collaboration with Matthews and Johnson, 1987) the participants rated how the main responsibility was shared for different duties at home. Figure 8, in which data from managers and clerical workers have been combined, shows that the women carried the main responsibility for laundry, shopping, cooking, sewing and mending, daily cleaning and

TOTAL WORKLOAD
WHO CARRIES THE MAIN RESPONSIBILITY ?

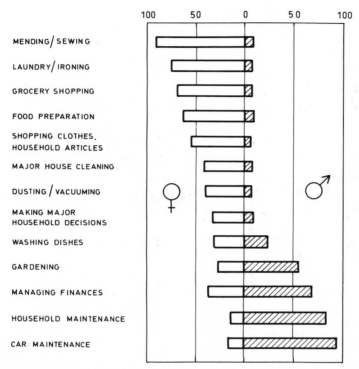

Figure 8. Percent of male and female subjects reporting carrying the main responsibility for different duties at home. (Based on Frankenhaeuser *et al.*, 1989.)

major house cleaning, whereas the men were responsible for the car and household maintenance, as well as finance and gardening. Thus, the division of labor followed the traditional pattern. Not only were women responsible for a greater number of activities at home but the nature of their responsibilities was such that their duties (e.g., cooking) had to be performed daily at a fixed time, whereas men's duties (e.g., managing money and fixing the car) had more flexibility (see Chapter 4).

The general picture was the same for managers and nonmanagers. However, combining the paid and unpaid work was more of a burden for the women managers, as shown (Figure 9) by answers to the question, How much does work outside paid work contribute to your total work load?

HOW MUCH DOES WORK OUTSIDE PAID
WORK CONTRIBUTE TO THE TOTAL WORKLOAD?

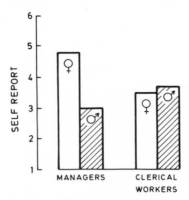

Figure 9. Self-reports of male and female managers and clerical workers of how much duties outside paid work contribute to their total work load (1 = very little; 7 = very much). (Based on Frankenhaeuser *et al.*, 1989.)

While the female clerical workers spent more hours in unpaid work than any other group, the female managers felt more torn between demands related to their profession and their family. "I wish I could split in two" is one of the expressions they used in interviews to describe their conflict.

Following the Volvo study the total work load questionnaire was developed further and given to 533 male and 551 female white-collar workers from different occupations (Mårdberg, Lundberg, & Frankenhaeuser, in press). The results confirm that it is the women managers who carry the heaviest total work load (Frankenhaeuser, Lundberg, & Mårdberg, submitted).

Androgyny and Competitiveness

According to self-estimates of masculine and feminine traits (as measured by a Swedish version of the Bem Sex Role Inventory), the women managers had an "androgynous profile," showing personality characteristics considered typical of men as well as characteristics typical of women. The women managers' masculinity scores were as high as those of their male colleagues and somewhat higher than the scores of the male clerical workers (Frankenhaeuser, 1989).

In line with this, women managers had the highest scores on Type A behavior (Figure 10), as determined by a videotaped structured interview

TYPE A BEHAVIOR

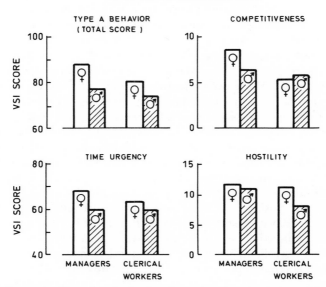

Figure 10. Scores for Type A behavior (total score) and each of three subcomponents (competitiveness, time urgency, hostility) in male and female managers and clerical workers. Scores were obtained by a videotaped structured interview (VSI). (Based on Frankenhaeuser *et al.*, 1989.)

(VSI) (Burell, Öhman, Ramund, Axelsson, & Fleischmann, 1991). Two observers made independent ratings of the VSI according to 35 criteria. On the subscale Competitiveness the difference between the women managers and the other groups reached significance. (For a detailed account see Lundberg, Hedman, Melin, & Frankenhaeuser, 1989a.)

Blood Pressure and Blood Lipids

The medical examination confirmed that all participants were in good health. All groups had normal blood pressure (systolic < 160 mm Hg, diastolic < 95 mm Hg). In agreement with established norms men had higher systolic pressure and lower heart rate than women under all conditions. (For details concerning group differences, see Frankenhaeuser *et al.*, 1989; Lundberg, Fredrikson, Wallin, Melin, & Frankenhaeuser, 1989b.)

Blood lipid values were within or close to the Swedish reference levels.

In agreement with these norms, men had higher low density lipoprotein (LDL) and lower high density lipoprotein (HDL) cholesterol than women. This was true when average values for male managers and nonmanagers were compared with the corresponding values for females. When managers and nonmanagers were analyzed separately (Figure 11), the female managers were shown to have as high total cholesterol and almost as high LDL levels as each of the two male groups. This was not true of the female clerical workers, who, in accordance with established norms, had lower LDL and total cholesterol levels than the men. This difference between the two groups of women is noteworthy, since high LDL levels are assumed to increase the risk for coronary heart disease. In contrast, HDL cholesterol, which is assumed to have protective properties, was significantly higher in women than in men regardless of occupational status. This suggests that women managers, while in some respects more similar to men than women in subordinate positions, nevertheless may retain some of the protective physiological characteristics considered typical of women.

In this connection it is interesting that Type A behavior was found to be positively correlated with LDL cholesterol in men but not in women. Figure 12 shows that Type A men had significantly higher LDL values than

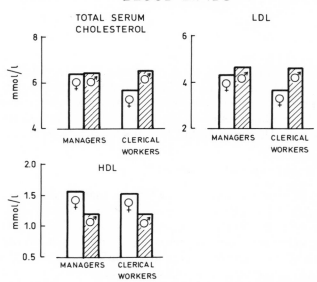

Figure 11. Serum cholesterol (total cholesterol, LDL and HDL cholesterol) in male and female managers and clerical workers. (Based on Frankenhaeuser *et al.*, 1989.)

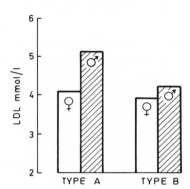

Figure 12. LDL cholesterol in Type A and Type B male and female employees. (Based on Lundberg *et al.*, 1989b.)

Type A women and Type B men and women. This may be interpreted as indicating that competitive women do not run the same health risks as do their male counterparts.

Psychosomatic Symptoms

Women reported significantly more psychosomatic symptoms than men, whereas there was no correlation between frequency of symptoms and occupational status. Figure 13 shows total scores (based on a questionnaire) for all men and all women, assessing gastrointestinal, musculoskeletal, cardiovascular, and mental symptoms over a 12-month period. (To

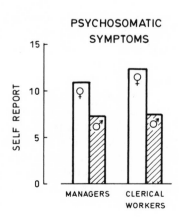

Figure 13. Self-reports of psychosomatic symptoms in men and women. (Based on Frankenhaeuser *et al.*, 1989.)

attain comparability between the sexes, symptoms in the female group associated with the menstrual cycle and menopause were excluded.) When age was taken into account, the sex difference was found to be due to the high frequency of symptoms in women above age 41. While psychosomatic symptoms and age were highly correlated in women, this was not the case in men, and below age 41 there was no difference between the sexes. Thus, the sex difference in psychosomatic symptoms was due entirely to the older women, who had twice as many symptoms as the younger women and all the men.

REACTIVITY AND "UNWINDING"

Since stress-induced increases in catecholamine output and blood pressure are regarded as risk factors for coronary heart disease, it is important to find out both how easily these arousal responses are triggered and how long they last. The underlying assumption here is that the more frequently these responses occur and the longer their duration, the greater will be the wear and tear on the cardiovascular system.

Stress exposure in the laboratory experiments that the Volvo employees underwent (for details see Lundberg, Melin, Fredrikson, Tuomisto, & Frankenhaeuser, 1990) provides an opportunity to compare reactivity patterns in the four groups of employees. As expected, the stress tests increased physiological arousal in all groups. Interactions between sex and occupation followed the same pattern as seen in our earlier studies (reviewed earlier this chapter). Thus, the women managers, in agreement with other groups of women in nontraditional occupations (engineers, bus drivers, and lawyers), exhibited a sharp rise in epinephrine output, similar to that of the two male groups. In contrast, the clerical women had a markedly weaker epinephrine response, typical of women in traditional roles. This is illustrated in Figure 14, which shows that while the epinephrine levels of the groups of women did not differ during resting conditions, the stress tests evoked a significantly larger response in the managerial group.

We may thus conclude that in acute stress situations women managers tend to be as reactive as men. This raises the question of how rapidly they unwind after a workday. Measurements taken at regular intervals during an ordinary day at work and during work-free conditions in the home environment showed moderate but consistent elevations of the arousal level of all groups at the workplace. (For a detailed account see Frankenhaeuser *et al.*, 1989.) This was expected and confirms earlier results. The interesting point was the "stress pattern" in the evening after work, when people are assumed to relax and unwind. Group comparisons showed marked sex

EPINEPHRINE EXCRETION

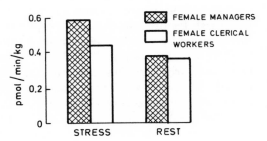

Figure 14. Epinephrine excretion in women managers and clerical workers during conditions of rest and laboratory-induced stress. (Based on Frankenhaeuser, 1989; Lundberg *et al.*, 1990.)

differences in the evening, particularly between female and male managers, as illustrated by the norepinephrine data presented in Figure 15. After 6 P.M. the male managers' norepinephrine level decreased sharply whereas the level in the female managers rose. Thus, according to this arousal indicator, the women managers tended to "wind up" in the evening while their male colleagues "wound down." Self-reports of tiredness and time pressure agreed with the physiological data. The picture was less clear for epinephrine, presumably because the marked diurnal variations in epinephrine release tend to obscure other influences.

CONCLUDING REMARKS

Until recently, knowledge about stress at work and its health consequences was based almost entirely on the study of men. Both epidemiological (e.g., Karasek, 1979; Kahn, 1981) and psychophysiological (e.g.,

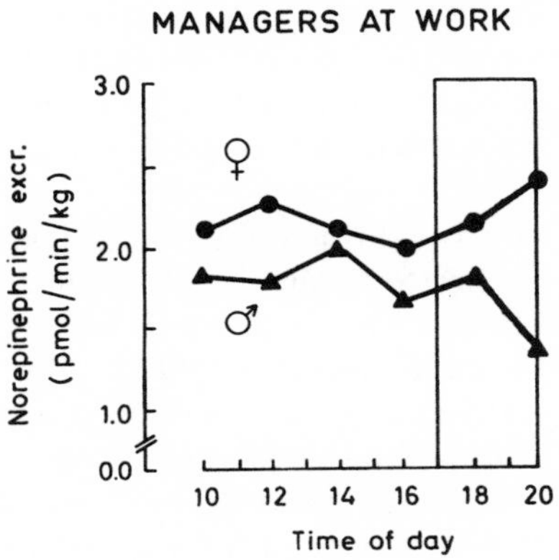

MANAGERS AT WORK

Figure 15. Norepinephrine excretion in male and female managers during and after a day at work. (Based on Frankenhaeuser *et al.*, 1989.)

Frankenhaeuser & Johansson, 1986) research identified work overload and underload, low autonomy, and poor social relations as major psychosocial risk factors. On the basis of psychophysiological studies, possible mechanisms by which stress can lead to health damage were identified (e.g., Frankenhaeuser, 1986). These mechanisms involve the neuroendocrine and cardiovascular reactions that are triggered by heavy work load, monotonous work, and low autonomy and are modulated as opportunities to exercise personal control increase.

The question now is whether, and to what extent, the results obtained in the study of men are valid for employed women. The research reviewed in this chapter points to sex similarities in some respects and differences in others. Psychophysiological studies of both sexes suggest that sex differences in acute stress responses as well as in more enduring functions (e.g., lipid metabolism) are diminishing as employment conditions and behavioral characteristics (e.g., competitiveness) become more similar. Likewise, personal control and social support have, in principle, the same buffering effect on both men and women.

However, there are major sex differences in stress exposure, that is, the demands and challenges to which men and women are exposed. The fact that the division of labor at home has remained essentially the same while women's employment situation has changed has led to a heavy total work load for employed women, as documented in several chapters in this volume (e.g., Chapters 4 and 5). (See also Lundberg & Palm, 1989.)

The Volvo study shows that the conflict between demands from paid work and duties at home is particularly strong among female managers (see Cooper & Davidson, 1982; Davidson & Cooper, 1983). The psychophysiological measurements, which are key components in our biopsychosocial approach, help to make these intrapersonal conflicts "visible." As already pointed out, rises in blood pressure and stress hormone release, when frequent and long-lasting, are believed to increase the risk for cardiovascular disease. Hence, the "slow unwinding" manifested in the women managers' high levels of stress hormones and blood pressure after a day at work illustrate how the use of psychophysiological techniques in research on working life can provide early warnings of long-term health risks.

In addition to personal control over the work situation, social support at the workplace is recognized as a strong buffer against harmful stress effects. This appears to be true, in particular, of women (Repetti, Matthews, & Waldron, 1989). The fact that the female managers at Volvo, unlike the women in subordinate positions, did not have the support of a strong network is also a matter of concern.

Finally, what do we know about the net effects on women's health of this multitude of interacting factors? In general, epidemiological studies (e.g., Baruch, Biener, & Barnett, 1987; Graves & Thomas, 1985; Waldron, Herold, Dunn, & Staum, 1982) do not show enhanced health risks in employed women (see also Chapter 2). Some studies draw attention to increased risks among certain groups of women (e.g., Alfredsson, Spetz, & Theorell, 1985; Chapter 10). In their recent review of research on effects of employment on women's health, Repetti *et al.* (1989) conclude that, on the average, the outcome is positive. The predominance of harmful as opposed to beneficial effects depends on factors such as the woman's martial status, her husband's contribution to home labor, her parental status, her attitude toward employment, and characteristics of her job.

The questions dealt with in this chapter have high priority today in the Scandinavian countries. Research-based knowledge provides arguments for the ongoing policy discussions about flexible working hours, division of labor at home, social support, and autonomy at work. The biopsychosocial approach opens up new possibilities to link these psychosocial issues to the occupational health of men and women.

ACKNOWLEDGMENTS

The research reviewed in this chapter was supported by grants from the Swedish Work Environment Fund, the J. D. & C. T. MacArthur Foundation Mental Health Network on Health and Behavior, the Swedish Medical Research Council, and the Swedish Council for Research in the Humanities and Social Sciences.

REFERENCES

Alfredsson, L., Spetz, C-L., & Theorell, T. (1985). Type of occupation and near-future hospitalization for myocardial infarction and some other diagnoses. *International Journal of Epidemiology, 14*, 378–388.

Baruch, G. K., Biener, L., & Barnett, R. C. (1987). Women and gender in research on work and family stress. *American Psychologist, 42*, 130–136.

Burell, G., Öhman, A., Ramund, B., Axelsson, Y., & Fleischmann, N. (1991). *Type A behavior in Sweden: Assessed by the videotaped structured interview.* Unpublished manuscript.

Collins, A. (1985). *Sex differences in psychoneuroendocrine stress responses: Biological and social influences.* Unpublished doctoral dissertation, University of Stockholm.

Collins, A., & Frankenhaeuser, M. (1978). Stress responses in male and female engineering students. *Journal of Human Stress, 4*, 43–48.

Collins, A., Hanson, U., Eneroth, P., Hagenfeldt, K., Lundberg, U., & Frankenhaeuser, M. (1982). Psychophysiological stress responses in postmenopausal women before and after hormonal replacement therapy. *Human Neurobiology, 1*, 153–159.

Cooper, C. L., & Davidson, M. J. (1982). *High pressure: Working lives of women managers.* London: Fontana.

Davidson, M. J., & Cooper, C. L. (1983). *Stress and the woman manager.* Oxford: Robertson.

Forsman, L., & Lindblad L-E. (1983). Effect of mental stress on baroreceptor-mediated changes in blood pressure and heart rate and on plasma catecholamines and subjective responses in healthy males and females. *Psychosomatic Medicine, 45,* 435–445.

Frankenhaeuser, M. (1979). Psychoneuroendocrine approaches to the study of emotion as related to stress and coping. In H. E. Howe & R. A. Dienstbier (Eds.), *Nebraska symposium on motivation* (pp. 123–161). Lincoln: University of Nebraska Press.

Frankenhaeuser, M. (1983). The sympathetic-adrenal and pituitary–adrenal response to challenge: Comparison between the sexes. In T. M. Dembroski, T. H. Schmidt, & G. Blumchen (Eds.), *Biobehavioral bases of coronary heart disease* (pp. 91–105). Basel, Switzerland: Karger.

Frankenhaeuser, M. (1986). A psychobiological framework for research on human stress and coping. In M. H. Appley & R. Trumbull (Eds.), *Dynamics of stress* (pp. 101–116). New York: Plenum.

Frankenhaeuser, M. (1988). Stress and reactivity patterns at different stages of the life cycle. In P. Pancheri & L. Zichella (Eds.), *Biorhythms and stress in the physiopathology of reproduction* (pp. 31–40). New York: Hemisphere.

Frankenhaeuser, M. (1989). Stress, health, job satisfaction. Stockholm: The Swedish Work Environment Fund.

Frankenhaeuser, M., Dunne, E., & Lundberg, U. (1976). Sex differences in sympathetic-adrenal medullary reactions induced by different stressors. *Psychopharmacology, 47,* 1–5.

Frankenhaeuser, M., & Johansson, G. (1986). Stress at work: Psychobiological and psychosocial aspects. *International Review of Applied Psychology, 35,* 287–299.

Frankenhaeuser, M., Lundberg, U., Fredrikson, M., Melin, B., Tuomisto, M., Myrsten, A-L., Bergman-Losman, B., Hedman, M., & Wallin, L. (1989). Stress on and off the job as related to sex and occupational status in white-collar workers. *Journal of Organizational Behavior, 10,* 4.

Frankenhaeuser, M., Lundberg, U., & Mårdberg, B. The total workload of men and women as related to occupational level and number and age of children. Manuscript submitted for publication.

Frankenhaeuser, M., Rauste-von Wright, M., Collins, A., von Wright, J., Sedvall, G., & Swahn, C-G. (1978). Sex differences in psychoneuroendocrine reactions to examination stress. *Psychosomatic Medicine, 40,* 334–343.

Graves, P. L., & Thomas, C. B. (1985). Correlates of midlife career achievement among women physicians. *Journal of American Medical Association, 254,* 781–787.

Johansson, G., Frankenhaeuser, M., & Magnusson, D. (1973). Catecholamine output in school children as related to performance and adjustment. *Scandinavian Journal of Psychology, 14,* 20–28.

Johansson, G., & Post, B. (1974). Catecholamine output of males and females over a one-year period. *Acta Physiologica Scandinavica, 92,* 557–565.

Kahn, R. L. (1981). *Work and health.* New York: Wiley.

Karasek, R. A. (1979). Job demands, job decision latitude and mental strain: Implications for job redesign. *Administrative Science Quarterly, 24,* 285–308.

Lundberg, U. (1983). Sex differences in behaviour pattern and catecholamine and cortisol excretion in 3–6-year-old day care children. *Biological Psychology, 16,* 109–117.

Lundberg, U., de Chateau, P., Winberg, J., & Frankenhaeuser, M. (1981). Catecholamine and cortisol excretion patterns in three-year-old children and their parents. *Journal of Human Stress, 7,* 3–11.

Lundberg, U., Fredrikson, M., Wallin, L., Melin, B., & Frankenhaeuser, M. (1989b). Blood lipids as related to cardiovascular and neuroendocrine functions under different conditions in healthy males and females. *Pharmacology, Biochemistry and Behavior, 33,* 381–386.

Lundberg, U., Hanson, U., Eneroth, P., Frankenhaeuser, M., & Hagenfeldt, K. (1984). Anti-androgen treatment of hirsute women: A study of stress responses. *Journal of Psychosomatic Obstetrics and Gynaecology, 3,* 79–92.

Lundberg, U., Hedman, M., Melin, B., & Frankenhaeuser, M. (1989a). Type A behavior in healthy males and females as related to physiological reactivity and blood lipids. *Psychosomatic Medicine, 51,* 113–122.

Lundberg, U., Melin, B., Fredrikson, M., Tuomisto, M., & Frankenhaeuser, M. (1990). Comparison between neuroendocrine measurements under laboratory and naturalistic conditions. *Pharmacology, Biochemistry & Behavior, 37,* 697–702.

Lundberg, U., & Palm, K. (1989). Total workload and catecholamine excretion in families with preschool children. *Work and Stress, 3,* 255–260.

Mårdberg, B., Lundberg, U., & Frankenhaeuser, M. (in press). The total workload of male and female white-collar workers: Construction of a questionnaire and a scoring system. *Scandinavian Journal of Psychology.*

Matthews, K. A., & Johnson, C. A. (1987, August). *Total work load and cardiovascular risk factors in women.* Paper presented at the Annual Meeting of the American Psychological Association, New York.

Repetti, R. L., Matthews, K. A., & Waldron, I. (1989). Effects of paid employment on women's mental and physical health. *American Psychologist, 44,* 1394–1401.

Rissler, A. (1985). Physiological stress indicators and their measurement at work in comparison to subjective reports. In J. J. Sanchez-Sosa (Ed.), *Health and clinical psychology* (pp. 21–35). Amsterdam: Elsevier.

de Schaepdryver, A. F., Hooft, C., Delbeke, M-J., & van den Noortgaete, M. (1978). Urinary catecholamines and metabolites in children. *The Journal of Pediatrics, 93,* 266–268.

Waldron, I., Herold, J., Dunn, D., & Staum, R. (1982). Reciprocal effects of health and labor force participation among women: Evidence from two longitudinal studies. *Journal of Occupational Medicine, 24,* 126–132.

II

Work and Family

Multiple Roles

4

The Forms of Women's Work

ROBERT L. KAHN

INTRODUCTION

This paper has four aims: (1) to propose the concept of productive activity as an alternative to conventional definitions of work, (2) to compare the patterns of productive activity of men and women throughout the life course, (3) to consider factors associated with those patterns as hypothetical causes or effects, (4) to discuss some implications of these findings for policy, especially with respect to national statistics.

THE FORMS OF WORK

To discuss the forms of women's work implies agreement on the definition of work itself and the forms that it takes for both men and women. Such agreement has by no means been achieved. Only among physicists, who long since settled on the definition of work as the product of force multiplied by distance, has the struggle among alternative conceptualizations been resolved. In the social sciences and in their predecessor field of social philosophy there is a large body of literature on the meaning of work in human affairs, but it is varied in orientation and almost all of it is undesirably narrow in conception. It seems to me to consist of four subliteratures, each dedicated to exploring a particular aspect of work and none taking much account of the others.

ROBERT L. KAHN • Survey Research Center, Institute for Social Research, University of Michigan, Ann Arbor, Michigan 48106-1248.

Work as Affliction

The first of these sub-literatures regards work as affliction. This is an ancient idea, reaching back at least to the biblical curse with which Adam and Eve were cast out of Eden: "In the sweat of thy face shalt thou eat bread." The underlying notion is that work is dissatisfying, even painful, and that it is undertaken only under compulsion, direct or indirect (economic). Quantitative evidence for this view of work comes almost entirely from the responses of people who hold jobs low in skill level, variety, and autonomy. Among unskilled workers in the steel and auto industries, for example, more than 80% say that they would not choose the same kind of work if they "had it to do over," and the vast majority say that they would not continue to work on their present jobs if they did not need the money (Kahn, 1981).

The following excerpt from an interview with a women in her mid-forties who works in a luggage factory, making molded inner linings for suitcases, typifies work as affliction:

> We have to punch in before seven. We're at our tank approximately one to two minutes before seven to take over from the girl who's leaving. The tank runs twenty-four hours a day.
>
> . . . . .
>
> The tank I work at is six-foot deep, eight-foot square. In it is a pulp, made of ground wood, ground glass, fiberglass, a mixture of chemicals, and water. It comes up though a copper screen felter as a form, shaped like the luggage you buy in the store.
>
> . . . . .
>
> In forty seconds, you have to take the wet felt out of the felter, put the blanket on—a rubber sheeting—to draw out the excess moisture, wait two, three seconds, take the blanket off, pick the wet felt up, balance it on your shoulder—there is no way of holding it without tearing it all to pieces, it is wet and will collapse—reach over, get the hose, spray the inside of this copper screen to keep it from plugging, turn around, walk to the hot dry dies behind you, take the hot piece off with your opposite hand, set it on the floor—this wet thing is still balanced on your shoulder—put the wet piece on the dry die, push this button that lets the dry press down, inspect the piece we just took off, the hot piece, stack it and count it—when you get a stack of ten, you push it over and start another stack of ten—then go back and put our blanket on the wet piece coming up from the tank . . . and start all over. Forty seconds. . . .
>
> . . . . .
>
> All day long is the same thing over and over. That's about ten steps every forty seconds about 800 times a day. . . .
>
> . . . . .
>
> I hope I don't work many more years. I'm tired. I'd like to stay home and keep house . . . [in] a place near the lake where I can have a little garden of my own and raise my flowers that I love to raise. (Terkel, 1974, pp. 289–293)

Work as Addiction

The literature of work as addiction, on the other hand, is relatively recent although the phenomenon itself is surely not. The term *addiction* seems to be applied to work in a metaphorical rather than a literal sense, implying that some people are tied to their work as though to a drug— working more than is required by their employer, more than is prescribed by social norms, perhaps more than is compatible with their performance of such other life roles as spouse, parent, and citizen. The term *workaholic* was coined to label this kind of dependency, and it has entered the common vocabulary as well as the research literature.

The president of a large radio broadcasting corporation in the United States described his well-rewarded and work-dominated life in ways that illustrate the meaning of work as addiction:

> My days starts between four-thirty and five in the morning, at home in Winnetka. I dictate in my library until about seven-thirty. Then I have breakfast. . . . The driver gets there about eight o'clock and oftentimes I continue dictating in the car on the way to the office. . . .
>
> . . . . .
> I will probably have as many as 150 letters dictated by seven-thirty in the morning. I have five full-time secretaries who do nothing but work for [me]. . . .
>
> . . . . .
> I get home around six-thirty, seven at night. After dinner with the family I spend a minimum of two and a half hours each night going over the mail and dictating. . . . Although I don't go to the office on Saturday or Sunday, I do have mail brought out to my home for the weekend. I dictate on Saturday and Sunday. When I do this on holidays, like Christmas, New Year's, and Thanksgiving, I have to sneak a little bit, so the family doesn't know what I'm doing. . . . (Terkel, 1974, pp. 390–393)

This company president may seem as driven by his dictating machine as the woman factory worker is by the assembly line, but their situations are very different. His work activities are varied, not monotonous; he is involved in the decisions that define his job and he receives a large salary. He has the power to delegate or share the excessive burdens of his office, but in some real sense he chooses not to do so. Work dominates his life, but he speaks as if he would be troubled and unhappy without it. Addiction seems a not unreasonable label by which to designate such a relationship to work. It seems likely, however, that the number of people so addicted is small, even if many of us can recognize in ourselves occasional tendencies in that direction.

Work as Fulfillment

The fulfilling aspects of work have been studied in some depth, primarily in surveys that ask people to identify the importance of different job characteristics and secondarily by searching out which of those characteristics determine overall job satisfaction. (See, for example, Locke, 1976; Quinn & Cobb, 1973; Robinson, Athanasiou, & Head, 1969; Smith, Kendall, & Hulin, 1969.) The consensus among employed men and women in these matters, irrespective of their satisfaction or dissatisfaction with their own jobs, is sufficient to provide a profile description of what makes work fulfilling. "A good job," our composite respondent tells us, "is one in which the work is interesting. I have a chance to use and develop my own special abilities, and I can see the results of my work. It is a job where I have enough information, enough help and equipment, enough time, and enough authority to get the work done properly. The supervisor is competent and my responsibilities are clearly defined. The people I work with are friendly and helpful; the pay is good and so is the job security."

Not many men or women describe their own jobs as meeting all these idealized standards, and still fewer have jobs that provide opportunities for continuing personal growth. Nevertheless, most people have come to terms with their jobs and call themselves more satisfied than dissatisfied. Most people who are working say they would like to go on doing so even if they had enough money to live comfortably without working, although unskilled workers do not agree, women give this response less often than men, and the percentage of people who give this answer seems to be declining, at least in the United States (Quinn & Staines, 1979; Kahn, 1984).

In combination, however, these findings suggest that work as paid employment occupies a central place in the lives of people who have it, on balance far more positive than negative. That conclusion has been disputed (Dubin, 1976) but not disproved, and the evidence in its favor continues to accumulate. People's overall assessment of the quality of their lives is predicted first of all by their satisfaction with family, but satisfaction with work comes second (Campbell, Converse, & Rodgers, 1976).

Beyond such generalizations differences in attitudes toward work depend substantially on the nature of the work that people do. Scientists, university professors, physicians, bankers, and people in other prestigious and highly rewarded occupations not only want to continue working but to continue at their present kind of work; 90% of them say that they would choose the same line of work if they "had it to do over again." Unskilled workers value working but not the kind of work they are doing, and the great majority would not choose the same kind of work if they "had life to live over again" (Kahn, 1981). The implication is that people recognize the importance of jobs in their lives both for economic and psychological reasons, but the ideal of work as fulfillment is approximated only at the top of the prestige hierarchy of occupations.

Work as Exchange

The view of work as exchange is essentially economic, and although less extreme than the view of work as affliction, it emphasizes the negative aspects of working. Bertrand Russell (1930) epitomized this conception of work in a typically trenchant and sweeping assertion: "In taking to agriculture mankind decided that it would submit to monotony and tedium in order to diminish the risk of starvation" (p. 90).

The transition from agricultural to industrial dominance, and now to occupations that seem neither agricultural nor industrial, has made the relationship of work to survival less direct, but the home truth remains, at the individual as well as the societal level. Paid employment involves exchange. The worker agrees, by written or oral agreement, or through silent understanding, to perform certain tasks at certain times in certain places, usually under the direction of certain persons. In exchange, the employer or someone representing the employing organization makes a commitment of money.

Economists concerned with such transactions refer to wages as inducements and to required labor as contributions, the implication of these paired terms being that providing such contributions of effort involves costs to the worker that must be overcome by extrinsic rewards. If the work is unpleasant, hazardous, or extreme in its physical demands, the physical and psychological costs of performance are obvious. But even if the work is none of these things, it involves what economists call "opportunity costs": the person who goes to a job forgoes the possibility of doing something else. How great these opportunity costs are depends on the pleasures foregone or postponed for the sake of work and on the characteristics of the work itself. Indeed, if a man or woman considers work a rescue from some even less attractive activity, the opportunity costs become negative and thus add to the attractiveness of the job.

The intangible rewards of the job complicate the exchange still further so that no single coinage can express the exchange adequately. As with other economic exchanges, the underlying idea is psychological, involving what the economists term "utility," or value to the individual, and the adequate measurement of disparate utilities has yet to be attained. Nevertheless, people speak of paid employment in terms that are quite consistent with the view of work as exchange. Some years ago, my colleagues and I included in a survey of employed men the following question: "In your opinion, what makes the difference between something you would call work and something you would not call work?" The answers emphasized the obligatory nature of work and the fact that it is paid, that it demands effort, and that it is productive. The first of these answers was the most common: once committed to the exchange, you do your job whether you feel like it or not and whether you like it or not. It is the fourth of these characteristics, however, the productivity of work, that seems to me most promising for definitional purposes.

Work as Productive Activity

I have become convinced that none of the four preceding approaches is adequate to understand work in modern societies. The first three—work as affliction, addition, or fulfillment—share the defect of defining the activity in terms of its effects on the individual. In addition, each of them directs us to different effects or outcomes. All these outcomes are among the possible consequences of work performance, and all of them occur. How often, how much, and why are empirical questions rather than definitional ones, however. The definition of work as exchange is more promising, but in practice if not in theory it has led to an exclusive concern with paid employment.

I propose instead that work be defined as productive behavior, that is, as any activity that adds to the stock or flow of valued goods and services. Whether the activity gives pleasure or pain to the worker and whether it is done for pay or for other reasons are significant questions, but they do not enter into the definition of work; nor does the question of whether the work product meets some standard of quality or ultimate societal benefit. If the activity generates valued goods or services, it is productive, and the magnitude of its productivity can be defined as the market value (actual or attributed) of the goods and services so generated minus the nonlabor costs involved in their production (House & Kahn, 1984).

Using the criterion of market value to define an activity as productive, as my colleagues and I have chosen to do, is admittedly time-bound and culture-bound. Whether it agrees or disagrees with other measures of value thus becomes an important question, one that can be addressed empirically. For example, gifted artists, unappreciated by the connoisseurs of their time, might nevertheless persist in assigning a high value to their own work if they were asked to assess its true worth. The difference between their subjective evaluation and the "objective" data of the market, and the consequences of such differences, would then become empirical questions.

This definition of work as productive activity offers several advantages over the others we have reviewed. First, it makes no untestable assumptions that a particular activity is productive; its productivity depends on whether or not it generates valued goods and services, which in turn is determined by actual or synthetic (attributed) market value. Second, this definition, and the market measures it implies, are independent of the perceptions of the individual engaged in the activity, and in this sense are objective. An individual's own perception of his or her productivity can of course be separately measured. We thus distinguish between objective and subjective productivity, both of which we hypothesize to be predictors of individual well-being. For example, the highly paid writer of television commercials may rate the value of his or her work lower than its market price, and the hardworking homemaker may rate her work more highly than the market rates for housework and child care. The approach I am advocating makes such differences visible and invites research on their causes and consequences.

A third advantage of defining work as productive activity is its inclusiveness. Unpaid activity that meets the definition of productivity is work no less than paid employment. It may take place in the home and in other informal settings as well as in organizations. Furthermore, the beneficiaries of unpaid work, so defined, may include the people who perform it. For example, the person who works unpaid with other members of the congregation to paint the local church is engaged in productive activity, the market value of which can be assessed in any of several ways. But so is the person who helps paint a neighbor's house, and the person who paints his or her own house is being no less productive, although admittedly less altruistic. All such activities meet the essential requirement of contributing to the supply of valued goods and services.

PATTERNS OF PRODUCTIVE BEHAVIOR
IN THE UNITED STATES

In utilizing this approach in empirical research on work and its consequences for well-being, my colleagues and I have attempted to measure in commensurate terms four major categories of activity hypothesized to meet the definition of productive behavior—paid employment, regular and irregular; unpaid work in the home, especially housework and the care of children; work done in voluntary organizations; and direct help provided to relatives and friends.

Within each of these categories the magnitude or quantity of productive behavior for each person engaged is measured in two main ways: number of hours and monetary value, actual or attributed. The measurement of time invested in different activity categories has been the subject of extensive methodological research and has been managed with demonstrable success in earlier large-scale surveys (Juster, 1975; Szalai & Andrews, 1980). Attribution of monetary value for activities that are not paid directly has also been the subject of methodological research, and various methods have been proposed and compared (Murphy, 1982; Peskin, 1983): specialist cost, both for specific activities and for activity patterns in combination; opportunity cost; and value added. My colleagues and I use a variation of the last of these, called the "foregone expense approach," in which the basic question is how much the individual or organization saved because the work was done without payment (Morgan, 1981).

It is our intention to develop an annual series of data for the United States showing the patterns of productive behavior for men and women over the life course, the ways in which those patterns are changing, and the consequences for health and the quality of life. Data from the first wave of this national longitudinal study are now available, and although they provide only a limited basis for inferences about cause and effect, they tell us much about the forms of women's work in themselves and in comparison to those of men.

Let us look first at patterns of participation in nine categories of behavior hypothesized to be productive—regular paid work, irregular work, housework, child care, home maintenance and related "do-it-yourself" activity, volunteer work in organizations, help to friends and relatives, and help to people with either chronic or acute problems (Table 1). Some of these activities are engaged in to some extent by the vast majority of adults; these include housework (broadly defined), home maintenance and related do-it-yourself activities, help of any kind given to friends and relatives, and paid employment. Other productive activities engage large minorities—child care, voluntary work in organizations of all kinds, and help given to people with acute problems. Few people are caring for someone with a chronic illness or disability, although the burden of providing such care can be very great for the few who have assumed it. And few people report irregular paid employment, although we must suspect underreporting of such activity because it often takes place outside the tax structure.

Table 1. Productive Activities among Adults 25 Years Old and Older by Sex

	Percentage participating			Hours during past year		
	Men		Women	Men		Women
Regular work	77.3	**	55.1	1749.7	**	971.5
Paid irregular work	19.8	**	11.4	12.5	**	7.1
Housework	91.1	**	99.4	377.9	**	1197.1
Child care	44.1		44.7	453.8	**	774.1
Home maintenance	92.4	**	81.9	105.9	**	66.5
Volunteer work	42.1	*	46.9	28.3		28.5
Help to friends and relatives	82.6		80.2	49.3	*	56.1
Help for chronic problems	13.4	*	17.1	11.7	**	19.8
Help for acute problems	35.9	**	42.9	16.4	**	26.5

Note. N = 3,617.
*p < .05. **p < .01

Participation by men and women in these various activities is not grossly different when we look only at the dichotomous question of participation or none at all and do not differentiate extent of participation. Men are more likely to be involved in paid work, but other participation rates are similar for men and women (Table 1, columns 1 and 2). When we differentiate extent of participation by measuring hours spent at each activity during the year, sharp differences between the sexes become apparent (columns 3 and 4). Women spend only about half as many hours at paid work, a fact that reflects both lower rates of participation and more part-time work arrangements, wanted and unwanted. But they spend twice as many hours in child care and three times as many in housework. Moreover, although the numbers are small, women spend significantly more time in all of the help-giving activities—to family and friends, and for chronic and acute problems (House & Kahn, 1985).

If we look at the patterns of paid work, unpaid work, and help giving in combination, the pattern of difference between the sexes is clear, and it persists throughout the life course (Figure 1). Men do more paid work; women do more unpaid work; and when we combine categories to get an estimate of total hours of productive activity, women do significantly more at every age from 25 through 75 and beyond.

The heavy investment of women in forms of work that are unpaid and their increasing involvement in paid employment as well imply a particularly heavy work load for employed women, unless one assumes a compensatory reduction in hours of unpaid work. Such trade-offs do occur,

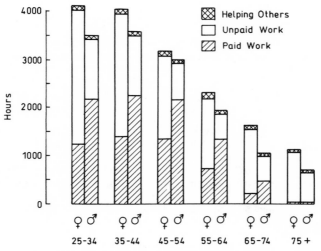

Figure 1. Annual hours of productive activity, by age and sex.

as voluntary organizations have learned to their sorrow, but the compensatory effects are limited (Table 2). Employed women work almost 4,000 hours per year in paid and unpaid forms of productive activity; that is, their workweek approaches 80 hours, assuming a two-week vacation. The corresponding total of all productive activities for men—about 3,400 hours annually—implies a workweek of about 68 hours. Both are busy schedules, but the differential of about 2½ hours of leisure per day between men and women is more than statistically significant.

These differences between the work patterns of men and women persist throughout the life course. When men are not engaged in paid employment, their total productive time drops drastically. Men over the age of 55 who are not working for pay, which is the majority circumstance, report only about 600 hours of productive activity per year. Nonemployed women in the same age groups work twice as many hours. For employed men and employed women, the differences are proportionally smaller, especially in the years after the responsibilities of child care are past in most families. In summary, women spend more hours productively than men do, and the differential between the sexes is sharpest among those men and women who are not employed for pay. The total work load is heaviest, however, among women who are employed (Figure 2).

Time is one of the major metrics for the assessment of work inputs; the other, at least in industrial societies, is money. The problem in using money values, of course, is the assignment of such values for unpaid work. Morgan (personal communication, August 30, 1980) has compared three methods of estimation: the first uses the direct response of each individual

Table 2. Total Productive Hours per Year,
by Age, Sex, and Employment Status

	All ages	25–34	35–44	45–54	55–64	65–74	75+
				Age group			
Men							
Employed	3405.9	3639.0	3709.4	3155.5	2800.0	2121.0	1138.6
Nonemployed	771.9	1356.0	1768.4	760.4	654.5	623.1	685.6
Women							
Employed	3903.6	4367.9	4281.0	3478.4	2934.6	2326.6	1818.1
Nonemployed	2217.0	3668.0	3411.1	2315.9	1736.2	1478.5	1097.3
Total							
Employed	3627.5	3936.1	3985.4	3295.4	2863.9	2218.4	1452.6
Nonemployed	1767.9	3310.5	3163.7	1997.4	1310.0	1164.2	930.8

Figure 2. Annual hours of productive activity by employment status and sex.

in answer to questions about the amount saved by voluntary and do-it-yourself work; the second uses imputed wage rates for all unpaid work, with the imputations based on actual wage rates for people comparable in age, gender, education, and other demographic characteristics; the third method values housework and child care at the average wage paid for unskilled service in the United States—$3.43 in 1986.

The first two methods give similar results; the third gives an evaluation about 25% lower. I have chosen to use the data generated by the second method of imputation, in which a synthetic wage rate for unpaid work is based on the demographic characteristics of the individual. This synthetic or imputed rate is then multiplied by the hours spent in each activity during the year, to yield an estimate of the annual dollar value of each category of unpaid work (Table 3; Figure 3).

The results show that housework, including the purchase and preparation of food, is the major form of unpaid work for both men and women throughout the life course. Child care bulks large in earlier years but reduces sharply in middle and old age, as would be expected. The dollar values reflect the grossly greater investment by women in these activities, blunted by the higher imputed hourly wage rates for the unpaid labor of men. This latter difference includes the effects of sex discrimination in the labor market.

Even so, the gross dollar value of women's unpaid work exceeds that of men by 28%–75% in all except the oldest age group. In the younger age groups (25–45 years), unpaid work is about 38% of the total dollar value of men's work but about 65% of women's. These differences peak in late middle age, when child care is substantially over but housework persists. And in old age there is increasing convergence, with unpaid work dominant for both sexes. Figure 3 reminds us of the relative dollar value, estimated as described above, of the various categories of unpaid produc-

Table 3. Estimated Annual Dollar Values of Various Productive Activities
Using Imputed Market Earning Potential, by Age and Sex, 1986

Gender/age	Housework	Child care	Do-it-yourself	Volunteer	Help others	Help chronic	Help acute	Irregular work
Men								
25–34	4,665	7,905	1,206	315	631	43	200	241
35–44	4,281	9,607	1,578	525	778	122	310	206
45–54	4,507	4,540	1,315	570	580	195	272	194
55–64	3,347	935	2,278	258	530	228	138	41
65–74	3,776	259	1,736	287	453	323	576	20
75+	2,871	162	486	140	226	102	87	3
Women								
25–34	8,563	10,300	470	168	426	105	220	65
35–44	10,239	10,033	689	388	565	158	301	105
45–54	11,040	3,330	859	336	627	248	340	58
55–64	9,135	748	542	223	551	250	206	15
65–74	8,909	418	511	251	389	187	250	12
75+	3,384	49	146	80	107	59	67	3
All	6,736	5,663	918	315	533	155	253	104

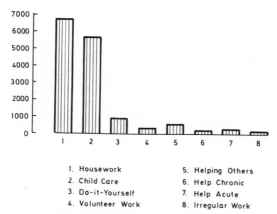

1. Housework   5. Helping Others
2. Child Care   6. Help Chronic
3. Do-it-Yourself   7. Help Acute
4. Volunteer Work   8. Irregular Work

Figure 3. Estimated annual dollar values of various productive activities, 1986.

tive behavior. It is interesting to speculate on the societal effects of increasing the amount of altruistic behavior—manifested both as voluntarism in organizations and as informal help to others—and on the question of how such behavior can be increased. The current situation, in the United States at least, is that the direct household inputs—child care and housework itself—account for about 85% of all unpaid work, as measured in dollars.

My colleagues and I, in the study titled "Americans' Changing Lives," have attempted some measurement of process and outcome benefits of paid and unpaid work in its various forms. Process benefits were measured by direct questions about the enjoyment of the activity, and outcome benefits by similarly direct questions about who is better off, and by how much, as a result of the activity. The results for both process and outcome benefits show less differentiation than we had hypothesized, both between the sexes and between activities (Figure 4). They also show a suspicious skewness toward the favorable end of the scale, and I therefore propose caution in their interpretation. The small differences that are apparent show slightly more favorable responses from women than from men regarding the enjoyment of all unpaid productive activities. Housework is least enjoyed of all activity categories, paid and unpaid. Child care ranks highest, although it may also be most vulnerable to biases of social acceptability.

The perceived benefits of productive activities to others (Figure 5) are similarly skewed toward the favorable end of the response scale and show little differentiation between the sexes and among the various activities.

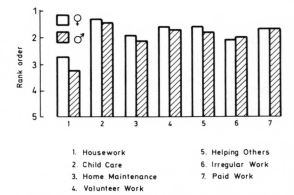

1. Housework   5. Helping Others
2. Child Care   6. Irregular Work
3. Home Maintenance   7. Paid Work
4. Volunteer Work

Figure 4. Enjoyment of productive activities, by activity category and sex.

CAUSES AND CONSEQUENCES OF PRODUCTIVE WORK

Definitive identification of the causes and consequences of productive activity must wait on successive waves of data from the same national sample of the adult population. Some interpretations can be made with confidence, however, from the cross-sectional data already in hand. This is especially true for the hypothesized demographic predictors of productive activity, since for these factors the direction of causality is clear. The importance of sex as a predictor of both form and amount of productivity is apparent in the comparative data for men and women presented earlier. Multiple classification analysis (Andrews, Morgan, Sonquist, & Klem,

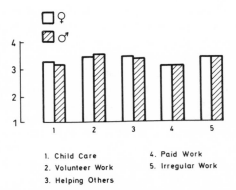

1. Child Care   4. Paid Work
2. Volunteer Work   5. Irregular Work
3. Helping Others

Figure 5. Perceived benefit of productive activities, by sex.

1973), assessing the strength of the relationship between sex and total hours of productive activity with age held constant, shows that sex is a significant predictor of almost every form of productive behavior.

It is strongest as a predictor of housework, where it alone explains almost 30% of the variance in hours of work, and it is a lesser but still substantial predictor of hours of child care; both are forms of productive behavior in which women's hours greatly exceed those of men. Sex is also a predictor of hours spent in paid work and in home maintenance, forms of productive behavior in which men report more hours than women. Only for the prediction of volunteer work does sex appear to be irrelevant. It would probably differentiate the kinds of volunteer activities in which people engage, but the data do not yet permit this distinction.

Multiple regression analyses, using more than 20 variables to predict the productive hours of men and of women separately, generate the predictive pattern summarized in Table 4. Regression coefficients smaller than .10 are omitted from the table even though the size of the population sample (3,617) makes them statistically significant. In combination the predictors explain from 4% to 51% of the variance in hours of productive activity for women and from 4% to 41% of the variance for men. Child care is the activity best predicted for women, paid work for men. For both men and women demographic factors predict productive activity more strongly than do measures of health, social contact, or personality.

Hours of paid work are predicted by age for both men and women and by education and marital status for women but not for men. The signs are opposed, however: education of women predicts positively to paid work and marital status predicts negatively.

Housework is not predicted by age; people do it almost all their lives. It is predicted by marital status for both men and women, but the effects are opposite: regardless of paid employment, marriage increases hours of housework for women and decreases them for men. It is the only predictor that has such opposite effects, and it reminds us of the power of sex roles in our society. Being employed for pay decreases hours of housework for both men and women. Increasing household size, on the other hand, increases hours of housework for women but not for men. Finally, hours of housework are negatively predicted by depression among men but not among women, perhaps because women are compelled by circumstances to do housework almost regardless of their emotional state. The summary picture is one in which women do most of the housework regardless of their other employment and their emotional state; for men housework remains more of an option, more responsive to their state of well-being and less responsive to household size.

Hours of child care are predicted by age and by number of persons in

Table 4. Prediction of Hours Spent in Productive Activities, by Sex

							Important predictors[b]							
		R^{2a}	Age	Marital Status	Education	Employment status	No. of persons in household	Home ownership	Health rating	Functional health	Informal social contacts	Formal social contacts	Physical activity	CES-D
Paid work	M	.41	-.46						.12	.13	-.12		-.10	
	F	.28	-.37	-.11	.17				.10					
Housework	M	.12		-.14		-.16								
	F	.18		.13		-.23	.20							.14
Child care	M	.35	-.29				.39							
	F	.51	-.46			-.15	.42							
Home maintenance	M	.16	-.10	.12				.25						
	F	.12						.20					(.14)	
Volunteer work	M	.21			.10							.37		
	F	.20										.39		
Informal help to others	M	.09	-.13										.13	
	F	.09									.18			
Help chronic problems	M	.04	.16	.10										
	F	.04	.11						-.11	.12				

Note. Variables are coded so that higher scores indicate a greater degree of the characteristic being measured.

[a]Amount of variance accounted for by multiple regressions that include as predictors age, race, marital status, education, employment status, family income, number of persons in household, urbanicity, home ownership, health rating, number of chronic conditions, functional health, verbal intelligence, cognitive impairment, informal social contacts, formal social contacts, physical activity, religious participation, three dummy variables for religious denomination, self-efficacy, depression, extraversion, fatalism.

[b]Shown are standardized regression coefficients .10 or larger.

Source: Americans' Changing Lives Study, Institute for Social Research, University of Michigan, 1986.

the household for both men and women and, negatively but less power-fully, by the paid employment of women. Other forms of productive activity are predicted less well by demographic factors, especially for women. Helping people with chronic problems is predicted by age, and it is the only form of productive activity for which age is a positive rather than a negative or negligible predictor. That finding is a reminder that disabled old people are often cared for by others of their own age, persons who, as the coefficient for health of the female caretakers implies, are not them-selves in robust health.

The relationship of productive activity to physical and psychological well-being is almost certainly complex, with initial well-being increasing the likelihood and the hours of productive behavior and productive activity in turn having positive effects on well-being. These hypotheses await testing with longitudinal data that will be analyzed in the future. The cross-sectional data that we have reviewed, however, imply that these relationships may not be strong. If present patterns are sustained, we must conclude that the forms of productive activity and their amount are determined substantially by sex roles, as reflected in demographic and household characteristics. In the United States, at least, the increasing proportion of women engaged in paid employment seems not to have produced complementary changes in the division of other labor between the sexes or in the flexibility of women's unpaid labor.

IMPLICATIONS FOR POLICY

The main purpose of this chapter is to begin the correction of a pervasive bias in our national statistics and, by extension, in national politics and policy. That bias consists in treating paid employment as if it were synonymous with all forms of productive activity. Thus, people who are employed for pay are typically described as working, and people not so employed are labeled nonworkers. Goods and services generated from paid employment are then treated as if they were all of the societal product, and unpaid societal contributions remain uncounted. The part, in short, is treated as if it were the whole. In literature, as synecdoche, this is done for dramatic effect and variety of language. In science the use of such partial or surrogate variables is usually a matter of expediency, that is, of inability to measure more fully the characteristic of interest. Too often, researchers and the consumers of research then treat the partial measure as if it were the whole, and it is this that constitutes bias. This is exactly what is done when paid employment is treated as if it were all of productive activity. The ramifications of this failure to include goods and services generated without pay are discriminatory, primarily against women because they are the major contributors of unpaid societal work. There are discriminatory implications for older people as well, who are regarded as totally unproductive after they leave the labor force. National debates about whether the United States can afford the economic burden of its growing elderly population, for example, attain credibility in part because they ignore the unpaid productive work of older men and women.

The relationship between national statistics and national policy is admittedly complex and interactive, but it is fair to say that modern industrial societies are substantially influenced in their policies by the content of their national statistics; in other words, we are more likely to pay attention to the things we count. In the United States prior to World War II there were no reliable data on rates of unemployment, and the national debate on policy in that domain was handicapped by Congressional arguments about the magnitude of the problem. Since 1942 the Bureau of the Census has collected comprehensive labor force data on a monthly basis, and they are widely used. The availability of such data does not eliminate debates over policy, but it enables them to begin with a foundation in fact.

We would like to see a national data base developed for unpaid productive activity of all kinds and collected on a basis that permits integration and comparison with data for paid employment. The research on which I have drawn for this paper is intended to promote such development although its primary orientation is to scientific description and hypothesis testing. I hope that by developing adequate measures of productive activity in its full range and demonstrating the utility of such measures we can also increase understanding of and appreciation for the forms of women's work.

REFERENCES

Andrews, F. M., Morgan, J. N., Sonquist, J. A., & Klem, L. (1973). *Multiple classification analysis.* Ann Arbor, MI: Institute for Social Research.

Campbell, A., Converse, P. E., & Rodgers, W. L. (1976). *The quality of American life.* New York: Sage.

Dubin, R. (Ed.). (1976). *Handbook of work, organization and society.* Chicago: Rand McNally.

House, J. S., & Kahn, R. L. (1984). *Productivity, stress, and health in middle and late life.* Proposal to the National Institute on Aging. Unpublished manuscript, Institute for Social Research, Ann Arbor.

House, J. S., & Kahn, R. L. (1985). Measures and concepts of social support. In S. Cohen and S. L. Syme (Eds.), *Social support and health* (pp. 83–108). Orlando, FL: Academic Press.

Juster, F. (Ed.). (1975). *Education, income, and human behavior.* New York: McGraw-Hill.

Kahn, R. (1981). *Work and health.* New York: Wiley.

Kahn, R. L. (1984). Productive behavior through the life course: An essay on the quality of life. *Human Resource Management, 23*(1), 5–22.

Locke, E. A. (1976). The nature and causes of job satisfaction. In M. D. Dunnette (Ed.), *Handbook of industrial and organizational psychology* (pp. 1297–1350). Chicago: Rand McNally.

Morgan, J. N. (1981). Behavioral and social science research and the future elderly. In S. B. Kiesler, J. N. Morgan, & V. K. Oppenheimer (Eds.), *Aging: Social change* (pp. 587–611). New York: Academic Press.

Murphy, M. (1982). The value of household work in the United States, 1976: Measuring Nonmarket Economic Activity [Special issue]. *BEA Working Papers*, (3). Bureau of Economic Analysis, U.S. Department of Agriculture.

Peskin, J. (1983). *The value of household work in the 1980s.* Paper presented at the American Statistical Association Meetings, Toronto.

Quinn, R. P., & Cobb, W., Jr. (1973). What workers want: Factor analyses of importance ratings of job facets. *The 1972–73 quality of employment survey.* Ann Arbor, MI: Institute for Social Research, University of Michigan.

Quinn, R. P., & Staines, G. L. (1979). *The 1977 quality of employment survey.* Ann Arbor, MI: Institute for Social Research.

Robinson, J., Athanasiou, R., & Head, K. (1969). *Measures of occupational attitudes and occupational characteristics.* Ann Arbor, MI: Institute for Social Research, University of Michigan.

Russell, B. (1930). *The conquest of happiness.* New York: Liveright.

Smith, P. C., Kendall, L. M., & Hulin, C. L. (1969). *The measurement of satisfaction in work and retirement.* Chicago: Rand McNally.

Szalai, A., & Andrews, F. (1980). *Quality of life: Comparative studies.* London: Sage.

Terkel, S. (1974). *Working.* New York: Random House.

5

Coping with Role Overload

CAMILLE WORTMAN, MONICA BIERNAT,
AND ERIC LANG

INTRODUCTION

In this chapter we highlight findings from a program of research on coping with role strain and role conflict. Earlier research from our laboratory has focused primarily on how people deal with stressful life events such as physical disability (e.g., Bulman & Wortman, 1977) or the loss of a loved one (see, e.g., Lehman, Wortman, & Williams, 1987). Long-term goals of this research program include elaborating the theoretical mechanisms through which stress has deleterious effects on subsequent health and functioning (see Silver & Wortman, 1980, or Kessler, Price, & Wortman, 1985, for reviews).

The work described in this chapter represents a shift from the investigation of acute life events to that of chronic role strains and conflict between roles. We begin the chapter by offering a theoretical rationale for this shift in focus. Second, we provide an overview of our research program, which includes three studies on coping with role strain and role conflict. Third, we focus in some detail on the initial findings from one of these studies, a four-wave longitudinal investigation of married women professionals with preschool children. Women professionals with young children provide an ideal group in which to investigate chronic role strain and conflict because they are likely to be experiencing high levels of

CAMILLE WORTMAN • Department of Psychology, SUNY at Stony Brook, Stony Brook, New York 11794-8790.   **MONICA BIERNAT** • Department of Psychology, University of Florida, Gainesville, Florida 32611.   **ERIC LANG** • American Institutes for Research, P.O. Box 1113, Palo Alto, California 94302.

objective stress in both the home and work domains. Young children place high demands on these women's time while they are still in the career-establishment phase. Furthermore, population data suggest that women are increasingly likely to postpone the birth of their first child until they have attained their educational goals. For this reason, women professionals with young children form a substantial proportion of the fastest growing segment of the labor force, namely, mothers with young children (Mott, 1982; U.S. Department of Labor, 1985). Therefore, it is particularly important to investigate how they can successfully combine work and family roles. We examine such issues as equality in division of labor between these women and their husbands; frequency of conflicts between work and family roles for women and men; consequences of role involvement for self-esteem and feelings of pride; problems created by trying to combine multiple roles and differences in how these problems are experienced by men and women; and, finally, "spillover" from the woman's work situation to her home life and to her husband. We conclude with a discussion of future research questions that we plan to pursue.

THEORETICAL BASIS FOR THE PROPOSED WORK

There are several reasons why we felt that a shift in focus from stressful life events to the study of chronic role-related strains would enhance our conceptual understanding of stress and coping processes. First, the literature suggests that chronic role strains have a much more deleterious effect on subsequent mental and physical health than life events (Kessler *et al.*, 1985). Moreover, persistent role strains, such as job pressure or conflict between work and family roles, are much more widely experienced than most stressful life events. Yet, with few exceptions (e.g., Pearlin, Lieberman, Meneghan, & Mullen, 1981), the mental health impact of exposure to role strains has not been investigated. By identifying the structural aspects of roles that may produce difficulties within and between roles and by examining the relationship between exposure to these role strains and subsequent impairment, our current work should help to expand what is known about the impact of stress.

Most studies in the stressful life events literature have focused on how people cope with a single catastrophic event, such as breast cancer or the death of a child. There is growing consensus, however, that in order to advance what is known about coping, it is important to look at the same individual in various contexts or situations (Kessler *et al.*, 1985). By examining how women experience and respond to specific problems in various role domains, the research should provide important information about flexibility and consistency across domains. Studies focusing on specific life events also tend to look at the process of coping with a particular stressful event in isolation. Little is known, at this point, about how people deal simultaneously with multiple problems or stressors. A major goal of the research is to shed light on the process through which people integrate, organize, and balance multiple roles.

Another advantage of moving beyond a focus on isolated life stressors is that there is growing evidence that stress can be transmitted from one situation to another, thus magnifying its effects. By studying individuals in various life roles, it is possible to examine the conditions under which stress is particularly likely to be transmitted, or to spill over, from one life domain or role to another, for example, from the work role to the family and vice versa.

Within the literature on stressful life events, stress and coping have generally been studied at the individual level. Several investigators have emphasized that coping is a dynamic process and that an individual's coping efforts should not be considered independently from the social context in which they occur. In the past, however, most studies have overlooked the fact that some people may habitually deal with stress in ways that have deleterious effects on others. In our current work we attempt to move beyond this individual perspective by examining how individuals' efforts to combine multiple roles influence the health and well-being of other members of their families.

OVERVIEW OF RESEARCH PROGRAM

To address these issues we have initiated a program of research designed to assess how individuals cope with chronic role strain and role conflict. At present three studies are in various stages of completion. These studies are depicted in Figure 1 and Table 1. In Study I we have focused on a group of individuals who are intensively involved with three life roles: marriage, career, and parenting. This study focuses on two groups of married women professionals with young children—professors and businesswomen—and their husbands. These women were interviewed four times over a 1-year period. Study II, which focuses on physicians, was undertaken for the purpose of examining differences between women and men who are intensively involved in their jobs. This longitudinal investigation has followed individuals from medical school through their early years of practice. Data have been collected at four points in time from the physicians and twice from their spouses.

In each of the aforementioned studies we have focused our attention

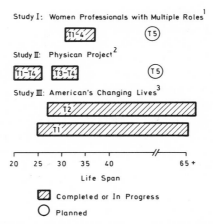

Figure 1. Research program on multiple roles: time points assessed.

[1] This project has been conducted by Camille Wortman, Monica Biernat, and Eric Lang in collaboration with Carol-Ann Emmons, Linda Beth Tiedje, and Geraldine Downey. Support was provided by the National Science Foundation and the National Institute of Mental Health.
[2] This project has been conducted by Camille Wortman in collaboration with Linda Grant and Holly Peters-Golden. Support was provided by the National Institute of Mental Health.
[3] This study represents a collaborative effort between Camille Wortman and Jim House, Ron Kessler, Robert Kahn, James Morgan, Regula Herzog, James Jackson, and Toni Antonucci. Funding was provided by the National Institute of Aging.

Table 1. Research Program on Multiple Roles: Description of Samples

	Study I Women professionals with multiple roles	Study II Physician project	Study III American's changing lives
N	140	200	3600
Sample	Professors and middle managers	Physicians	National probability sample
Sex	Women (and their spouses)	Men and women (and their spouses)	Men and women
Marital status	All married	Married and single	Married, single, divorced, widowed
Parental status	All with preschool children	Parents and non-parents	Parents and non-parents

on individuals who are involved in demanding occupations. We felt that such occupations were the most appropriate place to begin our inquiries into the impact of role strain and role conflict. As we accumulate information about coping with role strain, however, it will be important to determine whether our results generalize to individuals involved in nonprofessional occupations. It will also be important to compare people who are involved in multiple roles with people who are enacting fewer roles simultaneously. For these reasons we have begun a large-scale study (Study III) to explore the stresses and satisfactions associated with different role combinations and have interviewed a national probability sample of approximately 3,600 individuals at two points in time (see Figure 1 and Table 1).

STUDY 1: ROLE STRAIN AND CONFLICT IN MARRIED WOMEN PROFESSIONALS WITH YOUNG CHILDREN

In this chapter we focus on some preliminary findings from our study of married women professionals with preschool children. These women represent the prototypical case of heavy involvement in three major roles: work, marriage, and parenting. Hence, we felt that they would constitute an ideal population in which to examine the theoretical issues delineated earlier.

In addition to the attempt to clarify theoretical processes concerning stress and coping, there are compelling societal reasons for focusing attention on employed women with young children. Profound changes in the labor force participation rates of mothers with young children are creating one of the most significant social trends of this century (Presser & Baldwin, 1980). By the time their youngest child is 4 years of age, 60% of mothers are employed. Nearly half of all married women with children less than a year old now work outside the home, more than double the rate in 1970 (Hayghe, 1986). This trend reflects the "subtle revolution" (Smith, 1979) that has been taking place since the 1940s whereby the normative pattern of women's lives has been gradually transformed from one in which family (marriage, parenthood) and work roles were enacted sequentially to one in which family and work roles are enacted simultaneously. This transformation in women's lives has led to increased scientific and societal concern about the implications for health and well-being of combining multiple roles. Nonetheless, after more than a decade of research on multiple roles, we still know little about how the process of coping with multiple roles is played out in the lives of women and their families (Haw, 1982). The present study of women professionals with young children was undertaken to elucidate our knowledge of these processes.

Although men also combine multiple roles, there were many reasons for focusing our initial study on women. This decision was based on a careful review of empirical research that indicates that women experience greater inter-role conflict than men (Cleary & Mechanic, 1983; Holahan & Gilbert, 1979). We restricted our sample to women professionals with young children because, as noted earlier, these women form a substantial proportion of the fastest growing segment of the labor force—mothers of preschool children (U.S. Department of Labor, 1985)—and because these women are likely to possess a high degree of career commitment and work involvement. Women professionals are thus more likely to view work as another primary role, enhancing the likelihood of conflict between work and family roles. Moreover, the demanding nature of professional occupations and the potential for role overflow further increases the likelihood of inter-role conflict. Finally, survey data show that having a preschool child is associated with poorer mental health in employed women (see McLanahan & Adams, 1987, for a review). Employed mothers of preschoolers are also more likely than either fathers or mothers of older children to report spillover between work and family (Crouter, 1984), role-related tensions (Kelly & Voydanoff, 1985), and lower marital satisfaction (Staines, Pleck, Shepard, & O'Connor, 1978; White, Booth, & Edwards, 1986). These findings, taken together, suggest that the pressures of managing multiple roles are greatest and the psychological benefits from employment are least under conditions of heavy work and family responsibilities, that is, among married professionals with small children.

This research project had three specific goals. First, we sought to provide information about how women professionals with small children experience their multiple roles. In many prior studies, role occupancy has been linked to various mental and physical health outcomes, and there has been considerable debate about whether multiple roles affect mental health negatively (Coser, 1974; Goode, 1960; Merton, 1957) or positively (Marks, 1977; Sieber, 1974; Thoits, 1983; Verbrugge, 1983). Because only a few researchers (e.g., Barnett & Baruch, 1985; Baruch & Barnett, 1986; Pearlin *et al.*, 1981; Pleck & Staines, 1985; Repetti, 1987) have moved beyond a focus on role status to investigate women's perceptions of their roles, we know remarkably little about how multiple roles are experienced by the woman herself.

Second, we sought to explicate how objective stressors in one role influence role satisfaction and performance in other roles. In particular, we hoped to study how objective characteristics of the woman's work situation influence her experiences in marital and parental roles. Several authors (e.g., Aneshensal & Pearlin, 1987) have argued that research on this problem cannot progress unless efforts are made to describe the characteristics of particular job settings and to document their relationship to perceived job stress, role conflict, and performance in other roles. In most previous studies of working women it was not possible to address such issues, either because the women were recruited from a single profession (Hirsch & Rapkin, 1986) or because they were recruited from a wide variety of occupations differing on numerous characteristics (Pearlin *et al.*, 1981; Pleck & Staines, 1985; Ross, Mirowsky, & Huber, 1983), thereby yielding small numbers of women within any particular occupation. In our study women were recruited from two professions—professor and business executive—that were expected to differ markedly in job characteristics likely to affect role conflict and role overload. Thus, this study makes it possible to examine how such objective factors as time flexibility at work influence perceptions of role conflict, role overload, and functioning in the marital and parental roles.

Third, we sought to move beyond the individual perspective to see how women's efforts to integrate, organize, and balance multiple roles affect their husbands. With few exceptions (Bolger, DeLongis, Kessler, & Wethington, in press; Pleck, 1985; Ross *et al.*, 1983) past studies have focused only on the women themselves. Relatively little is known about how members of their families, particularly their husbands, perceive and react to their situations. In our study we questioned women's husbands explicitly in order to examine this issue.

Toward meeting these three goals we designed and executed a study focusing on 200 female business executives and university professors. We utilized a longitudinal design and collected data from the women, their husbands, and their employers. These occupations were selected because they were expected to differ on characteristics that may be related to role overload and role conflict. As a rule, businesswomen's work schedules allow them little flexibility in scheduling and thus may create more difficulties in integrating work and family roles than college professors' schedules. In contrast, college professors may have more choice over the projects they work on and even when and where they work. Academic life, however, is by its very nature "never finished"; there is always more that one could be doing. In this sense the work lacks "boundedness," a feature that might also present conflicts with home life. Because the two occupations were expected to differ on these and other structural aspects, the study permitted us to examine the impact of particular structural variables on role overload, role conflict, and spillover from work to family.

To be eligible for the study a woman had to be employed at least 30 hours per week, be married and currently living with her husband, and have at least one child 1 to 5 years of age. University professors were identified from lists of instructional faculty provided by the six largest universities in Michigan and in the Chicago area. Of the six universities contacted, all (100%) agreed to participate. Of the 116 eligible female professors identified, 107 (93%) agreed to participate. Businesswomen were selected from a stratified, random sample of companies with 50 or more employees in geographic proximity to the universities. The companies were selected from four occupations that tend to attract a significant number of women: law, banking, accounting, and advertising. Of the 104 companies contacted, 95 (90%) agreed to participate. Of the 98 eligible women identified, 93 (95%) agreed to participate.

Most prior studies of stress and coping have relied primarily on measures of perceived stresses. In the present study an effort was made to obtain as much objective information as possible about the stressors to which the women were exposed. For example, in the work domain, professors provided detailed information on how many students they were supervising and how many classes they were teaching. In the home domain, women were asked to count how many times their child awoke at night during the past week. As an added check on the reliability of the information a woman provided, her husband also provided information about her stresses in the marital and parental roles.

In the interviews an attempt was made to measure such coping resources as the women's personality characteristics, the coping strategies she utilized to deal with role overload and role conflict, and the social support available to her from her spouse, other family members, and friends. Outcomes included mental health, self-reported physical health, role strain and satisfaction, and role functioning. To move beyond the limits of self-report methodology regarding the assessment of functioning, information on the women's role functioning was collected not only from the women themselves but also from their spouses and employers. Objective indicators of functioning in the work role, such as citations, salary, and time until promotion, were also obtained.

The sociodemographic characteristics of the sample are as follows: Ninety-one percent of the women were white, 3% were black, and the remaining 6% were of other races. The mean ages of the women and their husbands were 35.0 years and 37.2 years, respectively. The couples had been married an average of 8.0 years. Fifty-six percent of the couples had one child, 33% had two children, 10% had three children, and 1% had four children. The children ranged in age from 13 months to 21 years. The median age of the children in single-child families was 2.5 years, in families with two children the median age was 4.9 years, and in families with three or more children the median age was 10.5 years. Eighty-four percent of the women and 68% of their husbands had graduate degrees. Fifty-eight percent of the husbands were employed in professional and technical occupations, 23% were managers, 13% were sales workers, and the remaining 6% were clerical workers, craftsmen, operatives, and service workers. The median total family income was in the category $70,000 to $74,999. The median income the women reported for themselves was in the category $30,000 to $34,999; the median income reported by their husbands was in the category $35,000 to $39,999.

Comparisons between the university professors and businesswomen showed that the professors were significantly older (M = 37.5 years) than the businesswomen (M = 32.6 years), $t(133) = 7.55, p < .01$. Professors had also been in their present jobs significantly longer (M = 5.0 versus 3.5 years), $t(132) = 2.90, p < .01$, and had been married significantly longer (M = 9.1 versus 7.0 years), $t(133) = 3.22, p < .01$. Of the academic women, 42.1% were at the assistant professor level, 27.1% at the associate, and 3.7% at the full professor level. The remaining 27.1% were in an "other" category (e.g., lecturers or research associates). A significantly greater proportion of the professors had college degrees (100% versus 70.6%), $\chi^2 (1, N = 114) = 32.83, p < .0001$. Although personal and spouse incomes were not significantly different for those two groups of women, the mean total family income of the university professors (M = $85,000 to $89,999) was significantly higher than that of the businesswomen (M = $70,000 to $74,999), $t(131) = 2.23, p < .05$.

FINDINGS OF THE STUDY

In this study one of our central areas of concern was how often our respondents experienced conflict between their work and family roles. Both women and their husbands were asked how often they had experienced conflicts between their work and family responsibilities during the past month. Husbands were also asked to report the frequency with which their wives experienced role conflict. Such conflicts were a common phenomenon for most women in this sample. Over 75% reported experiencing such conflicts every day, and the average frequency of role conflict was "two or three times a week" during the past month. Husbands reported experiencing conflict between work and family responsibilities significantly less than did their wives—an average of once a week during the past month, $t(111) = -6.02, p < .0001$. Although husbands said their wives experienced role conflict significantly more often than they themselves did, their estimation of their wives' role conflict was still significantly lower than their wives reported for themselves, $t(132) = -4.09, p < .0001$. These results suggest that women are in fact burdened by conflicts between work and family and that their husbands are not fully aware of that burden (see

Emmons, Biernat, Tiedje, Lang, & Wortman, in press, for a more detailed discussion).

To provide a context in which to interpret information about role conflict among these women professionals and their husbands, we next attempted to determine the extent to which their marriages were characterized by equality in terms of whose career takes precedence, provision of career support, and division of responsibility for household tasks. Regarding whose career takes precedence, more women said it was their husband's than said it was their own (34.1% vs. 24.4%); however, the largest group (41.5%) responded "both about the same." Similarly, over half of our respondents (59.3%) felt that they and their spouse supported each other's careers equally. Women who reported some inequity, however, were more likely to say that they provided more support for their husbands' careers than they received (23.0%); only 18% felt that they received more support from their husbands than they gave in return. Finally, the majority of women in our sample reported that their husbands engaged in each type of supportive behavior we studied "much of the time" or "almost always." Examples of supportive behaviors included listening to the wife talk about work-related problems, encouraging her to take advantage of professional opportunities, being understanding when she has to work extra hours, and performing extra household chores when she needs to devote more time to her work (Emmons *et al.*, 1990).

Prior studies of dual-career marriages have shown that although husband participation in household tasks and child care is gradually increasing (Pleck, 1985), wives still perform a disproportionate share of these duties (Bernardo, Shehan, & Leslie, 1987; Bryson, Bryson, & Johnson, 1978; Pleck, 1978, 1985; Weingarten, 1978; Yogev, 1981). To our knowledge, however, this is one of the first studies to focus on couples that include men and women of approximately equal status in terms of their education and job attainment. To assess division of labor among household tasks women were asked to indicate who took responsibility for, as well as who actually performed, six different household tasks—grocery shopping, planning meals, laundry, housecleaning, household finances, and repairs and maintenance (Biernat & Wortman, in press).[1] Figure 2 indi-

---

[1] Due to time constraints, husbands were not asked to provide detailed information about their involvement in household activities. However, on the detailed child care check list, husband and wife ratings correlated very highly ($r = .75$). We did obtain global assessments of each spouse's perceptions of his or her own and others' contributions to household chores. Here we found no significant differences between the reports of women and their husbands, with both spouses agreeing that the husband contributed between "too little" and "a satisfactory amount," and that the wife contributed between "a satisfactory amount" and "too much" to running the home.

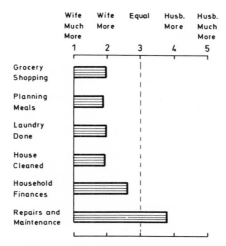

Figure 2. Division of responsibility for household tasks. Note: Wives indicated "who has responsibility for seeing to it that each of the tasks gets done."

cates that in all cases except for repairs and maintenance, women perceived that it was their responsibility, to a far greater extent than their husbands', to make sure that these tasks were accomplished. Women were also asked to indicate who actually performed these chores. The question asked: For each household chore listed below, please indicate how much of the time that chore is done by you and by your husband, by circling the appropriate number." The possible responses ranged from 1, "never or almost never," to 5, "all or most of the time." These data suggested greater equity than did the responsibility data. Women perceived themselves as doing a significantly greater amount of housecleaning and managing the finances relative to their husbands; they perceived general equality regarding grocery shopping and cooking and perceived their husbands as doing a significantly greater amount of laundry and household repairs than they did. Responses to open-ended questions suggested that women appreciated the help they received on these household tasks but felt burdened by being primarily responsible for the organization and management of the household. Many seemed to resent the implicit assumption that the housework is really their responsibility and that when the husband participates, he is doing the wife a favor for which she should be grateful.

Figure 3 provides the women's assessments of the division of child care activities between spouses. The results indicate that the burden of child care falls much more heavily on the women in our sample than on their

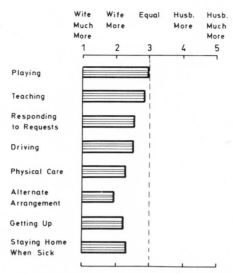

Figure 3. Wives' assessment of division of child care activities between spouses.

husbands. In general, the husbands in our sample agreed that their wives contributed much more to child care than they did (Biernat & Wortman, in press, will have a more detailed discussion). Interestingly, husbands were more likely to participate in the more enjoyable aspects of child care (e.g., playing, teaching the child about the world). Husbands were far less likely to participate in the child's physical care or to engage in such burdensome aspects of child care as getting up in the middle of the night, making alternative arrangements when the child care provider is unavailable, or staying home when the child is sick. Responses to open-ended questions suggested that women perceive their husbands as willing to perform specific tasks in connection with the children if they are asked. As with household tasks, however, many women disliked having to request a "fair share" of input from the husbands. As one mother put it, "He never volunteers to read her a bedtime story. This puts me in the position of having to nag him or do it myself. I'd rather just do it myself." Wives often seemed reluctant to confront their husbands about inequities in child care, although some admitted to trying to manipulate the situation in subtle ways. One of our respondents mentioned that during meals her 2-year-old son would typically request "more juice" on a regular basis. This mother made it a practice to "ignore" the first several requests in hopes that through such "passive-aggressive" behavior she could get her spouse to contribute more.

To our knowledge, the women in our sample represent one of the most well educated and accomplished groups to be followed in a study of this sort. The women appeared to be as involved in their jobs and to experience as many demands from their job as did their husbands. For this reason we felt it would be important to ascertain these women's feelings about the inequitable distribution of labor that exists within their marriages. Do they resent the lack of participation from their spouses, whose work responsibilities are no greater than their own? Despite the inequalities reported above, only about a quarter of the women in our sample said that their husbands contributed "too little" to household chores and child care. The majority (62.8%) described their husbands as doing a "satisfactory amount," and 13.3% said that their husbands contributed "too much." In evaluating their husband's contribution to the household perhaps women don't use equality as the standard of comparison. Instead, they may compare their husbands to other men—fathers, brothers, perhaps husbands of friends. If a woman's husband is more helpful and supportive than other men, she may feel lucky and fortunate even if his contribution is not equal to her own.

Once we had documented these patterns of inequity among our married professional women and their husbands, we felt it was important to explore the consequences of these sex differences in household responsibilities. As a result of investing more time and energy in the marital and family roles, do women experience more pride in their performance or greater feelings of competence in these domains than do their spouses? Recent analyses by Biernat and Wortman (in press) suggest that, in fact, most women are rather critical of themselves. Table 2 summarizes each spouse's evaluation of his or her own role performance in the marital and parental roles. On a five-point scale ranging from 1, "not at all true," to 5, "very true," women were significantly more likely than their husbands to agree that they were "not as good a spouse" as they would like to be and that they "felt guilty about not being a better spouse." Women were also less likely than their husbands to agree with the statement "I am a good spouse." Similarly, on two of the three questions asked about the parental role, women were significantly more self-critical than their spouses were. They were more likely to agree, for example, that they were "not as good a parent" as they would like to be.

Women in the sample were much more critical of their own functioning in the various roles than their husbands were of them. We measured functioning within each role with three items designed to tap how well

Table 2. Each Spouse's Evaluation of Own Role Performance

	Wife rates self	Husband rates self	p
Spouse role			
Not as good as would like	2.65	2.41	.05
Feel guilty about not being better	2.81	2.54	.05
Am a good spouse	3.70	4.15	.001
Parent role			
Not as good as would like	2.71	2.33	.001
Feel guilty about not being better	2.44	2.09	.001
Am a good parent	3.35	3.27	NS

Note. The range of the scale was from 1, "not at all true," to 5, "very true."

during the preceding month the woman handled responsibilities, made good decisions, and got along with people involved in the role. Response scales had five points, ranging from 1, "very poorly," to 5, "exceptionally well." Perceived success at managing multiple roles was measured on a five-point scale ranging from 1, "much worse than other women," to 5, "much better than other women." Table 3 indicates that when each spouse was asked to rate the woman's functioning as a wife, on household tasks, and on child care, as well as her success at balancing multiple roles, the women were more harsh in each case than were their husbands. Women rated themselves about average or "all right" in each case while their husbands rated them as doing better than average or "very well."

In interpreting these results one question that might be raised is whether the women in our sample were just more discerning or critical in general than their husbands were. Although we did not collect extensive data to address this issue, we did ask the women to rate how well their husbands performing as parents and compared this to the husbands' own ratings. Wives rated their husbands significantly higher on this item than

Table 3. Evaluation of Wife's Role Performance

Wife's functioning	Wife rates self	Husband rates wife	p
As a wife	3.24	3.52	.001
On household tasks	3.22	3.44	.01
On childcare	3.68	3.97	.001
How well wife balances roles	3.49	4.15	.001

the husbands rated themselves (Ms = 3.41, 3.27, respectively), $t(138)$ = 2.33, $p < .05$. Similarly, as noted earlier, when each spouse was asked to describe the husband's contribution to household chores and to child care, we found no mean differences, with both spouses reporting the husband contributed between "too little" and "satisfactory amount" to these tasks. Taken together, these data suggest that the married women professionals in our study apply harsh standards to their own performance in the marital and parental roles but not to the performance of their husbands.

Related to this point is a surprising pattern of correlations we have found between amount of child care performed relative to the spouse (an index of the six child care items) and role performance evaluations. Among women, the more child care performed, the more likely they were to report feelings of not being a good enough parent (r = .17), not being a good enough spouse (r = .21), and feeling guilty about not being a better spouse (r = .17), all $p < .05$. Among men, amount of child care involvement was unrelated to these self-evaluations. It seems, then, that not only do women perform the majority of necessary child care but the extent of this performance is directly related to the self-criticism we have noted. The causal direction of this relation is unclear: it is plausible that feeling guilty about not being a good parent might lead the mother to more intensive child care involvement. That this does not occur among men in perhaps another manifestation of differences in sex-role socialization. We are currently attempting to untangle the link between child care and self-evaluation, with an eye toward understanding the husband's role in the process.

The women in our study also appear to apply high standards to evaluating their homes. Women were asked to indicate how often they experienced each of several home-related problems as a result of trying to balance the demands of a career, a marriage, and a family. Responses to these questions were made on a five-point scale that ranged from "never" to "all the time." Husbands were also asked to indicate how often they encountered these problems as a result of their wives' trying to balance the demands of a career, marriage, and family. For women, problems like not having enough time to tackle big projects like cleaning out the garage, not being able to keep up with little projects and errands, and not having enough time to keep the house as clean as they would like it to be were major stressors. The majority of women reported being bothered often or all the time by such problems. In contrast, their husbands were far less likely to experience these issues as problems. Husbands may use more lenient standards than their wives do to evaluate the day-to-day operation of the household. In contrast, the women may be socialized to expect near perfection. As one respondent put it, "I guess it bothers me not to be perfect. Things are very different from what I grew up thinking it would be like . . . like having a nice clean house, a house you're proud to invite people in to see, and well-cooked meals . . . it's all different."

Up to this point we have summarized data pertaining to women's and men's involvement in multiple roles as well as to the consequences of this involvement. However, it is important to determine how individuals' experiences in marital and parental roles are influenced by the structural characteristics of the work role. At present the two major areas of interest that we are pursuing in our analyses are (1) the impact of structural characteristics of the woman's work environment on her functioning and well-being and (2) "spillover" between work and family domains. As noted earlier, we chose two groups of professionals—academics and business-women—because we expected them to be characterized by different sorts of stressors. It was expected, for example, that businesswomen would be stressed by having a less flexible schedule whereas academics would be stressed by the open-ended, "never-finished" quality of academic work. Specifically, we were interested in documenting these and other differences in the structural characteristics of these two occupations. We then planned to assess whether these two groups of women differed in the amount of spillover from one role domain to another and, if so, whether such spillover was related to specific characteristics of the women's jobs. We were also interested in the husbands' perceptions of spillover from their wives' jobs into their own lives. Finally, we investigated the relationship between these women's occupations and their mental health or well-being, as well as the mental health and well-being of their husbands.

Before discussing our preliminary findings let us take a few moments to describe how we are conceptualizing spillover (see Lang, 1988, for a more detailed discussion). In recent years this term has come to represent the influence of conditions or experiences in one role domain on conditions or experiences in another role domain. Drawing from earlier theoretical work on spillover processes (e.g., Crouter, 1984), we delineated two constructs: spillover stress and spillover strain. Spillover stress refers to reports of objective instances of conflict between work and family. We assessed objective conflicts spilling over from work to family (e.g., missing a family-related activity because of work or travel) as well as those spilling over from family to work (e.g., missing a work-related function because of family responsibilities). Spillover strain refers to subjective feelings of distress caused by spillover from work to family (e.g., "When I'm with my family, I'm bothered by things at work I should be doing") and from family to work (e.g., "When I'm at work, I'm bothered by things at home I should be doing"). Spillover from work to personal relaxation was also investigated (e.g., "When relaxing, I'm bothered by all the things at work that I should be doing"). We developed multi-item indices to assess each of these constructs (Lang, 1988).

We first conducted statistical tests to determine whether the two occupational groups differed in structural characteristics that might be related to spillover.[2] As predicted, the two occupational groups were found to differ on job flexibility (e.g., "How much choice do you have over which days you work?"), with academics reporting significantly greater job flexibility. Academics also reported significantly lower scores on a scale developed to assess "boundedness" (e.g., "My job allows me to put aside work concerns when I leave my office for the day") and more overload (e.g., "The amount of work I have to do interferes with how well my work gets done"). In addition, academics reported somewhat more job involvement (e.g., "I live, eat, and breathe my job"), although this difference fell short of statistical significance. Interestingly, however, businesswomen worked significantly more hours per week. These occupational differences are summarized in Table 4. Contrary to our expectations, there were no differences between the two groups on the amount of authority or control the women experienced in the work environment, with both groups reporting high control. Similarly, there were no group differences in reports of conflict with coworkers or for work ambiguity, with both groups reporting low levels. Finally, there were no differences between academics and businesswomen in reports of sex discrimination on the job, as both groups reported a moderate to low incidence of this.

We next related the three job stressors on which the academic and businesswomen differed to various marital functioning and mental health outcomes of each spouse. To assess marital satisfaction and strain we utilized three-item scales drawn from Pearlin and Schooler (1978). These ask respondents how often they have experienced positive feelings (e.g., happiness, enjoyment) and negative feelings (e.g., unhappiness, frustration, or anger) in a life role. Sexual satisfaction was assessed by a three-item index designed to tap satisfaction with the quality and frequency of marital sex. Depression was assessed through a 13-item subscale of the Hopkins Symptom Checklist (Derogatis, Lipman, Rickels, Illinhuth, & Covi, 1974). We also used the total psychiatric symptomatology score.

The wife's job overload was associated with her reports of increased marital strain ($r = .18, p < .05$), decreased satisfaction with sex ($r = .19, p < .01$), increased depression ($r = .27, p < .001$), and increased psychiatric

---

[2]Our job stress scales are still being developed by the research staff. The scales described here are based on our a priori decisions about structural job characteristics. We are currently taking an empirical approach to scale development, based largely on factor analysis; thus, future reports from this project may use slightly different indices.

Table 4. Ocupational Differences: Work Role

	Academics	Businesswomen	p
Job involvement	2.53	2.28	NS
Hours worked	46.6	55.79	.001
Work characteristics			
Flexibility	3.51	2.51	.001
Boundedness	1.71	2.13	.001
Overload	3.73	3.44	.02

Note. The range of the scale was from 1, "characteristic not true to the job,"
to 5, "characteristic very true of the job."

symptoms (the Hopkins Symptom Checklist, $r = .29, p < .0001$). The wife's overload also significantly predicted husband's depression ($r = .23, p < .01$) and symptoms ($r = .21, p < .05$). Similarly, "unbounded" work demands were related to the wife's decreased satisfaction with sex ($r = -.16, p < .05$), increased depression ($r = .23, p < .01$), and increased symptomatology ($r = .22, p < .01$) but not with any husband outcomes. Finally, lack of job flexibility, the stressor characterizing business careers, was unrelated to either spouse's mental or overall functioning.

Our next step was to examine the two occupational groups to determine whether they differed in coping resources. In terms of personality, we found no differences in self-esteem, as measured by Rosenberg's (1965) scale, or in mastery, as measured by Pearlin's scale (see Pearlin *et al.*, 1981). We did find significant differences in two personality dimensions: learned resourcefulness, which refers to a repertoire of skills that assist a person in regulating his or her distress so that it does not interfere with performance (Rosenbaum, 1984), and hostility or mistrust of others, as assessed by the Cook-Medley (1954) Hostility Scale. Academic women were found to be significantly more resourceful and significantly less cynical than the businesswomen. The academic women also received more support from their spouses for their career. Finally, as noted earlier, academic women were earning significantly more money than the businesswomen.

In summary, we find that the academics and businesswomen report different types of stressors, with businesswomen having less flexibility, and academics experiencing more job overload and more problems keeping their work within bounds. We find that the academics have more resources available to cope with these stressors. Given this pattern of results, we were interested in determining whether the two groups differed on spillover. Table 5 presents occupational differences in spillover stress and strain. Even though the academic women have more time flexibility and more resources and even though they work significantly fewer hours per week

Table 5. Occupational Differences in Spillover: Stress and Strain

	Academics	Businesswomen	p
Stress			
Work → Family	2.65	2.30	.01
Family → Work	2.38	1.83	.001
Strain			
Work → Family	2.80	2.52	.001
Family → Work	2.83	2.67	.08
Work → Relaxation	2.99	2.48	.001

than the businesswomen, the academic women report more problems with spillover stress and strain. As shown in Table 5, academic women report significantly more objective conflicts spilling over from work to family as well as from family to work than do businesswomen. Similarly, academics experience more distress or strain than businesswomen as a result of spillover between work and family and spillover between work and relaxation.

Next we conducted analyses to determine whether these occupational differences in stressors and in spillover would influence husbands' outcomes. We examined each husband's subjective perceptions of spillover from his wife's work life to his life. We also examined such outcomes as marital strain and satisfaction, sexual satisfaction, and depression. These findings are summarized in Table 6. Here it can be seen that the husbands of academic women were more likely to agree that their quality of life suffers because of the wife's job, and they were more likely to report marital strain and problems with sexual satisfaction, and heightened criticism of the wife's performance as a mother. Interestingly, the wives generally agreed with these assessments about the marriage: academic women were

Table 6. Occupational Differences in Spillover: Husband's Outcomes

	Academics	Businesswomen	p
Spillover perceptions			
Relationship with wife suffers because of her job	2.42	2.02	.01
My quality of life suffers	2.02	1.69	.03
Marital strain	2.27	1.95	.03
Sexual satisfaction	3.16	3.44	.03
Critical of wife as mother	2.03	1.75	.02
Depression (SCL)	1.72	1.55	.03

significantly more likely to report marital strain and problems with sexual satisfaction than were businesswomen. Finally, husbands of academic women were more likely to report depression than husbands of businesswomen.

Of course, these analyses are preliminary, and it is too early to conclude that characteristics of the wife's work environment are causing these difficulties for the husband and the marriage. At present we are developing some causal models to explicate the relationships among the variables. While this work is in the early stages, some of our initial findings appear promising. For example, we have found that while the objective instances of spillover from the wife's work to her family are positively predictive of husband's depression, the wife's subjective distress from spillover negatively predicts husband's depression. As a result of this counterintuitive pattern of findings, we attempted to identify those conditions under which women's objective spillover stress is likely to get translated into marital strain. In so doing we discovered that a powerful determinant of spillover strain is marital commitment: women who are highly committed to their marriage tend to become more distressed when work spills into family life. In a causal model including the wife's spillover stress and strain and her marital commitment, we can account for 61% of the variance in the husband's depression (Lang, 1988). One interpretation of these data is that if a woman is strongly committed to her marriage, she is likely to become upset when work intrudes and, once upset, engage in compensatory behaviors that reduce her husband's distress.

SEX DIFFERENCES IN COMBINING WORK AND FAMILY: PRELIMINARY ANALYSES OF DATA FROM THE PHYSICIAN STUDY

The data reported in the previous section of this chapter suggest that women experience and cope with competing demands between work and family very differently than do their husbands. Women tend to take far more responsibility for household activities and child care, and they experience more role conflict than their husbands. However, this greater investment in the family is not reflected in higher evaluations of their performance. In contrast to their husbands' positive evaluations of their performance as wives and mothers, women judge their performance in the marital and family roles rather harshly and are critical of how things are going at home.

Because our study of married women professionals was designed to focus primarily on women, the data from which sex differences could be examined was somewhat limited. To explore sex differences in combining work and family more fully, we turned our attention to our study of physicians. We have collected data from approximately 200 physicians at four points in time: twice during the medical school years and twice in the early practice years. Data were also collected from the physician's spouse at two points in time during the early practice years. On the basis of results of our study with married women professionals, we decided to select men and women for our physician study who were heavily involved in multiple roles, that is, those physicians and their spouses who were involved in equally demanding jobs and had small children.

Drawing from our data, we had no problem identifying women in the sample whose husbands worked full-time in a demanding profession and who had small children. However, we were surprised to find that almost none of the male physicians in our sample had wives who fit into this category. Less than a quarter of the male physicians were married to a woman who worked full-time, and less than 20% were married to women whose careers were of equal status to their own. The most common pattern was for male physicians to marry nurses, medical technicians, or elementary school teachers who quit working or who worked only part-time once children were born. For males in our sample the status hierarchy in the workplace was carried over into the home. In contrast, virtually all of the female physicians in our sample were married to men who worked full-time, and over 90% were married to men who were working in a profession at least equal in status to their own (e.g., businessmen, lawyers, architects, or other physicians).

Given this information, it is perhaps not surprising that the most typical child care arrangement in the male physician households was one in which the wife watched the children or where child care was shared by the wife and a babysitter or day-care provider. In contrast, female physicians tended to rely almost exclusively on babysitters or day-care providers.

All of the physicians from our study were graduates from the University of Michigan Medical School. Hence, both men and women were subjected to the same selection criteria and the same training program. Nonetheless, by the early years of practice, they had arranged their lives very differently. In these couples, involvement in household work and child care was determined largely by gender.

FUTURE RESEARCH DIRECTIONS

Our study of women professionals began with three general goals, which we have addressed at some level in this chapter. How do multiple-role women experience their lives? It is clear that simultaneous participation in three major life roles produces substantial degrees of conflict between roles in addition to the demands within each domain. Despite our sample's high educational and career achievement, we find that the responsibilities of running a home and caring for children are placed largely in women's hands. Their response to this heavy involvement at home is criticism of themselves but general satisfaction with their husbands' contributions. Anecdotal evidence suggests that women professionals, subject to traditional sex-role socialization, are strongly influenced by standards of home performance set by women who did not work outside the home. They also have not come to expect equity in household responsibility within their own marriages, even though their out-of-home demands equal or exceed those of their husbands.

Our second major goal was to investigate how stress in one role influences satisfaction in other roles. We documented differences in the type and amount of job stress and spillover experienced by academics and businesswomen and found that certain aspects of the job, namely, high degree of overload and lack of boundedness, are related to increased marital strain, decreased sexual satisfaction, and high degrees of psychological distress. In short, stressors of a woman's job can have substantial impact on her functioning within another domain, marriage, and on her own and her husband's overall mental health. These analyses are at an early stage, but we believe the issue of spillover between roles and between spouses will be an exciting area for further investigation.

A third goal of this project was to move the stress and coping literature from an individual to an interpersonal perspective. The findings summarized in this chapter reflect such a perspective. We have further shown that a wife's experiences of spillover stress and strain and her level of marital commitment can account for a substantial amount of variance in her husband's depression. Clearly, the marital dyad provides a rich arena for investigation of the give and take of stresses and satisfactions. To understand a single individual's level of stress and response to that stress, it is extremely important to assess what his or her partner contributes to the situation. For example, Bolger *et al.* (1990) describe at a day-to-day level the compensation that occurs when one spouse has a difficult day at work and brings that stress home. The compensatory actions of the second spouse, for example, her or his heavier involvement in child care, could not be understood without learning that the first spouse retreated from child care that day in response to the work stress. We feel that this type of dyadic interchange deserves future research emphasis.

We began this program of research with a theoretical interest in stress and coping processes. As the research has progressed, however, we have become fascinated by the sex differences that have emerged in our study of how work and family roles are managed. For women involved in demanding careers, combining work and family is particularly challenging. The option of having a spouse whose career takes second place and who takes major responsibility for the household and the children is the norm for men in demanding professions. Unfortunately, this option is not typically available or socially acceptable for women. Hence, women must cope with intense demands both at work and at home—and with their own harsh standards of performance in the home domain.

Our goal for future research will be to explore the antecedents and consequences of inequities in household responsibilities and child care. Such findings are often regarded as implicating the man for not taking more responsibility for home tasks. However, it is important to gain greater insight into why women are so accepting of the inequitable patterns of involvement that exist. Do women behave in ways that unwittingly discourage more participation from their husbands? Perhaps women's use of a "superwoman" coping strategy, a highly endorsed style characterized by "trying to do everything," combined with their high standards for performance lead men to withdraw. Women may also send signals that "all is well," further encouraging men's minimal involvement in running the home.

On the other hand, we have little understanding of how men feel about the inequities in performance of household duties. Why do these men continue to "let" their wives take care of them and the home? How would the men in our sample react if their wives attempted to relinquish more household duties? It would be surprising if they cheerfully picked up the slack, no questions asked. We have some evidence that when a woman does divest herself of responsibilities at home, presumably by assigning chores to her husband, he responds by reporting that she is not fulfilling her role as a spouse. He does not, however, increase his involvement in child care. In fact, very few women in our sample used divestment or delegating as a coping strategy at home or at work. This suggests a nonproductive cycle whereby women may initially delegate responsibility to the husband but are made to feel, in turn, that this indicates poor role performance; furthermore, delegating responsibility does not alter the husband's involvement. Delegation may then not appear to be a viable coping option, which leaves the women once again bearing primary responsibility for running the home. In addition, despite their financial resources, only 57% of the couples in this sample employed paid domestic help beyond their child care arrangements. Apparently, these couples are unable to overcome the behaviors dictated by their deep-rooted value systems concerning the woman's proper role in the home.

In this study, we explored the impact of the inequitable distribution of labor regarding housework and child care on women themselves. An issue that cannot be addressed in this study but that represents an important goal for subsequent work concerns the impact of such dual-career work patterns on children. Are children benefited or harmed by the greater involvement of their employed mothers than their employed fathers in the day-to-day aspects of their physical care? Some of our respondents commented that they did more than their share of the child care because they felt that they typically relate to the child in a way that is more loving and nurturant. If fathers increase their involvement in child care, will children receive less nurturance than they receive from their mothers? Will the children benefit in other ways from more involvement on the part of their fathers?

The lives of married women professionals with young children are complicated "juggling acts" that require them to face conflicting role demands and time shortages on a regular basis. In this chapter we have taken a preliminary step toward understanding how these women experience their roles and toward explicating the processes through which women's chronic role stress influences their experiences in other roles, spills over into other roles, and affects their husbands' well-being. It is our hope that enhanced awareness of these processes will help to clarify how women and men who are equally involved in their work can relate more as equal partners at home.

ACKNOWLEDGMENTS

Work on this paper was supported by grants BNS8807327 and BNS8417745 from the National Science Foundation and from grant MH40255-01 from the National Institute of Mental Health. The research was based at the Institute for Social Research at the University of Michigan, Ann Arbor, Michigan. The authors are grateful to Geraldine Downey, Carol-Ann Emmons, and Linda Beth Tiedje for the many contributions they have made to the study of professional women on which this chapter is based. The authors also thank Kate McGonagle for her helpful comments on an earlier version of this manuscript.

REFERENCES

Aneshensel, C. S., & Pearlin, L. I. (1987). Structural contexts of sex differences in stress. In R. C. Barnett, L. Biener, & G. K. Baruch (Eds.), *Gender and stress* (pp. 75–95). New York: Free Press.

Barnett, R. C., & Baruch, G. K. (1985). Women's involvement in multiple roles and psychological distress. *Journal of Personality and Social Psychology, 49,* 135–145.

Baruch, G. K., & Barnett, R. C. (1986). Role quality, multiple role involvement, and psychological well-being in midlife women. *Journal of Personality and Social Psychology, 51,* 578–585.

Bernardo, D. H., Shehan, C. L., & Leslie, G. R. (1987). A residue of tradition: Jobs, careers, and spouses' time in housework. *Journal of Marriage and the Family, 49,* 381–390.

Biernat, M., & Wortman, C. B. (in press). The sharing of home responsibilities between professionally employed women and their husbands. *Journal of Personality and Social Psychology.*

Bolger, N., DeLongis, A., Kessler, R. C., & Wethington, E. (1990). The microstructure of daily role-related stress in married couples. In J. Eckenrode & S. Gore (Eds.), *Stress between work and family* (pp. 95–115). New York: Plenum.

Bryson, R., Bryson, J. B., & Johnson, M. F. (1978). Family size, satisfaction and productivity in dual-career couples. *Psychology of Women Quarterly, 3,* 167–177.

Bulman, R. J., & Wortman, C. B. (1977). Attributions of blame and coping in the "real world": Severe accident victims react to their lot. *Journal of Personality and Social Psychology, 35,* 351–363.

Cleary, P. D., & Mechanic, D. (1983). Sex differences in psychological distress among married people. *Journal of Health and Social Behavior, 24,* 111–121.

Cook, U., & Medley, D. (1954). Proposed hostility and pharisaic-virtue scales for the MMPI. *Journal of Applied Psychology, 38,* 414–418.

Coser, R. L. (1974). The complexity of roles as a seedbed of individual autonomy. In R. L. Coser (Ed.), *The family.* New York: St. Martin's Press.

Crouter, A. C. (1984). Spillover from family to work: The neglected side of the work–family interface. *Human Relations, 37,* 425–442.

Derogatis, L. R., Lipman, R. S., Rickels, K., Illinhuth, E. H., & Covi, L. (1974). The Hopkins Symptom Checklist (HSCL). *Modern Problems in Pharmacopsychiatry, 7,* 79–110.

Emmons, C. A., Biernat, M., Tiedje, L. B., Lang, E., & Wortman, C. B. (1990). Stress, support, and coping among women professionals with preschool children. In J. Eckenrode and S. Gore (Eds.), *Stress between work and family* (pp. 61–93). New York: Plenum.

Goode, W. J. (1960). A theory of role strain. *American Sociological Review, 25,* 483–496.

Haw, M. A. (1982). Women, work, and stress: A review and agenda for the future. *Journal of Health and Social Behavior, 23,* 132–144.

Hayghe, H. (1986). Rise in mothers' labor force activity. *Monthly Labor Review, 109,* 43–45.

Hirsch, B. J., & Rapkin, B. D. (1986). Multiple roles, social networks, and women's well-being. *Journal of Personality and Social Psychology, 51,* 1237–1247.

Holahan, C. K., & Gilbert, L. A. (1979). Inter-role conflict for working women: Career versus jobs. *Journal of Applied Psychology, 64,* 86–90.

Kelly, R. F., & Voydanoff, P. (1985). Work/family role strain among employed parents. *Family Relations, 34,* 367–374.

Kessler, R. C., Price, R. H., & Wortman, C. B. (1985). Social factors in psychopathology: Stress, social support, and coping processes. *Annual Review of Psychology, 36,* 531–572.

Lang, E. L. (1988). *Role conflict and work/family spillover: Comparing academic and nonacademic multiple-role women.* Unpublished doctoral dissertation, University of Michigan.

Lehman, D. R., Wortman, C. B., & Williams, A. F. (1987). Long-term effects of losing a spouse or a child in a motor vehicle accident. *Journal of Personality and Social Psychology, 52,* 218–231.

Marks, S. (1977). Multiple roles and role strain: Some notes on human energy, time and commitment. *American Sociological Review, 42,* 921–936.

McLanahan, S., & Adams, J. (1987). Parenthood and psychological well-being. *Annual Review of Sociology, 13,* 237–257.

Merton, R. K. (1957). *Social theory and social structure* (rev. ed.). New York: Free Press.

Mott, F. L. (1982). *The employment revolution: Young American women of the 1970's.* Cambridge: MIT Press.

Pearlin, L. I., Lieberman, M. A., Meneghan, E. G., & Mullen, J. T. (1981). The stress process. *Journal of Health and Social Behavior, 22,* 337–356.

Pearlin, L. I., & Schooler, C. (1978). The structure of coping. *Journal of Health and Social Behavior, 19,* 2–21.

Pleck, J. H. (1978). The work-family role system. *Social Problems, 24,* 417–427.

Pleck, J. H. (1985). *Working wives, working husbands.* Beverly Hills: Sage.

Pleck, J. H., & Staines, G. L. (1985). Work schedules and family life in two-earner couples. *Journal of Family Issues, 6,* 61–82.

Presser, H. B., & Baldwin, W. (1980). Child care as a constraint on employment: Prevalence, correlates, and bearing on the work and fertility nexus. *American Journal of Sociology, 85,* 1202–1219.

Repetti, R. L. (1987). Linkages between work and family roles. In S. Oskamp (Ed.), *Applied social psychology annual: Vol. 7. Family processes and problems* (pp. 98–127). Beverly Hills: Sage.

Rosenberg, M. (1965). *Society and the adolescent self-image.* Princeton, NJ: Princeton University Press.

Rosenbaum, M. (1984). A model for research on self-regulation: Reducing the schism between behaviorism and general psychology. In I. M. Evans (Ed.), *Paradigmatic behavior therapy: Critical perspectives on applied social behaviorism.* New York: Springer.

Ross, C. E., Mirowsky, J., & Huber, J. (1983). Dividing work, sharing work, and in-between: Marriage patterns and depression. *American Sociological Review, 48,* 809–823.

Sieber, S. D. (1974). Toward a theory of role accumulation. *American Sociological Review, 39,* 567–578.

Silver, R. L., & Wortman, C. B. (1980). Coping with undesirable life events. In J. Garber & M. E. P. Seligman (Eds.), *Human helplessness: Theory and applications* (pp. 279–340). New York: Academic Press.

Smith, R. E. (1979). *The subtle revolution.* Washington, DC: The Urban Institute.

Staines, G. L., Pleck, J. H., Shepard, L. J., & O'Connor, P. (1978). Wives' employment status and marital adjustment: Yet another look. *Psychology of Women Quarterly, 3,* 90–120.

Thoits, P. A. (1983). Multiple identities and psychological well-being: A reformulation and test of the social isolation hypothesis. *American Sociological Review, 48,* 147–187.

U.S. Department of Labor. (1985). *The United Nations decade for women, 1976–1985: Employment in the United States.* Washington, DC: U.S. Department of Labor, Women's Bureau.

Verbrugge, L. (1983). Multiple roles and physical health of women and men. *Journal of Health and Social Behavior, 24,* 16–30.

Weingarten, K. (1978). The employment pattern of professional couples and their distribution of involvement in the family. *Psychology of Women Quarterly, 3,* 43–52.

White, L. K., Booth, A., & Edwards, J. N. (1986). Children and marital happiness—why the negative correlation. *Journal of Family Issues, 7,* 131–147.

Yogev, S. (1981). Do professional women have egalitarian marital relationships? *Journal of Marriage and the Family, 43,* 865–871.

6

The Relationship between Women's Work and Family Roles and Their Subjective Well-Being and Psychological Distress

ROSALIND C. BARNETT AND NANCY L. MARSHALL

OVERVIEW

The aim of this chapter is to assess the effects of women's work and family roles (both the occupancy and quality of these roles) on their mental health.[1] Although there is general concern about the impact of multiple roles on women's mental health, most of the available research examines the impact of individual roles such as that of mother (by itself) or paid employee (by itself). For example, we know that mothers report more symptoms of distress than nonmothers (Barnett & Baruch, 1985; Veroff, Douvan, & Kulka, 1981). Similarly, findings suggest that occupancy of the paid-employee role is associated with high subjective well-being and low psychological distress (Baruch, Biener, & Barnett, 1987; Brown & Harris, 1978; Thoits, 1983).

[1]See Barnett & Baruch, 1987, for a review of this literature.

ROSALIND C. BARNETT AND NANCY L. MARSHALL • Center for Research on Women, Wellesley College, Wellesley, Massachusetts 02181.

111

In those studies of women that do consider both employment and family roles, it is usually assumed that women have family roles and attention is focused on the impact of adding the employee role to the family roles. In contrast, the study reported in this chapter starts with the fact of women's employment and asks about the effects on mental health of family-role occupancy and family-role quality.

Our approach also differs sharply from that characterizing mainstream research on men and mental health, which is striking for its neglect of the fact that male workers also function in nonworkplace roles. For example, many of the major studies of the stress-illness relationship in men do not even report their subjects' partnership or parental status (see, e.g., Rosenman, Brand, Jenkins, Friedman, Straus, & Wurm, 1975). This one-dimensional view is most assuredly due to the dual assumptions that the employee role is men's most salient role and that men's family roles are benign. (These assumptions have been challenged by empirical findings; see Farrell & Rosenberg, 1981; Pleck, 1985.)

Although there is some previous research on the effect of family-role occupancy on the relationships between employment and health, it is generally quite limited. Furthermore, most of it has focused on physical rather than mental health. For example, there is evidence to suggest that for women family-role occupancy moderates the negative effects of workplace stressors on cardiovascular disease (Haynes & Feinleib, 1982). Also, some studies suggest that family-role occupancy conditions the physical health enhancing effects of employment[2] (Waldron & Jacobs, 1988; Waldron & Jacobs, 1989). With respect to subjective well-being, some studies find a beneficial effect of employment for all women, regardless of marital or parental status (Baruch, Barnett, & Rivers, 1984).

Even less attention has been given to the potentially more interesting questions concerning the effects of family-role quality (a subjective variable) on the relationships between workplace roles and mental health outcomes. Role quality refers to the relative rewards and concerns a woman experiences in a given role. A woman's role quality will be positive as long as her level of reward exceeds her level of concern. Accordingly, role quality can be enhanced by reducing concerns, that is, stressors, or by increasing rewards. There is general agreement that role quality is an important predictor of mental health.

In our approach to the relationship between role quality and mental health, we focus equally on positive mental health, that is, subjective well-

---

[2]In the absence of longitudinal data it is, of course, possible that women with better mental health select themselves into the paid-labor force. Ingrid Waldron and her associates (Waldron & Jacobs, 1988; Waldron & Jacobs, 1989) demonstrate such social selection with respect to the relationship between employment and physical health.

being, and negative mental health, that is, anxiety and depression. This dual focus has not been prevalent in mainstream research, which has focused primarily on the stress–illness relationship. A major reason for this imbalance is the reliance on the medical model, which equates positive mental health with the absence of symptoms and consequently ignores the existence of subjective well-being as a distinct construct with its own correlates. In contrast, research within the area of personality psychology, as well as the adult development literature in general, strongly supports a two-dimensional model (Bryant & Veroff, 1984; Diener, 1984; Diener & Emmons, 1985). The underlying premise is that well-being is more than just the absence of symptoms; it is the presence of positive affect.

According to the dual focus view, knowing that a woman reports few symptoms of anxiety and depression tells us only that she is not experiencing psychological distress; it does not tell us that she is experiencing subjective well-being. Being symptom-free is not the same as enjoying positive well-being.

In this chapter, we take the following positions: (1) women's mental health is a complex construct consisting of at least two dimensions, positive mental health, that is, subjective well-being, and negative mental health, that is, psychological distress; (2) these two dimensions, although negatively correlated, are not merely the mirror image of one another; (3) each dimension has a unique relationship to the aspects of work and nonwork roles addressed in this chapter, namely, work rewards, work concerns, family-role occupancy, and family-role quality; and (4) a full understanding of the effects of employment on women's mental health requires both joint consideration of women's work and family roles and separate consideration of the positive and negative mental health dimensions.

The chapter is organized into three sections. In the first, we identify those aspects of work that are related to each of the two mental-health dimensions. As you will see, the findings indicate that virtually the same aspects of work predict to both dimensions. Moreover, psychological distress and subjective well-being are correlated at $r = -.57$, indicating that each measure explains 32% of the variance in the other. On the basis of these data, one might conclude that mental health is unidimensional. However, as the data presented in the second and third sections of the chapter indicate, there is strong support for a two-dimensional model of mental health when we consider the joint effects of women's work and family roles.

In the second section of the chapter, we look at family-role occupancy and its effects on the relationship between rewards and concerns at work and the experience of well-being or distress. In the third, we examine family-role quality and its impact on the relationship between the work factors and the two mental-health dimensions. The findings reported in these two sections challenge the unidimensional model of mental health. In brief, the effects on well-being of the work and family variables are independent. More specifically, in every instance the relationship between the work factors and well-being is unaffected by the family-role variables, that is, occupancy and quality. In contrast, the relationship between psychological distress and the work factors is conditioned by family-role occupancy and, in certain instances, by family-role quality. In short, employed women who occupy family roles are less vulnerable to the effects of particular work factors, and employed mothers with challenging jobs are protected from the distress-exacerbating effects of troubled relationships with their children. Only when we look at women in the context of their multiple roles do we see that the two mental-health dimensions are not merely opposite ends of the same construct.

THE STUDY

Data for this chapter come from the first wave of a 3-wave longitudinal study of a disproportionate, stratified, random sample of 403 Massachusetts women, ages 25 to 55, who were employed at least half-time at the start of the study in one of two health care professions—social work and licensed practical nursing. These two professions were selected on the basis of three criteria: (1) they are female professions; (2) they are high-strain professions, that is, presumably characterized by high-job demand and low-job control; and (3) they are professions with public licensure records, thereby allowing for the identification of populations from which to draw a random sample.

Understanding the relationship between work rewards and concerns and mental-health states among employees in service occupations, such as social work and licensed practical nursing, is of particular importance at this time, since these occupations are part of the fastest growing sector of the American economy. In the next decade, a 26% increase in health-service workers is projected (The Association of Schools of Public Health, 1988). More generally, 9 out of every 10 new jobs in the next decade will be in the service sector, and this sector will continue to employ an increasingly large percentage of women. For example, whereas women represented 44% of the labor force in 1985, they constituted 61% of service-industry employees (Marshall, Barnett, Baruch, & Pleck, in press).

All the respondents in this study lived within a 25-mile radius of Boston and were drawn randomly from the registries of the two given professions. Data were collected from the fall of 1985 to the spring of 1986. Respondents were interviewed in their homes or offices by a trained interviewer. The interviews lasted about 2 hours and covered the rewards and concerns in each of the woman's major social roles, that is, partner, parent, and paid worker; the women were also rated as indices of psychological distress and subjective well-being. Respondents were paid a fee of $10 for participating.

Within the two occupations, the sample was stratified on race, parental status, and partnership status (women who were either married or living with a partner were defined as "partnered") (see Table 1). The mean age of the sample was 39.5 years (SD = 7.4). Approximately half of the sample was partnered (n = 194, 49.1%), and roughly half had children (n = 227, 56.3%). The ages of the respondents' children ranged from less than 1 year to over 30 years, and the median family size was 2.0 children. Most of the mothers were not caring for young children; only 15% had children under the age of 6. In contrast, 45% of the mothers had children 18 years or older. Sixty-one women (15.3%) were black and 342 (84.7%) were white. On average, the women had been working in their respective occupations for 11 years (the range was 2 to 35 years) and at their current jobs for 6 years. They worked 38 hours per week on average, and 80% worked the same schedule on a regular basis. The mean individual income in 1985 was $24,400 (SD = $2,700).

Measures of Mental Health

Psychological distress was assessed by the anxiety and depression subscales of the SCL-90-R, a frequency of symptoms measure (Derogatis, 1975). (The SCL-90-R is a 90-item revision of an earlier measure, the Hopkins Symptom Check List.) Subjects indicated on five-point scales (from 0 = "not at all" to 4 = "extremely") how often in the past week they were bothered by each of 10 symptoms of anxiety and 13 symptoms of depression. The decision to combine the scales into a psychological distress score was based on a correlation of .80 between the scales and on the similarity in the pattern of correlations between the anxiety and depression scales and the other variables of interest in the study. The SCL-90-R has high levels of both internal consistency and test–retest reliability. In

Table 1. Sample Design

| | Partnership status | | | |
| | Partnered | | Nonpartnered | |
Parental status	LPN	SW	LPN	SW
Parent	59	64	42	64
Nonparent	18	57	36	63

Note. n = 403.

this sample coefficient alpha was .88 for depression and .89 for anxiety. These figures are similar to those reported by Derogatis (1983). Satisfactory test–retest correlations (.82 for depression and .80 for anxiety) have also been reported (Derogatis, 1983). For this sample, mean scores for the depression and anxiety scale were .72 and .53, respectively. These scores are within one standard deviation of the mean score for a normative sample of 494 nonhospitalized adult females.

Subjective well-being was assessed by responses to a 14-item positive-affect scale developed by the Rand Corporation (Davis, Sherbourne, Peterson, & Ware, 1985). The women were asked to respond on six-point scales (from 1 = "none of the time" to 6 = "all of the time") to such items as, "How often in the past month did you feel relaxed and free of tension?" and "How often in the past month did you expect in the morning to have an interesting day?" In this sample, Cronbach alpha was .94, which is essentially identical with the .96 figure given by Veit and Ware (1983), who also report a 1-year test–retest correlation of $r = .64$. The mean per-item score on subjective well-being was 3.6 for this sample, which is within one standard deviation of the mean for the normative sample.

As expected, the two mental-health measures were negatively correlated ($r = -.57$, $p < .001$). The moderate strength of the correlation is consistent with both the premise that subjective well-being and psychological distress are not merely redundant measures and with the search for factors that account for the relatively high percent (i.e., 68%) of unexplained variance.

I. WHICH ASPECTS OF WORK ARE RELATED TO MENTAL-HEALTH MEASURES?[3]

Karasek and his colleagues have identified the combination of high "demand" and low "decision latitude" (i.e., control) as strongly associated with several stress-related health problems (Karasek, Schwartz, & Theorell, 1982). (Demand, that is, "psychological demand," refers to such work-related feelings as not having enough time to do one's work, having conflicting demands on the job, and having to work fast. According to Karasek, decision latitude refers to two constructs: skill discretion and decision authority. Workers with a high level of skill have control over which specific skills to use to accomplish a task. Thus, this combination of

[3]Certain aspects of the paid-employee role, such as challenge and decision authority, have been identified as rewarding. Other aspects have been identified as problematic, e.g., overload, low control, boredom. Rewarding aspects and those that are problematic may, in turn, be related to mental health. However, most of the literature on job conditions has focused on identifying work stressors, not mitigators of stress or work rewards.

constructs is often labelled "control" [Karasek & Theorell, 1990, p. 58].) These studies have had a major effect on shaping the research paradigm for the study of the stress—illness relationship, among men as well as women. However, they were done with all male samples (see, e.g., Karasek, Schwartz, & Theorell, 1982; Caplan, Cobb, French, Van Harrison, & Pinneau, 1975), as were almost all of the early theory-building studies concerning the relationship between work conditions and stress-related health measures. In this section we identify the work factors that women experience as "rewarding" and as "of concern."

The instrument we used to assess work rewards and work concerns was empirically derived from the open-ended responses of roughly 100 employed women. They were asked to tell us about the rewarding and the problematic aspects of their jobs. Their responses were tape-recorded, transcribed, and content-analyzed. On the basis of frequency of response, 25 work-reward and 25 work-concern items were identified (see Baruch & Barnett, 1986, for a fuller discussion). These items constitute the scales used in this study.[4]

To identify which aspects of work are related to women's mental health, the sample was divided into random halves. Exploratory work, guided by previous research, was conducted on the responses of one-half of the sample to 25 work-reward and 25 work-concern items.[5] Confirmatory factor analyses were then performed on the responses of the other half of the sample.

Six work-reward factors were identified in one half of the sample and confirmed in the other half: Helping Others, Decision Authority,[6] Challenge, Supervisor Support, Recognition, and Satisfaction with Salary. Five work-concern factors were identified and confirmed: Overload, Dead-End Job, Hazard Exposure, Poor Supervision, and Discrimination. Table 2 lists the items constituting each factor. (The details of the confirmatory factor analyses are discussed in Barnett & Marshall, 1990.)

Main Effects of Work Rewards and Work Concerns

To identify those work-reward and work-concern factors that have mental-health consequences, we estimated separate regression models

[4] These scales have very satisfactory psychometric properties. Test—retest correlation coefficients (over a 1- to 3-month period) were .88 for work rewards and work concerns; Cronbach alphas were .88 for work rewards and .89 for work concerns.

[5] The work-reward and work-concern scales are available upon request from the authors.

[6] The term *decision authority* is used because the items constituting this factor correspond closely to those identified by Karasek *et al.* (1982), who also uses this term. The four items constituting Karasek's decision-authority scale are (1) freedom as to how one works; (2) allows a lot of decisions; (3) assist in one's own decision; and (4) have say over what happens.

Table 2. Work-Reward and Work-Concern Factors

Work-reward factors	Mean	Standard deviation
Helping Others		
1. Helping others	3.42	.69
2. Being needed by others	3.13	.77
3. Having an impact on other people's lives	3.23	.71
Decision-Authority		
1. Being able to make decisions on your own	3.30	.72
2. Being able to work on your own	3.24	.75
3. Having the authority you need to get your job done without having to go to someone else for permission	2.98	.86
4. The freedom to decide how to do your work	3.24	.74
Challenge		
1. Challenging or stimulating work	2.93	.80
2. Having a variety of tasks	3.12	.79
3. The sense of accomplishment and competence you get from doing your job	2.99	.79
4. The job's fitting your interests and skills	2.99	.80
5. The opportunity for learning new things	2.91	.86
Recognition		
1. The recognition you get	2.53	.83
2. The appreciation you get	2.75	.80
Work-concern factors		
Overload		
1. Having too much to do	2.43	.94
2. The job's taking too much out of you	2.15	.93
3. Having to deal with emotionally difficult situations	2.35	.93

Note. n = 403.

with the two mental-health measures as outcomes and the six reward factors entered simultaneously as predictors. We then estimated regression models with the five work-concern factors entered simultaneously as predictors.

In order to control for the relationship between background characteristics and the mental-health measures, all models included the following control variables: socioeconomic status,[7] age, race, and per capita income.[8]

[7]Socioeconomic status was determined by summing scores for occupation (2 = social worker, 1 = licensed practical nurse) and years of education. This model of SES was based on results from a principle components analysis indicating that these two variables contributed equally to the first component.

[8]Since roughly 30 women did not provide per capita income data, the number of subjects in the following regressions is less than 403.

Social workers and licensed practical nurses (LPNs) were included in a single model on the basis of preliminary analyses indicating no differences between the two occupations in the relationships of the independent variables to the mental-health measures.

With well-being as the mental-health measure, four work-reward factors emerged as significant: Helping Others, Challenge, Decision Authority, and Recognition. With psychological distress as the health measure, three work-reward factors were significant: Helping Others, Challenge, and Decision Authority. The set of significant work-reward and work-concern factors differed only slightly for the two measures. Thus, Supervisor Support and Satisfaction with Salary contributed to the level of reward a woman experienced at work; however, neither had an independent impact on her level of distress or well-being. Interestingly, for both well-being and distress, Overload was the only work concern that remained significant when all five work concerns were entered into the same regression model. Although Poor Supervision, Hazard Exposure, Discrimination, and a Dead-End Job contributed to the level of concern women reported in their paid jobs, none of these factors was uniquely associated with either well-being or distress. In short, not all work rewards or concerns are equal in their ability to affect mental-health measures; some work rewards and concerns may be associated with job satisfaction but have no mental-health consequences.

These findings suggest that the narrowing of attention to the two workplace dimensions of "demand" and "decision latitude" may be premature. It is important to note that these two dimensions are concerned with tasks and pressures, not with the interpersonal aspects of the workplace. (The same comment applies to two of the other dimensions that Karasek identifies as problematic, namely, noxious stimuli and hazard exposure; the exceptions are supervisor and coworker support.) To the extent that women compared to men experience different aspects of work as rewarding or problematic, the search for workplace sources of stress and mitigators of stress will need to be broadened to include these aspects.

Interactions between Work Rewards and Concerns

The presence of work rewards, such as Decision Authority or Helping Others, may buffer the impact of Overload on mental health. Conversely, low levels of reward may exacerbate the impact of Overload. To explore these possibilities, we estimated both main and interaction-effects models by creating interaction terms with Overload and each of the work-reward factors, for example, Overload × Helping Others, Overload × Decision Authority, Overload × Satisfaction with Salary. (We focus exclusively on Overload, since it was the only work-concern factor that remained signifi-

Table 3. Work-Reward and Work-Concern Factors and Health Measures

	Psychological distress		Subjective well-being	
	B[a]	SE[b]	B[a]	SE[b]
Socioeconomic status	−0.02	0.26	−0.32	0.25
Age	−0.12	0.08	−0.02	0.08
Race	−4.23*	1.67	1.40	1.68
Per capita income	0.04	0.06	0.09	0.06
Helping Others	−3.80***	1.14	4.54***	1.18
Decision Authority	−4.19***	1.04	2.51**	0.95
Overload	5.15***	0.85	−3.25***	0.87
Overload × Helping Others	−4.89***	1.31	3.07*	1.33
R^2 = .29				

Note. n = 372.
[a]Unstandardized regression coefficients.
[b]Standard error of the regression coefficients.
*p < .05. **p < .01. ***p < .001.

cant when the effects of all four work-concern factors were estimated simultaneously).

Higher rewards from Decision Authority were associated with lower psychological distress, as can be seen in Table 3.[9] (Nonsignificant terms, other than controls, were dropped from the final model.) It is interesting to note that Challenge, which had been significantly associated with psychological distress in analyses that included only work-reward factors, failed to remain significant when Overload was included in the regression model.

Of great importance is the significant interaction between Overload and Helping Others. As can be seen in Figure 1, under conditions of low concern[10] about work Overload, the rewards of Helping Others have little relationship to psychological distress. However, under conditions of high concern about work Overload, high rewards from Helping Others are associated with lower psychological distress—a classic buffering relationship (Cohen & Wills, 1985). The converse of such a buffer is also apparent in Figure 1: low rewards from Helping Others exacerbates the relationship between work Overload and psychological distress.

With subjective well-being as the mental-health measure, Helping Others and Recognition were positively associated and Overload was negatively associated (see Table 3). As was the case with distress, Challenge—which had been significantly related to well-being in analyses

[9]Tolerance statistics were computed for all regressions to test for collinearity. Results indicated no collinearity problems.
[10]High and low concerns or rewards were defined as plus or minus one standard deviation from the mean.

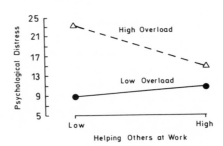

Figure 1. Interaction of work Overload and Helping Others at work on psychological distress.

without the work-concern factors—failed to remain significant when Overload was included in the regression model. Once again, the interaction between Helping Others and Overload was significant, as shown in Figure 2. We again find a buffering effect of Helping Others: when concerns about work Overload are low, Helping Others has relatively little impact; when concerns about work Overload are high, rewards from Helping Others improves well-being.

Before proceeding, it is important to keep in mind that the data reported in this chapter are based on self-reports. It is possible, therefore, that response bias may account for the pattern of findings. The interpretative issues are especially difficult when we are dealing with subjective evaluations of role quality. For example, it may be that women who enjoy high subjective well-being (compared to those who do not) are more rewarded from Helping Others at work, less concerned about work Overload, and experience their family roles more positively. However, examination of the magnitude of the zero-order correlations indicates only modest correlations between the two mental-health measures and the work-role quality and family-role quality indices. With well-being, r's range from $-.29$ to $.50$, with a mean correlation of $r = .30$. With psychological distress, r's ranged from $-.39$ to $.38$, with a mean correlation of $r = .29$.

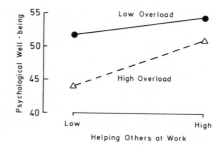

Figure 2. Interaction of work Overload and Helping Others at work on psychological well-being.

Thus, there is little direct evidence to suggest that response bias played a major part in the pattern of results.

With this caveat in mind, we can answer the first of the three questions addressed in this chapter. The data indicate that subjective well-being and psychological distress are related similarly to specific work-reward and work-concern factors. Concern about work Overload is associated with low subjective well-being and high psychological distress. That is, women who are concerned about "having too much to do," concerned that the job's "taking too much out" of them, and concerned about "having to deal with emotionally difficult situations" are at risk for a diminished sense of well-being and greater distress. At the same time, for women employed in these health-care occupations, rewards from "being needed by others," "helping others," and "having an impact on other people's lives" buffer the negative impact of work overload; high rewards from Helping Others mitigate the effect of work Overload. To paraphrase a frequently expressed sentiment, "The hassles at work are all the more intolerable if I can't help someone."

On the basis of these findings one might question the premise that mental health is two-dimensional. However, 68% of the variance between the two measures was unaccounted for, and even though the specific work-reward and work-concern factors associated with the two outcomes were highly similar, the regression models accounted for a larger proportion of the variance in psychological distress than in well-being (29% vs. 18%). Thus, we turn in the following sections to an examination of women's nonworkplace roles and role quality in order to discover whether there are significant and meaningful differences in the pattern of relationships between these two mental-health measures and the combination of role occupancy and role-quality variables.

II. DOES FAMILY-ROLE OCCUPANCY AFFECT THE RELATIONSHIP BETWEEN THE MENTAL-HEALTH MEASURES AND THE WORK-REWARD AND WORK-CONCERN FACTORS?

This question is of central importance in understanding the relationship between women's experience in the labor force and their experience of subjective well-being and distress. To illustrate, the mental-health benefit of having a job that allows women to interact with others in emotionally meaningful ways may be greater for single than for partnered women. And women who are mothers may be more or less vulnerable than women who are not mothers to the mental-health effects of specific work factors. We believe that our understanding of the stress–illness relationship in both women and men will be furthered if such interactions between roles are taken into account.

Table 4. Family-Role Occupancy and Psychological Well-Being

	B^a	SE^b
Socioeconomic status	−0.30	0.25
Age	−0.05	0.10
Race	1.91	1.67
Per capita income	0.10	0.07
Helping Others	4.18***	1.17
Recognition	2.35*	0.95
Overload	−3.63***	0.85
Overload × Helping Others	2.47†	1.31
Parent-role occupancy	0.93	1.66
Partner-role occupancy	3.59**	1.22
Parent-role occupancy × partner-role occupancy	−0.26	2.41
$R^2 = 0.20$		

Note. $n = 370$.
[a]Unstandardized regression coefficients.
[b]Standard error of the regression coefficients.
*$p < .05$. **$p < .01$. ***$p < .001$.
†$.05 < p < .10$

To determine whether family-role occupancy tells us any more about the relationships between work factors and each of the mental-health measures, we looked separately at the main effects of partner-role and parent-role occupancy. We then examined the interaction of each family-role occupancy variable with the work-reward and work-concern factors to assess whether the relationship between work rewards and concerns and the mental-health measures differed for women who were parents or partners and those who were not. To generate these interaction terms, dummy variables were created for parental status (0 = nonparent, 1 = parent) and partnership status (0 = single, 1 = partnered).

Subjective Well-Being

With subjective well-being as the mental-health measure, family-role occupancy does not affect the relationship between well-being and the work rewards and concerns. Although partner-role occupancy was significantly related to well-being, none of the interaction terms between family-role occupancy and any of the work-reward or work-concern factors was significant. (The final model, showing only the significant predictors, is presented in Table 4.[11]) Thus, regardless of whether an employed health-

[11]Although not shown in Table 4, none of the three-way interaction terms between partner-role and parent-role occupancy and each of the work-reward and work-concern factors was significant.

care provider is partnered or not, the rewards of Helping Others and Recognition at work are related to high well-being, concern about work Overload is associated with a diminished sense of well-being, and there is a tendency for Helping Others at work to condition the negative well-being effects of work overload. This pattern held true regardless of whether the partnered women had children or not.

Parent-role occupancy was unrelated to subjective well-being. The well-being scores of women without children were indistinguishable from those of women with children, and there were no interactions between parent-role occupancy and any of the work factors.

Psychological Distress

With psychological distress as the mental-health measure, the results were very different. Family-role occupancy variables conditioned the relationship between certain work factors and psychological distress.

With regard to parent-role occupancy and psychological distress (see Table 5), the interaction between Decision Authority and parent-role occupancy was significant. As can be seen in Figure 3, psychological distress among women without children, compared to women with children, was much more reactive to the rewards of Decision Authority at work. Childless women experience high distress when decision authority is low and low distress when Decision Authority is high. In contrast, among employed mothers, psychological distress is relatively unrelated to Decision Authority. Stated differently, the fewer roles a woman occupies, the

Table 5. Parent-Role Occupancy and Psychological Distress

	B^a	SE^b
Socioeconomic status	−0.07	0.26
Age	−0.15	0.10
Race	−4.03*	1.66
Per capita income	0.08	0.06
Helping Others	−3.88***	1.14
Decision Authority	−4.21***	1.04
Overload	4.99***	0.85
Overload × Helping Others	−4.49***	1.31
Parent-role occupancy	1.09	1.62
Parent-role occupancy × Decision Authority	4.67*	1.94
$R^2 = 0.31$		

Note. $n = 371$.
[a]Unstandardized regression coefficients.
[b]Standard error of the regression coefficients.
*$p < .05$. **$p < .01$. ***$p < .001$.

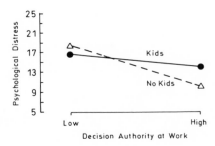

Figure 3. Interaction of parent-role occupancy and decision authority at work on psychological distress.

more important Decision Authority is to her level of psychological distress. Overload at work and the rewards of Helping Others, in contrast, have similar effects on women, whether or not they have children.

Partner-role occupancy conditioned the relationship between psychological distress and Helping Others at work (see Table 6). Compared to partnered women, the distress of single women is more reactive to this work reward, as can be seen in Figure 4.

Among single women, there is an inverse relationship between psychological distress and rewards from Helping Others. When these rewards are high, distress is low; when they are low, distress is high. In contrast, the psychological distress of partnered women is relatively unaffected by the level of reward from Helping Others at work. Once again, for women without family roles psychological distress, but not well-being, is more dependent on the presence or absence of particular work rewards.

Table 6. Partner-Role Occupancy and Psychological Distress

	B^a	SE^b
Socioeconomic status	0.03	0.26
Age	−0.13	0.08
Race	−4.08	1.67
Per capita income	0.05	0.06
Helping Others	−3.51**	1.14
Decision Authority	−4.28***	1.04
Overload	5.01***	0.84
Overload × Helping Others	−4.58***	1.31
Partner-role occupancy	−1.03	1.19
Partner-role occupancy × Helping Others	5.10*	2.07
$R^2 = 0.31$		

Note. $n = 371$.
^{a}Unstandardized regression coefficients.
^{b}Standard error of the regression coefficients.
*$p < .05$. **$p < .01$. ***$p < .001$.

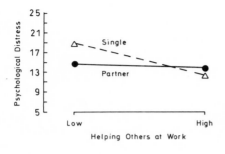

Figure 4. Effect of interaction of subjects' partner-role occupancy and the rewards of Helping Others at work on subjects' psychological distress.

Thus, with respect to the relationship between psychological distress and work rewards and concerns, all women are not the same. While women with and without family roles are at risk from high Overload at work and reap mental-health benefits from some work rewards, other work rewards are more important to single than partnered women and more important to women without children than those who are mothers.

In sum, the answer to the question about the effects of family-role occupancy on the relationship between the mental health measures and the work rewards and work concerns is: It depends on which mental-health measure and which family role. The findings reported in this section support the premise that subjective well-being and psychological distress are separate constructs, each having a distinct pattern of associations between the work factors and family-role occupancy.

III. DOES FAMILY-ROLE QUALITY AFFECT THE RELATIONSHIP BETWEEN MENTAL-HEALTH MEASURES AND WORK-REWARD AND WORK-CONCERN FACTORS?

How are the effects on mental-health measures of work rewards and concerns affected by family-role quality? Can a problematic job offset the positive effects of good family relationships? Can a job that is experienced as rewarding mitigate the negative-health effects of a poor relationship with one's partner or children? Conversely, can troubled relationships with partners or children attenuate the mental-health benefits of work rewards? Such questions, which are potentially more interesting than those concerning the effect of family-role occupancy, have received even less research attention.

To address these important questions, we developed measures of partner-role and parent-role quality. As will be remembered, each woman in the study was interviewed about the rewards and concerns she was experiencing in each of her major family roles; each woman received a total reward and a total concern score for each family role. Partner-role quality was operationalized as the difference between the reward and the concern scores for the partner role, parent-role quality, as the difference between the reward and the concern scores for the parent role. (See Barnett & Marshall, 1988, for a discussion of this score.) Since only women who occupied a role received a role-quality score, the following analyses were performed on subsamples; the effect of partner-role quality was estimated among the 187 women who were partnered and the effect of parent-role quality was estimated among the 211 women were mothers.

We first estimated separate main-effects regression models for each mental-health measure with the control variables, the work factors, and the appropriate family-role quality scores as predictors. We also created interaction terms to test whether the relationship between the health measures and the work reward and concern factors differed by the level of family-role quality. Finally, for each subsample, we tested whether occupancy of the other social role affected these relationships; for example, among parents we tested the main and interaction effects of being partnered or not on the relationship between the parent-role quality and the mental-health measures.

Subjective Well-Being

Not surprisingly, parent-role quality was a significant predictor of well-being. After controlling for the effects of parent-role quality, however, Helping Others at work remained significant while the other work factors were only marginally significant, as was the interaction between Helping Others and Work Overload. (Table 7 shows the final model with only significant independent variables.) Interestingly, parent-role quality did not interact with any of the work rewards or with Overload. Thus, for example, the positive association between Helping Others at work and well-being is not lost among women with troubled relationships with children. Moreover, the interaction between parent-role quality and partner-role occupancy was not significant. Thus, the relationship between parent-role quality and subjective well-being was the same for employed mothers who were partnered or single.

Indeed, up to this point in the analyses single mothers have been indistinguishable from partnered mothers. Yet there is a widely held belief that single mothers are at particularly high risk for stress-related health problems. The lack of significant differences between partnered and single mothers may well be due to the inclusion of the control variables: SES, age, race, and per capita income. It is possible that the vulnerability ascribed to single mothers is attributable primarily to low SES and low per

Table 7. Parent-Role Quality and Well-Being

	B^a	SE^b
Socioeconomic status	−0.57†	0.33
Age	−0.18	0.13
Race	1.13	2.07
Per capita income	0.29**	0.10
Recognition	2.19†	1.30
Helping Others	5.02***	1.75
Overload	−2.30*	1.22
Overload × Helping Others	4.11†	2.16
Parent-role quality	3.19**	1.01
R^2 = .24		

Note. n = 211.
[a]Unstandardized regression coefficients.
[b]Standard error of the regression coefficients.
*p < .05. **p < .01. ***p < .001.
† .05 < p < .10.

capita income, not to the absence of a partner per se. It is also important to remember that the mothers in this sample did not have young children; the vulnerability of single mothers may be more apparent among those with young children.

With respect to the partnered women, concerns about work Overload were associated with a diminished sense of well-being and rewards from Helping Others were associated with high well-being, even after controlling for the strong effect of partner-role quality (see Table 8). In this subsample, Recognition at work and the interaction between Helping Others and Overload were only marginally significant ($p < .10$) after controlling for the effect of partner-role quality.

It is again noteworthy that none of the interactions between partner-role quality and the work factors was significant. Thus, Helping Others and Recognition at work were associated with high well-being and Overload with low well-being, regardless of whether the woman's relationship with her partner was good or bad. Moreover, neither parent-role occupancy nor the interaction of partner-role quality and parent-role occupancy were significant. In other words, among partnered women, the relationships between well-being and both work Overload and Helping Others at work were unaffected by either the quality of the partner relationship or parent-role status or the interaction between the two.

For partnered women, then, the effects on well-being of work rewards and concerns and family-role quality are independent. If relationships between women and their partners are good, the women's sense of well-being is high; if the women's jobs are "good," that is, with abundant rewards from Helping Others and receiving Recognition and low in work

Table 8. Partner-Role Quality and Well-Being

	B^a	SE^b
Socioeconomic status	−0.42	0.30
Age	−0.01	0.10
Race	2.95	2.28
Per capita income	0.07	0.06
Recognition	1.97[†]	1.13
Helping Others	3.33*	1.44
Overload	−3.06**	1.02
Overload × Helping Others	3.01[†]	1.72
Partner-role quality	5.47***	0.83
$R^2 = .39$		

Note. $n = 187$.
[a]Unstandardized regression coefficients.
[b]Standard error of the regression coefficients.
*$p < .05$. **$p < .01$. ***$p < .001$.
[†] $.05 < p < .10$.

Overload, their sense of well-being is high. Having a bad job does not detract from the well-being advantage women enjoy as a result of having a rewarding partnership; conversely, if their relationship with their partner is troubled, women can still derive a well-being advantage from having a good job.

In sum, with respect to well-being, for all employed women the effects of multiple-role occupancy are independent. Both employed partnered women and employed mothers benefit from multiple-role involvement because the arenas of work and family make independent contributions to their well-being.

Psychological Distress

In the subsample of parents, rewards from Helping Others at work and concerns about work Overload made significant contributions to mothers' psychological distress, even after taking into account the quality of their experiences as mothers. However, the interaction of Overload and Helping Others was not significant in this subsample because of the reduced degrees of freedom.

As expected, employed women who have positive relationships with their children report low levels of psychological distress. The question of interest here is whether parent-role quality interacts with any of the work rewards or with work Overload. Indeed, the interaction between Challenge and parent-role quality was significant, as can be seen in Table 9.

For employed mothers, high rewards from Challenge at work buffered the impact on distress of a difficult parenting experience, as shown

Table 9. Parent-Role Quality and Psychological Distress[a]

	B[b]	SE[c]
Socioeconomic status	−0.46	0.33
Age	−0.02	0.13
Race	−4.87*	2.06
Per capita income	−0.06	0.10
Helping Others	−3.25†	1.72
Challenge	0.30	1.75
Overload	4.18***	1.18
Parent-role quality	−2.67**	1.00
Parent-role quality × Challenge	4.29*	1.78
$R^2 = 0.19$		

Note. n = 210.
[a]This analysis was supported by a grant from the National Centre for Management
Research and Development, School of Business Administration, University of Western
Ontario, Canada. The grant was awarded to Rosalind C. Barnett and is discussed in
Barnett, Marshall, and Sayer (1991).
[b]Unstandardized regression coefficients.
[c]Standard error of the regression coefficients.
*$p < .05$. **$p < .01$. ***$p < .001$.
†$.05 < p < .10$

in Figure 5. In fact, the psychological distress of women with troubled
parent–child relationships is no worse than that of women with good
relationships—provided they are in challenging jobs. In other words, if
there are problems with children, a job with rewards from Challenge fully
compensates women for the distress-exacerbating effects of a stressful
parenting experience. Given popular beliefs about the spillover between
home and work, it is noteworthy that we found no interaction between
Overload at work and parent-role quality. Thus, the impact on psychological distress of difficulties in the parent-role are not compounded by
Overload at work.

Moreover, the negative impact on psychological distress of poor relationships with children and work-related Overload accrue equally to single
and to partnered mothers. Stated differently, after controlling for the

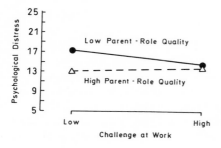

Figure 5. Interaction of parent-role quality
and challenge at work on psychological distress.

Table 10. Partner-Role Quality and Psychological Distress

	B^a	SE^b
Socioeconomic status	0.25	0.32
Age	−0.29**	0.10
Race	−5.89*	2.34
Per capita income	0.06	0.06
Helping Others	0.81	1.47
Decision Authority	−4.10**	1.27
Overload	3.96***	0.98
Overload × Helping Others	−3.27†	1.74
Partner-role quality	−4.59***	0.88
$R^2 = 0.41$		

Note. $n = 185$.
[a]Unstandardized regression coefficients.
[b]Standard error of the regression coefficients.
*$p < .05$. **$p < .01$. ***$p < .001$.
† $.05 < p < p$ .10.

effects of SES, race, age, and per capita income, employed single mothers are at no greater risk of psychological distress from concerns about their relationships with their children or from Overload at work than are employed partnered mothers. And mothers, regardless of whether they are partnered or single, are protected by challenging jobs from the psychological distress associated with troubled parent–child relationships.

Among partnered women, partner-role quality did not affect the relationship between the work factors and distress. As seen in Table 10, we found no interaction between Overload at work and partner-role quality, indicating that the impact on distress of difficulties with one's partner are not compounded by Overload at work. In addition, none of the interactions with the work-reward factors reached significance at the $p < .05$ level, indicating that the impact of rewards at work on distress are independent of the quality of the partner-role.

Of great interest are two findings concerning the effect on psychological distress of occupying two family roles in addition to the paid-employee role.[12] First, the positive association between good partner-role quality and low psychological distress was significantly more pronounced among women who did not have children, as can be seen in Figure 6. When a woman's relationship with her partner was troubled, her distress was higher if she did not have children than if she did.[13] Here again, the fewer roles a woman occupies, the greater impact problems in any role have on her mental health.

[12]In the interests of brevity the regression models are not presented.
[13]This effect is not apparent under conditions of high partner-role quality.

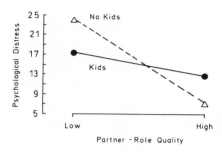

Figure 6. Interaction of partner-role quality and parent-role occupancy on psychological distress.

Second, there was a tendency for the psychological distress of employed women who occupied both the role of partner and of parent to be less reactive to Overload at work than was the distress of employed partnered women who were not parents, after controlling for partner-role quality (see Figure 7). To illustrate, under conditions of high-work Overload, employed partnered women experienced more distress if they did not have children than if they did. This seemingly counterintuitive finding fits the model emerging from these data, namely, that the fewer roles a woman occupies, the greater the impact each has on her psychological distress. This model suggests a mechanism by which women in general benefit from multiple-role involvement, that is, multiple-role occupancy protects women by reducing the negative impact of particular stressors on their mental health.

It is important to remember that the analyses reported here are cross-sectional, so we are unable to determine the direction of effect. While we use a theoretical model that posits that women whose jobs are more rewarding will be less distressed, it is possible that women who are less distressed find their jobs more rewarding. Longitudinal analyses are necessary to clarify such issues.

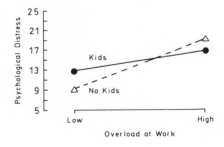

Figure 7. Interaction of parent-role occupancy and overload at work on psychological distress among partnered women.

DISCUSSION AND CONCLUSIONS

The major findings of this chapter are the following: (1) work rewards and work concerns, and their interactions, need to be included in models relating the paid-employee role to mental-health states; (2) there may be gender differences in those aspects of the paid-employee role that are experienced as rewarding and those that cause a person concern; and (3) analyses aimed at estimating the effects on women's mental health of their multiple roles (i.e., employee, partner, and parent) indicate significantly different patterns of relationships for two dimensions of mental health—subjective well-being and psychological distress.

Mental health is affected by both the presence of work concerns and the absence of work rewards. Subjective well-being and psychological distress are both associated with concerns about Overload at work and by the presence of rewards from Helping Others and having the Authority to make decisions about your work. Improvements in mental health can, therefore, be achieved by reducing concerns or increasing rewards. Moreover, rewards from Helping Others at work buffer the negative mental-health effects of work Overload. In the absence of rewards from Helping Others at work, the negative effects of Overload go unchecked, at least for women in the helping professions. It is important to note that while having a job high in rewards from Helping Others was central to the mental health of the women in our study, there are undoubtedly many more women who work in jobs characterized by Overload than there are women whose jobs provide them with the rewards of Helping Others.

The importance for women's mental health of rewards from Helping Others at work raises the possibility of gender differences in the work-related rewards and concerns that are associated with mental health measures. Work by Haw (1982) and by Johnson and Hall (1988) reaches a similar conclusion. The model generated on male samples by Karasek and his associates received only modest support in the present study. Whereas Overload (or Demand in Karasek's model) was a consistent predictor of both low well-being and high psychological distress, Decision Authority (an aspect of Decision Latitude/Control in Karasek's model) was associated only with distress and only among women without children. (However, the work of LaCroix and Haynes, 1987, confirmed the Karasek model in a sample of female employees.) In contrast, Helping Others at work emerged as a consistent predictor of the degree of well-being and psychological distress in this sample of employed female health-care providers. Mainstream research on men and work (and research within that tradition with female samples) has not addressed this aspect of the paid-employee role. However, it is not possible from our data to disentangle the effects of gender from those of the particular occupations we studied. It may be that

Helping Others is an important work reward for all employed women; alternatively, Helping Others may be a reward particular to people (men and women) in health-care occupations or perhaps in service occupations in general. In any case, the findings indicate the importance of including the reward of Helping Others in future studies of the relationship between work and health.

When we consider the effects of family-role occupancy and quality on the relationships between the work factors and women's mental health, different patterns emerge for the two dimensions of mental health. It appears that each dimension is associated with a process by which women can benefit from multiple roles. In the case of subjective well-being, the relationships between the work factors (rewards and concerns) and family roles are independent. Family-role occupancy benefits the well-being of employed women in two ways: first, partnered women report higher well-being than single women; second, the quality of experience in each role—worker, partner, parent—makes an independent contribution to subjective well-being. Thus, women benefit by having separate arenas in which to enhance well-being.

In contrast, with psychological distress as the measure of mental health, the relationships are interactive. Family-role occupancy reduces the vulnerability of employed women to the psychological distress associated with low rewards in certain aspects of work. With respect to family-role quality, the existence of interactive effects raises the possibility for rewards in one arena to mitigate or exacerbate the negative effects of the experience of stress in the other. Indeed, employed mothers with troubled relationships with their children are protected from negative distress-exacerbating consequences, provided that their jobs are challenging.

In conclusion, the findings presented here demonstrate that women's mental health reflects a combination of their experiences in their multiple roles. If we are to understand the contribution of workplace rewards and concerns to women's mental health, we must include simultaneous study of family-role occupancy and family-role quality. After all, women (and men) function in the worlds of work *and* of the family, and their mental health reflects their experiences in both arenas.

ACKNOWLEDGMENTS

The data reported in this paper are from the first wave of a three-wave, longitudinal, interview study, funded by the National Institute of Occupational Safety and Health (#OHO 1968).

We extend our deepest appreciation to our late colleague, Grace Baruch, for her consistent wisdom and help in making this work possible. We also extend our thanks to the project coordinator, Nathalie Thompson and to the interviewers, without whose dedication the project would never have been completed: Carol Anello, Joyce Buni, Krista Comer, Connie Counts, Susan Gates, Marjorie Bahlke Harrison, Michele Meagher, Celia Morris, Judith Shangold, Jane Scherban, Sandra Walker, Marsha Wise, and Marcia Wells.

Correspondence concerning this article should be addressed to Rosalind C. Barnett, Center for Research on Women, Wellesley College, Wellesley, MA 02181.

REFERENCES

The Association of Schools of Public Health and the National Institute for Occupational Safety and Health. (1988). *Proposed national strategies for the prevention of leading work-related diseases and injuries: Part 2.* Washington, DC: Author.

Barnett, R. C., & Baruch, G. K. (1985). Women's involvement in multiple roles and psychological distress. *Journal of Personality and Social Psychology, 49,* 135–145.

Barnett, R. C., & Baruch, G. K. (1987). Social roles, gender, and psychological distress. In R. C. Barnett, L. Biener, & G. K. Baruch (Eds.), *Gender and stress* (pp. 122–143). New York: Free Press.

Barnett, R. C., & Marshall, N. (1988a). *Clarification of the role-quality concept.* Working Paper #192, Wellesley College Center for Research on Women, Wellesley, MA.

Barnett, R. C., & Marshall, N. (1989). *Factor structure of the rewards and concerns in women's three major social roles.* Unpublished manuscript.

Barnett, R. C., Marshall, N., & Sayer, A. (1990). *Positive spillover effects from job to home: A closer look.* Unpublished manuscript.

Baruch, G. K., & Barnett, R. C. (1986). Role quality, multiple role involvement, and psychological well-being in midlife women. *Journal of Personality and Social Psychology, 51,* 578–585.

Baruch, G. K., Barnett, R. C., & Rivers, C. (1984). *Lifeprints: New patterns of love and work for today's women.* New York: New American Library.

Baruch, G. K., Biener, L., & Barnett, R. C. (1987). Women and gender in research on work and family stress. *American Psychologist, 42,* 130–136.

Brown, G. W., & Harris, T. (1978). *Social origins of depression: A study of psychiatric disorder in women.* New York: Free Press.

Bryant, F., & Veroff, J. (1984). Dimensions of subjective mental health in American men and women. *Journal of Health and Social Behavior, 25,* 116–135.

Caplan, R. D., Cobb, S., French, J. R. P., Van Harrison, R., & Pinneau, S. R. (1975, April). *Demands and worker health: Main effects and occupational differences* (HEW Publication NIOSH #75-160). U.S. Government Printing Office.

Cohen, S., & Wills, T. A. (1985). Stress, social support and the buffering hypothesis. *Psychological Bulletin, 98,* 310–357.

Davies, A. R., Sherbourne, C. D., Peterson, J. R., & Ware, J. E., Jr. (1985). *Scoring manual: Adult health status and patient satisfaction measures used in Rand's health insurance experiment* (WD-2742-HHS). Washington, DC: Department of Health and Human Services.

Derogatis, L. R. (1975). *The SCL-90-R.* Baltimore, MD: Clinical Psychometrics.

Derogatis, L. R. (1983). *Description and bibliography for the SCL-90-R and other instruments of the psychopathology rating scale series.* Baltimore, MD: Johns Hopkins University School of Medicine.

Diener, E. (1984). Subjective well-being. *Psychological Bulletin, 95*, 542–575.

Diener, E., & Emmons, R. A. (1985). The independence of positive and negative affect. *Journal of Personality and Social Psychology, 47*, 1105–1117.

Farrell, M. P., & Rosenberg, S. D. (1981). *Men at midlife*. Dover, MA: Auburn.

Haw, M. A. (1982). Women, work and stress: A review and agenda for the future. *Journal of Health and Social Behavior, 123*, 132–144.

Haynes, S. G., & Feinleib, M. (1982). Women, work, and coronary heart disease: Results from the Framingham 10-year follow-up study. In P. Berman & E. Ramey (Eds.), *Women: A developmental perspective* (NIH Publication No. 82-2298, pp. 79–101). Washington, DC: U.S. Government Printing Office.

Johnson, J. V., & Hall, E. M. (1988). Job strain, work place social support, and cardiovascular disease: A cross-sectional study of a random sample of the Swedish working population. *American Journal of Public Health, 78*, 1336–1342.

Karasek, R. A., Schwartz, J., & Theorell, T. (1982). *Job characteristics, occupation and coronary heart disease: Final report* (Contract # R-01-0H00906). Washington, DC: National Institute of Occupational Safety and Health.

Karasek, R., & Theorell, T. (1990). *Healthy work: Stress, productivity, and the reconstruction of working life*. New York: Basic Books.

LaCroix, A. Z., & Haynes, S. G. (1987). Gender differences in the health effects of workplace roles. In R. C. Barnett, L. Biener, & G. K. Baruch (Eds.), *Gender and stress* (pp. 96–121). New York: Free Press.

Marshall, N. L., & Barnett, R. C. (1990). *Development of the job-role quality scales*. Working Paper #207, Wellesley College Center for Research on Women, Wellesley, MA.

Marshall, N., Barnett, R. C., Baruch, G. K., & Pleck, J. (in press). More than a job: Women and stress in caregiving occupations. In J. A. Levy & H. Z. Lopata (Eds.), *Current research on occupations and professions* (Vol. VI, pp. 266–277).

Pleck, J. H. (1985). *Working wives/working husbands*. Beverly Hills, CA: Sage.

Rosenman, R. H., Brand, R. J., Jenkins, C. D., Friedman, M., Straus, R., & Wurm, M. (1975). Coronary heart disease in the Western Collaborative Group Study: Final follow-up experience of 8-1/2 years. *Journal of the American Medical Association, 233*, 872–877.

Thoits, P. A. (1983). Multiple identities and psychological well-being: A reformation and test of the social isolation hypothesis. *American Sociological Review, 48*, 174–187.

Veroff, J., Douvan, E., & Kulka, R. A. (1981). *The inner American*. New York: Basic Books.

Viet, C. T., & Ware, J. E. (1983). The structure of psychological distress and well-being in general populations. *Journal of Consulting and Clinical Psychology, 51*, 730–742.

Waldron, I., & Jacobs, J. (1988). Effects of labor force participation on women's health—new evidence from a longitudinal study. *Journal of Occupational Behavior, 36*, 871–883.

Waldron, I., & Jacobs, J. (1989). Effects of multiple roles on women's health: Evidence from a national longitudinal study. *Women and Health, 15*, 3–19.

III

Work Load and Cardiovascular Health

7

Women, Work-Related Stress, and Smoking

MARGARET A. CHESNEY

Cigarette smoking, marketed to women first as glamorous and later as liberated (Davis, 1987), has become the single greatest threat to the health of women in Western industrialized countries. The prevalence of smoking among women and the health effects of this important risk behavior are reviewed in the first section of this chapter. Research that explores the relationships among work, stress, psychological distress, and women's smoking, in keeping with the theme of this volume, is then discussed. A model integrating these factors will be presented, and data from the Women and Health Study, a work-site-based investigation of women and work, will be examined in light of this model. In the final section implications of the model for smoking cessation programs in industry will be discussed.

PREVALENCE OF CIGARETTE SMOKING AMONG WOMEN

Early in the twentieth century cigarette smoking, although common among men, was rare among women (United States Department of Health and Human Services, 1980). In 1955 the National Cancer Institute provided the first reliable estimates of the prevalence of smoking in the United States (United States Department of Health and Human Services,

MARGARET A. CHESNEY • Prevention Sciences Group, School of Medicine, University of California, San Francisco, California 94105.

1988). This survey showed the prevalence of smoking among women to be 24.5%, whereas the prevalence among males was 52%. The percentage of women smokers rose as the years passed to a peak of 34.1% in 1965 while the percentage of men was 53%. Similar increases in the prevalence of smoking are seen in other industrialized nations (Berggren & Sjoestedt, 1981; Graham, 1987). For example, a questionnaire survey of 17,594 Swedish women between 19 and 65 years of age indicated a sixfold increase in cigarette consumption from 1920 to 1980 (Berggren & Sjoestedt, 1981). Since 1965, with the increasing evidence of adverse health consequences of smoking, the prevalence of smoking among women in the United States dropped to 28% in 1985. Over the same 20-year period the percentage of adult males smoking decreased to 33% (Remington, Forman, Gentry, Marks, Hogeline, & Trowbridge, 1985).

These trends in smoking prevalence over the last several decades have resulted in a convergence in the proportion of males and females currently smoking (Biener, 1988). In the United States among adolescents and in some groups of professionals the rate of smoking among women surpasses that of males (Dicken & Bryson, 1978; Eyres, 1973; Sorenson & Pechacek, 1986; United States Department of Health and Human Services, 1980). The convergence in gender prevalence of smoking has been attributed to a number of factors, including the introduction of filtered and low-tar cigarettes (Silverstein, Feld, & Kozlowski, 1980) and the careful targeting of advertising to women (Davis, 1987; United States Department of Health and Human Services, 1980). The impact of advertising is particularly evident among adolescents. Until 1979 the prevalence of smoking among adolescent girls was rising steadily (United States Department of Health and Human Services, 1980). Although some recent data suggest that initiation of smoking among adolescent girls may be on the decline (Cleary, Hitchcock, Semmer, Flinchbaugh, & Pinney, 1986), data continue to indicate a greater prevalence of cigarette smoking for adolescent females than for males.

Gender differences in smoking cessation rates have contributed to the convergence of gender smoking rates for men and women. Although not observed by all researchers (Waldron, in press), there is evidence indicating that the rate of smoking cessation is lower for women regardless of age (Stoto, 1986). This rate is thought to reflect a lower interest in quitting among women observed in large community surveys (Blake, Pechacek, Klepp, Folsom, Jacobs, & Mittelmark, 1984; Frerick, Aneshensel, Clark, & Yokopenic, 1981) and a greater likelihood among women to relapse after smoking cessation (Gritz, 1980). Biener (1988) suggests that women's lower success in efforts to stop smoking, of particular relevance to this chapter, is due to the fact that "women, more than men, rely on cigarettes as a method of dealing with negative affect"; Biener believes that "this reliance makes them either less motivated or less able to stop smoking" (p. 338). The prevalence of smoking among women is not only marked by a convergence in gender smoking rates but is also seen in a convergence in health consequences of smoking for men and women.

HEALTH CONSEQUENCES OF SMOKING

Cigarette smoking is one of the leading risk factors for cardiovascular disease, the leading cause of death among adult women in industrialized countries. Each year this disease accounts for approximately one-half of all deaths in the United States. According to the United States Department of Health and Human Services (1983), the risk of coronary heart disease is increased by two and one-half times for adults who smoke one pack of cigarettes per day compared to their nonsmoking counterparts. For example, in a study of 121,964 nurses between 30 and 55 years of age, smokers were found to have a threefold risk of myocardial infarction compared to women who never smoked (Willett, Hennekens, Bain, Rosner, & Speizer, 1981). This increased risk was not explained by history of hypertension, diabetes, high cholesterol or familial history of cardiovascular disease. The effect of cigarette smoking on risk of nonfatal first myocardial infarction was evaluated in a study of 4,397 women under 50 years of age admitted to 155 hospitals in the mid-atlantic New York and Boston regions of the United States (Rosenberg, Miller, Kaufman, Helmrich, Vad de Carr, Stoley, & Shapiro, 1983). Compared to women who had never smoked, the age-adjusted Relative Risk for infarct among current smokers was 5.5. For heavy smokers, that is, women who smoked 35 or more cigarettes per day, the Relative Risk was 8.3. Among the women who had suffered an infarct smoking prevalence was 85%, compared to 53% for the controls (i.e., women admitted to the hospital for disorders other than infarct). The authors estimated that about 65% of nonfatal first infarctions could have been prevented if the women had not smoked. In a similar study Slone and colleagues (1981) estimated that among women under 50 with no other risk factors 70% of the myocardial infarctions could be attributed to smoking.

Cigarette smoking has also been found to be related to the extent of coronary occlusion (Barboriak, Anderson, & Hoffman, 1984). In a study of 797 female heart disease patients, angiographically documented coronary occlusion was scored from 0 to 300, with 300 representing those cases with all three main branches occluded. The mean occlusion score for the 215 women who smoked at least one pack per day for 20 years was 101 whereas the score for nonsmokers was 54. This difference was maintained after adjusting for the standard risk factors and was more pronounced in women under 50 years of age. These findings were compared with published data on men and indicated that cigarette smoking exerts proportionately more risk for coronary occlusion in female heart disease patients than it does in male heart disease patients.

There is also evidence that cigarette smoking enhances the risk for cardiovascular disease associated with the use of oral contraceptives (Salonen, 1982). In a longitudinal study of 2,653 women in eastern Finland, women who both used oral contraceptives and smoked had a 7.2-fold risk of myocardial infarction compared to nonsmokers and nonusers of oral contraceptives. Women who smoked but did not take oral contraceptives had a 2.6-fold crude risk of acute infarction while women who used oral contraceptives had a 1.3-fold risk compared to women who neither smoked or used oral contraceptives.

Menopause

Epidemiologic evidence suggests that women are relatively protected from heart disease prior to menopause. Cigarette smoking may exert additional indirect risk because it is associated with an earlier onset of menopause (Hartz, Kelber, Borkowf, Wild, Gillis, & Rimm, 1987; Kannel & Thomas, 1982). It is estimated that women who smoke reach spontaneous menopause 1 to 2 years earlier than nonsmokers. For example, in a survey of 5,645 women from Denmark heavy smokers between 47 and 51 years of age (more than 14 cigarettes per day) experienced menopause significantly earlier than nonsmokers (Andersen, Transbol, & Christiansen, 1982; Bailey, Robinson, & Vessey, 1977). This earlier onset has been found to persist after taking into account obesity, age at last pregnancy, and use of oral contraceptives (Daniell, 1978; Van Keep, Brand, & Lehert, 1979). Research in the United States and Sweden (Jick, Porter, & Morrison, 1977) suggests that the relationship between smoking and age at menopause is inverse and linear. That is, the more the woman smokes, the earlier the age of onset. Research investigating this issue of dose-dependent risk placed the median age of spontaneous menopause at 50, 49, and 48 for nonsmokers, moderate smokers, and heavy smokers, respectively (Jick et al., 1977).

Cancer

The impact of the increase in smoking prevalence among women over recent decades is reflected in increased disease-specific mortality rates. Most well known is the effect of smoking on cancer deaths among women. While death rates due to lung cancer have risen in the United States for both men and women, the rise has been steeper among women. From 1950 to 1977 the increase was 250% for women, compared to 200% for men (United States Department of Health and Human Services, 1983). Although the absolute number of cancer deaths continues to be greater among men than women, this gender difference is expected to decline as the gender prevalence of smoking converges (Russell & Epstein, 1987). Similar patterns in prevalence, incidence, and mortality are seen for laryngeal cancer, which has also been associated with cigarette smoking.

Lung Disease

Chronic obstructive pulmonary disease (COPD) provides another indication of the health effects of the increased rates of smoking among women. As with lung cancer, rates of death due to COPD in the United States have been rising. In the year between 1982 and 1983, for example, the increase in number of COPD deaths rose from 56,900 to 62,000. The impact of women's smoking rates is reflected in a decrease in the ratio of male to female COPD deaths, which in 1970 was 4.3:1 and by 1980 fell to 2.36:1. Given the fact that COPD results from chronic damage to lungs from smoking for years (Harris, 1983; United States Department of Health and Human Services, 1984), increases in COPD morbidity and mortality rates are expected to continue.

Fetal Health

Cigarette smoking is not only associated with health risks for women but is associated with risk for fetal health. Research has established that the birth weight of infants born to smoking mothers is 200 grams less, on average, than that of infants born to nonsmoking mothers (United States Department of Health and Human Services, 1980). Compared to nonsmoking mothers, women who smoke experience a higher incidence of spontaneous abortions, increased fetal and neonatal deaths, and a greater probability of preterm births (Russell & Epstein, 1988). Unfortunately, despite national campaigns to encourage pregnant women to stop smoking, it is estimated that 70% to 75% of women who smoke continue to do so during pregnancy (United States Department of Health and Human Services, 1980).

Summary of Health Consequences of Smoking for Women

In summary, cigarette smoking is an important risk factor for cardiovascular disease, cancer, lung disease, and fetal morbidity and mortality.

The observed rise in the number of women who smoke and in its associated health consequences are reflected in increased health care costs. The increases are predictable given that smokers use the health care system at least 50% more than nonsmokers. The costs associated with smoking extend beyond health to the social sector. For example, in the work setting the costs include higher rates of absenteeism among smokers and an estimated reduction in productivity of 30 minutes per day per smoker on the job (Luce & Schweitzer, 1978; Shimp, 1986). In the next section of this chapter the relationship between smoking and employment is discussed.

SMOKING AND WORK

In the United States, surveys in 1955 and 1970 indicated that employed women were slightly more likely than full-time homemakers to be smokers (Haenszel, Shimkin, & Miller, 1956; Waldron, 1980). In more recent surveys little or no difference in the prevalence of smokers has been found between employed women and full-time homemakers (Waldron & Lye, in press). In a thorough review of this relationship Waldron points out that the relationship between smoking and employment is a complex one influenced by a number of factors, including the adverse impact smoking has on health that results in some workers leaving the labor force, the higher smoking rates among unemployed persons of lower socioeconomic status, and the lower smoking cessation rates among the unemployed. Although the literature does not suggest that working leads to smoking, labor force participation may play a role in increasing stress. Stress, discussed in the next section of this chapter, is associated with increased smoking rates and difficulties in smoking cessation. Thus, there may be relationships between labor force participation and the prevalence of smoking that are explained by work-related stress factors.

THE WOMEN AND HEALTH STUDY

My associates and I conducted a large cross-sectional study of work, stress, and smoking in women at a large industrial firm in the San Francisco Bay area. Some attention will be paid here to describing the study, because data from this study will be presented throughout this chapter. Women employed by a large industrial firm in the San Francisco Bay area and wives of men employed in the same firm were invited to participate in a study of work and health. In order to increase the similarity between the employed women and the homemakers, the majority of the working women we chose for the study were married. The women in the sample were divided into three groups based upon their work status: professional or salaried working women, women working at an hourly wage, and homemakers.

The prevalence of cigarette smoking was significantly different among the three work status groups. A higher percentage of working women compared to homemakers smoked cigarettes. Specifically, 29% of hourly-wage working women were smokers, compared to 22% of the salaried working women and 17% of the homemakers. By comparison, a study of salaried working men conducted in the same industrial firm showed a 23% smoking rate. Thus, while the smoking rates were similar for professional men and women, more hourly-wage working women were smokers. The reason that a higher percentage of smokers was found among the working women compared to the homemakers is not known. Unlike the unemployed women in the studies reviewed by Waldron and Lye (in press), the homemakers in the Women and Health Study were all married to working men and reported not working out of choice. The women in a number of the studies Waldron reviewed included those from lower socioeconomic groups. Another explanation may be that smoking rates are associated with environmental stress. As discussed in the next section, higher levels of stress were reported by the working women in the Women and Health Study than by the homemakers, and perhaps the homemakers in our study experienced less environmental stress than the women of lower socioeconomic status included in the studies reviewed by Waldron and Lye (in press).

STRESS A

Cigarette smoking has long b
for both men and women. It has
that they smoked more heavily v
assisted them in coping (Linn &
Health and Human Services, 19
studies lend support to this rel
Schachter, Silverstein, Kozlows
ple, smoking patterns were m
presented with a high and a l
When confronted with a high-
cantly more cigarettes and to
sented with the low-stress co
The relationship betwee

contributing factor to gender differences in smoking rates. Biener and her associates (1988) suggest that the higher rate of smoking observed among female compared to male professionals may reflect a greater level of stress experienced by the women. This line of research argues that the greater level of stress is associated with smoking because smoking is a behavioral style of coping with stress. Recent research on job-related stress indicates that workers are at the most risk for stress-related illness when their jobs involve high demands and low control over aspects of the work situation (Karasek, 1979). In support of this hypothesis work environments characterized by high demands and low control have been found to be significantly associated with smoking status for professional women (but not for professional men) (Biener, 1988). In addition to this support for the proposed relationship between work stress and smoking in the United States, similar associations of smoking rates to high job demands coupled with low control were found in a study of white collar workers in Sweden (Karasek, Lindell, & Gardell, in press). One of the gender differences observed was a stronger association between job stress and cigarette smoking among women than among men.

Job stress research often focuses on stress of work as synonymous with gainful employment. Graham (1987), using data from the General Household Survey in Great Britain, points out that the prevalence of smoking may be highest in an often understudied group, that is, in low-income women. Graham shed light on this topic with an intensive study of 57 mothers, the majority of whom did not work outside the home. As with other women, smoking rates for these women were related to the level of self-reported stress of daily work. Smoking rates were higher among the single mothers than among those living with partners. Interviews indicated that smoking was used as a way of coping with stress. Graham noted that while the women limited expenses associated with food and clothing, they continued to purchase cigarettes and suggested that this exception was made because smoking was an important means of coping.

In studies of employed women, level of stress has been associated with increased smoking rates. For example, nurses who smoked cigarettes ported higher levels of job stress than nonsmoking nurses (Tagliacozzo ghn, 1982). The Women and Health Study provides an opportunity ine the relationship between smoking and stress for women in categories. Both working women and homemakers completed stionnaires that included items drawn from the Fra- tudy concerning stressors in their work. Homemakers uestions in relation to their work in the home. These reflect three sources of work stress: time pressure, work staying with a person so that she was thinking about it after working hours; see Chapter 3, this volume), and job strain. The percentage of women reporting these sources of stress in each of the three work status groups is presented in Table 1. As shown in the table, a significantly greater proportion of working women than home-makers reported each of the three sources of job stress, namely, time pressure, difficulty unwinding, and job strain. While there was no difference between the groups of working women in the proportion reporting time pressure, a significantly greater proportion of the salaried women reported difficulty unwinding and job strain than of the women who worked for an hourly wage.

The Women and Health Study indicates that there may be differences in the relationship between various job stress factors and smoking between working women and homemakers. Homemakers who reported time pressure in their daily work activities were significantly more likely to be smokers than homemakers who did not report time pressure. No relationship was observed between this job stress factor and smoking for the working women. Conversely, working women who reported job strain were significantly more likely to be smokers than working women who did not report job strain. No relationship was observed between the strain of housework and smoking for homemakers. There was no relationship between difficulty unwinding and smoking for any of the work status groups. That stronger relationships weren't observed between job stressors and cigarette smoking may have been due to the fact that environmental stressors alone may not elicit a coping response if it does not first induce a stress response such as negative affect in the person.

SMOKING AND AFFECT REGULATION

There is a growing body of literature that indicates that smokers use cigarettes to cope with negative affect. In fact, reducing negative affect is the primary reason for smoking reported by a large percentage of ciga-

Table 1. Women and Health Study: Proportion of Women Reporting Sources of Job Stress

Women	Time pressure (%)	Difficulty unwinding (%)	Job strain (%)
Salaried workers	67	57	45
Hourly wage workers	66	35	31
Homemakers	46	16	24

rette smokers (Pomerleau, Adkins, & Pertschuk, 1978). It is interesting to note that there is evidence that there may be a causal association between negative affect, distress, and neuroticism during childhood and incidence of smoking as an adult. Specifically, prospective studies have shown that individuals who show higher levels of negative affect and neurotic personality characteristics in childhood have a greater tendency toward smoking as adults (Cherry & Kiernan, 1976; Lerner & Vicary, 1984; Seltzer & Oechsli, 1985).

There may be gender differences in the degree to which smoking is used for management of negative affect, with women using smoking to cope with stress and negative affect more than men (Biener, 1988; Russell & Epstein, 1987). Women are more likely to state that they smoke in response to negative affect and that stressful events are associated with returning to smoking after having stopped (Frith, 1971; United States Department of Health and Human Services, 1980). Biener astutely points out that these gender differences may be due to women's greater propensity to report negative mood states. There has been one laboratory study that manipulated mood and indicated that women, more than men, smoked only during upsetting films (Ikard & Tomkins, 1973). There are data on the physiological effects of nicotine that support the role this substance might play in affect regulation; specifically, smoking reduced perception of or sensitivity to arousal in female smokers whereas the opposite was true for male smokers (Epstein, Dickson, McKenzie, & Russell, 1984).

The Women and Health Study permits an examination of the relationship between negative mood and smoking. All subjects in this study completed self-report questionnaires that included the Center for Epidemiological Studies Depression Scale (CES-D) (Radloff, 1977), a symptoms scale adapted from the Symptom Distress Checklist (Derogatis, 1977) and the Anger-In Subscale of the State Trait Anger Expression Inventory (Spielberger, 1988). Smokers scored significantly higher than nonsmokers on both the CES-D and the Tension Symptoms Scale (see Table 2). Since these data are cross-sectional, it is not possible to describe the smoking as

Table 2. Comparison of Smokers and Nonsmokers on Negative Mood in the Women and Health Study

	Current smokers	Nonsmokers	p
Depression	8.0	6.4	<.001
Tension	4.8	3.7	<.01
Anger-in	15.1	14.6	n.s.

a response to the negative mood states. However, the data indicate that women who are smokers are more likely than nonsmokers to report higher levels of depression and tension. There were no significant differences among the work status groups in this relationship between smoking and higher levels of depression and tension symptoms. There were no differences between smokers and nonsmokers in anger-in, anger that is felt but not expressed.

If smoking is a coping style for negative mood, one might argue that smokers should have lower levels of depression and tension symptoms than nonsmokers. Folkman and Lazarus (1988) point out that the relationship between emotional states and coping behaviors is not unidirectional and static. The style or type of coping behavior has an effect on emotions. For example, a "problem-focused" coping style is focused on eliminating the stressors that gave rise to the emotion. This coping style will, according to Folkman and Lazarus, neutralize distress. On the other hand, "escape-avoidance" coping strategies are less likely than problem-focused strategies to produce a lasting beneficial effect because they do not resolve the situation or otherwise address the stressor that gave rise to the emotion. Smoking is among a number of behaviors, including drug and alcohol use, that Folkman and Lazarus characterize as "escape-avoidance" coping strategies. Research has shown that these strategies, while providing a brief reprieve from the negative emotion, are related to increased depression (Folkman, Lazarus, Gruen, & DeLongis, 1986; Vitaliano, Russo, Carr, Maiuro, & Becker, 1985) and psychosomatic symptoms (Benner, 1984). The findings from the Women and Health Study, linking cigarette smoking to higher levels of depression and tension symptoms, are consistent with the literature on coping.

A MODEL OF STRESS, DISTRESS, AND SMOKING

The foregoing findings can be integrated into a model of smoking as a behavior for coping with stress and the negative mood states that stress engenders. This model is presented in Figure 1. Specifically, this model suggests that environmental stresses provoke negative mood states such as depression, anxiety, and anger in the person undergoing the stress. The stress and negative mood state elicit coping responses. One such coping response is smoking a cigarette. This model is relevant to smoking cessation and is consistent with the stress-coping model of relapse following smoking cessation (Shiffman & Shumaker, 1986). Traditionally, smoking cessation programs place an emphasis on breaking the smoking "habit" without attention to the instrumental role smoking may play for the

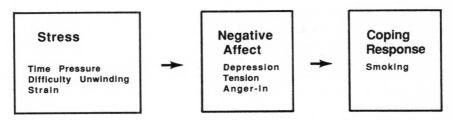

Figure 1. Proposed model of environmental stress, negative affect, and smoking as a coping response.

participant's coping with stress. Thus, programs designed to assist individuals to stop smoking would benefit from integrating this model and teaching subjects alternative strategies for managing stress. This model is not unique to smoking. Environmental stress and negative emotional states predict relapse for a variety of addictive behaviors and resulting conditions, including smoking, alcoholism, and obesity (Brownell, Marlatt, Lichtenstein, & Wilson, 1986).

The Women and Health Study data provide an opportunity to explore the validity of this model. According to the model, both negative mood and stress should be related to smoking, and, in fact, self-reports of women who smoke reach higher levels of certain indices of job stress and negative mood than do those of nonsmokers. The proposed model further suggests that job stress is related to negative mood. In the Women and Health Study women reporting job stress scored significantly higher on the depression and tension symptom scales. These relationships were observed for each of the three sources of job stress—time pressure, difficulty unwinding, and job strain—and for each of the work status groups. Salaried working women and homemakers who reported time pressure or difficulty unwinding were likely to score higher on the third negative mood state examined, "anger-in," than their counterparts who did not report these sources of stress. Thus, consistent with the model, these data indicate that there is a network of significant relationships among job stress, negative mood, and cigarette smoking.

There is evidence from the Women and Health Study that job stress and mood combine in their relationship to cigarette smoking. The relationship of these variables to smoking was examined in a series of multiple logistic analyses. When the stress and mood variables were analyzed together for the entire sample of women, the resulting chi square ($\chi^2 = 23.98$, $p = .0005$) was significantly larger than those resulting from the analysis of the job stress variables ($\chi^2 = 13.63$, $p = .003$) or the negative mood variables ($\chi^2 = 13.18$, $p = .004$) alone. Of the work status groups, a significant difference was observed between the data generated from the self-reports of working women and the homemakers in terms of the predictive model. For working women, two job stress variables—Time Pressure and Job Strain—and Tension Symptoms, a mood variable, contributed significantly to the ability of the model to predict smoking. For homemakers, only Time Pressure contributed significantly to the predictive model.

Thus, the research literature and the data from the Women and Health Study support the proposed model and suggest that cigarette smoking is used by women to cope with stress and negative mood. The implications that this model has for smoking cessation programs for women are discussed in the concluding section of this chapter.

IMPLICATIONS FOR SMOKING CESSATION PROGRAMS

Little attention in smoking cessation research has been paid to the development of smoking cessation programs for women (Russell & Epstein, 1988). The evidence of gender differences in smoking behavior implies that gender-specific smoking cessation programs might be beneficial. However, even in the absence of gender differences, it would appear profitable to design smoking cessation programs with attention to the variables that are related to smoking prevalence, that maintain smoking behavior, and that increase the likelihood of relapse.

Work site smoking cessation programs would be particularly appropriate for women, given the prevalence of smoking among employed women. Work site health promotion programs are often endorsed because of their convenience to the participant. Given the foregoing information showing the relationship between work-related time pressure and smoking among women, it would be imperative that participation in a smoking cessation program not increase time pressure. In addition, smoking cessation programs need to be designed to coincide with the work schedules of women outside the professional ranks, given the prevalence of smoking among women who work for an hourly wage. Although the prevalence of smoking among homemakers in the Women and Health Study was less than that of employed women, creative approaches to smoking cessation programs for homemakers are also needed. As with work site–based strategies, these cessation programs need to be sensitive to the restrictions and constraints experienced by homemakers (such as those studied by Graham, 1987) who lack resources.

The proposed model of smoking as a coping behavior also has implications for smoking cessation programs. The evidence that women report smoking as a coping strategy for stress and negative affect suggests that programs that focus on reducing stress and negative affect would be superior to programs that emphasize breaking the smoking habit. Such a program was evaluated in a study comparing approaches to enhance maintenance of smoking cessation (Russell, Epstein, Johnston, Block, & Blair, 1988). In this study a behaviorally oriented maintenance strategy that included group support and self-control strategies for coping with relapse situations was superior neither to an exercise nor to an attention-control condition in maintaining smoking cessation but was associated with an improvement in mood scores that was not seen in the other two groups. Perhaps more successful might be programs that approach smoking from a more comprehensive perspective and provide women with training in problem-solving coping strategies as more effective alternatives to smoking. Placing such programs at the work site would be beneficial because the work site is likely to be an environment in which the new alternative coping strategies will need to be practiced.

Cigarette smoking is the single greatest public health threat for women. This chapter opened with a review of the prevalence of smoking among women, a prevalence that makes even more distressing the evidence of the effects of smoking on morbidity and mortality among women. An evaluation of the literature, supported by data from the Women and Health Study, exposes a network of relationships between work-related stresses, negative affect, and smoking among both working women and homemakers. This network suggests a model that regards smoking as an ineffective strategy for coping with stress and negative affect. On the basis of this model, it appears that the design of smoking cessation programs for women must include the teaching of alternative strategies for coping with work-related stress and the distress it engenders and that conducting smoking cessation programs for women in the work setting is appropriate.

ACKNOWLEDGMENTS

This research was supported by a grant to the author from the National Institute of Mental Health. The work was conducted by the author when she was at SRI International (formerly Stanford Research Institute) and was carried out in collaboration with George Black, M.P.H., Michael Hecker, Ph.D., Nanette Frautschi, Ph.D., and Marcia Ward, Ph.D. The author wishes to extend her appreciation to her colleagues for their assistance in gathering the data cited herein.

REFERENCES

Andersen, F. S., Transbol, I., & Christiansen, C. (1982). Is cigarette smoking a promotor of menopause? *Acta Medica Scandinavica, 212,* 137–139.

Bailey, A., Robinson, D., & Vessey, M. (1977). Smoking and age of natural menopause. *Lancet*, ii, October 1, 722.

Barboriak, J. J., Anderson, A. J., & Hoffmann, R. G. (1984, March). *Smoking and coronary artery occlusion in female heart patients*. Paper presented at the American Heart Association Conference on Cardiovascular Disease Epidemiology, Tampa, FL.

Benner, P. (1984). *Stress and satisfaction on the job: Work meanings and coping of midcareer men*. New York: Praeger.

Berggren, G., & Sjoestedt, S. (1981). Smoking habits among women illustrated by a study in Oestergoetland. *Lakartidningen, 78*, 2596–2597.

Biener, L. (1988). Coping and adaptation. In R. C. Barnett, L. Biener, & G. K. Baruch (Eds.), *Gender and stress* (pp. 332–349). New York: Free Press.

Blake, S. M., Pechacek, T., Klepp, K., Folsom, A., Jacobs, D., & Mittelmark, M. (1984). Gender differences in smoking cessation strategies. Paper presented at the Society of Behavioral Medicine, Philadelphia.

Brownell, K. D., Marlatt, G. A., Lichtenstein, E., & Wilson, G. T. (1986). Understanding and preventing relapse. *American Psychologist, 40*, 765.

Cherry, N., & Kiernan, D. E. (1976). Personality scores and smoking behavior. A longitudinal study. *British Journal of Preventive and Social Medicine, 30*, 123–131.

Cleary, P. D., Hitchcock, J. K., Semmer, N., Flinchbaugh, L. J., & Pinney, J. M. (1986). *Adolescent smoking: Research and health policy* (Discussion Paper Series). Cambridge, MA: Institute for the Study of Smoking Behavior and Policy.

Daniell, H. W. (1978). Smoking, obesity, and the menopause. *Lancet*, ii, August 12, 373.

Davis, R. M. (1987). Current trends in cigarette advertising and marketing. *New England Journal of Medicine, 316*, 725–732.

Derogatis, L. R. (1977). Symptom Checklist-90: Manual I. Baltimore: Johns Hopkins University Press.

Dicken, C., & Bryson, R. (1978). Psychology in action, the psychology of smoking. *American Psychologist, 33*, 504–507.

Epstein, L. H., Dickson, B. E., McKenzie, S., & Russell, P. O. (1984). The effect of smoking on perception of muscle tension. *Psychopharmacology, 83*, 107–133.

Eyres, S. J. (1973). Public health nursing section report of the 1972 APHA Smoking Survey. *American Journal of Public Health, 63*, 846–852.

Folkman, S., & Lazarus, R. S. (1988). The relationship between coping and emotion: Implications for theory and research. *Social Science and Medicine, 26*, 309–317.

Folkman, S., Lazarus, R. S., Gruen, R., & DeLongis, A. (1986). Appraisal, coping, health status, and psychological symptoms. *Journal of Personality and Social Psychology, 50*, 571–579.

Frerick, R. R., Aneshensel, C. S., Clark, V. A., & Yokopenic, P. (1981). Smoking and depression: A community survey. *American Journal of Public Health, 71*, 637–640.

Frith, C. (1971). Smoking behavior and its relation to the smoker's immediate experience. *British Journal of Social Clinical Psychology, 10*, 73–78.

Graham, H. (1987). Women's smoking and family health. *Social Science and Medicine, 25*, 47–56.

Gritz, E. (1980). Problems related to use of tobacco by women. In O. J. Kalant (Ed.), *Alcohol and drug problems in women* (pp. 487-543). New York: Plenum.

Haenszel, W., Shimkin, M. B., & Miller, H. P. (1956). Tobacco smoking patterns in the United States. *Public Health Monographs, 45*, 1–105.

Harris, J. E. (1983). Cigarette smoking among successive birth cohorts of men and women in the United States during 1900–1980. *Journal of the National Cancer Institute, 71*, 473–479.

Hartz, A. J., Kelber, S., Borkowf, H., Wild, R., Gillis, B. L., & Rimm, A. A. (1987). The association of smoking with clinical indicators of altered sex steroids: A study of 50,145 women. *Public Health Reports, 102*, 254–259.

Ikard, F. F., & Tomkins, S. (1973). The experience of affect as a determinant of smoking behavior: A series of validity studies. *Journal of Abnormal Psychology, 81,* 172–181.

Jick, H., Porter, J., & Morrison, A. A. (1977). Relation between smoking and age of natural menopause. *Lancet,* i, June 25, 1354.

Kannel, W. B., & Thomas, H. E. J. (1982). Sudden coronary death: The Framingham study. *Annals of the New York Academy of Sciences, 383,* 3–21.

Karasek, R. (1979). Job demands, job decision latitude, and mental strain: Implications for job redesign. *Administrative Science Quarterly, 24,* 285–305.

Karasek, R., Lindell, J., & Gardell, B. (in press). Work and non-work correlates of illness and behavior in male and female Swedish white-collar workers. *Journal of Occupational Medicine.*

Lerner, J. V., & Vicary, J. R. (1984). Difficult temperament and drug use: Analyses from the New York Longitudinal Study. *Journal of Drug Education, 14,* 1–7.

Linn, M. W., & Stein, S. (1985). Reasons for smoking among extremely heavy smokers. *Addictive Behaviors, 10,* 197–201.

Luce, B. R., & Schweitzer, S. O. (1978). Smoking and alcohol abuse: A comparison of their economic consequences. *New England Journal of Medicine, 298,* 569–571.

Pomerleau, O., Adkins, D., & Pertschuk, M. (1978). Predictors of outcome and recidivism in smoking cessation treatment. *Addictive Behaviors, 3,* 65–70.

Radloff, L. (1977). The CES-D Scale: A self-report depression scale for research in the general populations. *Applied Psychological Measurement, 1,* 385–401.

Remington, P. L., Forman, M. R., Gentry, E. M., Marks, J. S., Hogeline, G. C., & Trowbridge, F. L. (1985). Current smoking trends in the United States. *Journal of the American Medical Association, 253,* 2975–2978.

Rose, J. E., Ananda, S., & Jarvik, M. E. (1983). Cigarette smoking during anxiety-provoking and monotonous tasks. *Addictive Behaviors, 8,* 353–359.

Rosenberg, L., Miller, D. R., Kaufman, D. W., Helmrich, S. P., Vad de Carr, S., Stoley, P. D., & Shapiro, S. (1983). Myocardial infarction in women under 50 years of age. *Journal of the American Medical Association, 250,* 2801–2806.

Russell, P. O., & Epstein, L. H. (1988). Smoking. In E. A. Blechman & K. Brownell (Eds.), *Behavioral medicine for women* (pp. 369–383). Elmsford, NY: Pergamon.

Russell, P. O., Epstein, L. H., Johnston, J. J., Block, D. R., & Blair, E. (1988). Effects of physical activity as maintenance for smoking cessation. *Addictive Behaviors, 13,* 215–218.

Salonen, J. T. (1982). Oral contraceptives, smoking and risk of myocardial infarction in young women: A longitudinal population study in Eastern Finland. *Acta Medica Scandinavica, 212,* 141–144.

Schachter, S., Silverstein, B., Kozlowski, L. T., Herman, C. P., & Liebling, B. (1977). Effects of stress on cigarette smoking and urinary pH. *Journal of Experimental Psychology, 106,* 24–30.

Seltzer, C. C., & Oechsli, F. W. (1985). Psychosocial characteristics of adolescent smokers before they started smoking: Evidence of self-selection. A prospective study. *Journal of Chronic Diseases, 38,* 17–26.

Shiffman, S., & Shumaker, S. A. (1986). Models of smoking relapse: Task force report. *Health Psychology, 5,* 13–27.

Shimp, D. M. (1986). Nonsmokers' rights in the workplace: A new look. *American Lung Association Bulletin, 3,* 3–6.

Silverstein, B., Feld, S., & Kozlowski, L. T. (1980). The availability of low-nicotine cigarettes as a cause of cigarette smoking among teenage females. *Journal of Health and Social Behavior, 21,* 383–388.

Slone, D., Shapiro, S., Kaufman, D. W., Rosenberg, L., Miettinen, O. S., & Stolley, P. D. (1981).

Risk of myocardial infarction in relation to current and discontinued oral contraceptive use. *New England Journal of Medicine, 305,* 420–424.

Sorenson, G., & Pechacek, T. (1986). Occupational and sex differences in smoking and smoking cessation. *Journal of Occupational Medicine, 28,* 360–364.

Spielberger, C. D. (1988). *The State Trait Anger Expression Inventory (STAXI).* Odessa, FL: Psychological Assessment Resources.

Stoto, M. A. (1986). *Changes in adult smoking behavior in the United States: 1955–1983* (Discussion Paper Series). Cambridge MA: Institute for the Study of Smoking Behavior and Policy.

Tagliacozzo, R., & Vaughn, S. (1982). Stress and smoking in hospital nurses. *American Journal of Public Health, 72,* 441–448.

United States Department of Health and Human Services. (1980). *The health consequences of smoking for women: A report of the surgeon general* (DHHS Publication No. 5396). Washington, DC: U.S. Government Printing Office.

United States Department of Health and Human Services. (1983). *The health consequences of smoking—cardiovascular disease: A report of the surgeon general* (USDHHS Publication No. PHS 84-50204). Washington, DC: U.S. Government Printing Office.

United States Department of Health and Human Services. (1984). *The health consequences of smoking—chronic obstructive lung disease: A report of the surgeon general* (DHHS Publication No. PHS 84-50205). Washington, DC: U.S. Government Printing Office.

United States Department of Health and Human Services. (1988). *The health consequences of smoking. Nicotine addiction: A report of the surgeon general* (USDHHS Publication No. CDC 88-8406). Washington, DC: U.S. Government Printing Office.

Van Keep, P. A., Brand, P. C., & Lehert, P. (1979). Factors affecting the age at menopause. *Journal of Biosocial Science, 6,* 37–55.

Vitaliano, P. P., Russo, J., Carr, J. E., Maiuro, R. D., & Becker, J. (1985). The ways of coping checklist: Revision and psychometric properties. *Multivariate Behavior Research, 20,* 3–26.

Waldron, I. (in press). Patterns and causes of gender differences in smoking. *Social Science and Medicine.*

Waldron, I. (1980). Employment and women's health. *International Journal of Health Services, 10,* 435–454.

Waldron, I., & Lye, D. (in press). Employment, unemployment, occupation and smoking. *American Journal of Preventive Medicine.*

Willett, W. C., Hennekens, C. H., Bain, C., Rosner, B., & Speizer, F. E. (1981). Cigarette smoking and non-fatal myocardial infarction in women. *American Journal of Epidemiology, 1123,* 575–582.

Wills, T. A., & Shiffman, S. (1985). Coping and substance use: A conceptual framework. In S. Shiffman & T. A. Will (Eds.), *Coping and substance use* (pp. 3–24). New York: Academic Press.

8

The Effect of Job Demands, Job Control, and New Technologies on the Health of Employed Women

A Review

SUZANNE G. HAYNES

INTRODUCTION

During the last four decades women have entered the work force at a rapid pace. In 1988, 56.5% of all American women were in the paid labor force, with an expected rise to 61.5% by the year 2000 (Spain, 1988). Despite the steady increase in women's participation in the work force, clerical occupations have remained the job category held by the largest proportion of women since 1950. In that year 27.4% of all employed women were employed in clerical occupations whereas 33.8% of women were employed in these jobs in 1980 (Bianchi & Spain, 1986). Using the Bureau of Labor Statistics estimates, Hunt and Hunt (1987) have estimated that clerical work will increase by 26.5% for both sexes between 1982–1995. Among women clerical workers the greatest increases between 1984–1995 are expected to occur in computer operators (46.1%), switchboard operators (28.7%), and order clerks (19.2%), jobs that are to a great extent related to the use of computers (Hartmann, Kraut, & Tilly, 1986).

SUZANNE G. HAYNES • National Cancer Institute, Bethesda, Maryland 20892.

The substantial role of clerical work in women's employment, particularly work involving computer technology, raises serious questions for the future health of women workers. Traditionally, workers engaged in clerical work report underutilization of skills and abilities, lack of autonomy, low levels of responsibility, sustained attentional demands, and social isolation (Mackay & Cox, 1984).

A recent report by Strober and Arnold (1987) found further disturbing trends for women moving into computer-related occupations:

1. Computer engineering, computer specialty work, computer programming, and other technical computer work employ few women. On the other hand, data entry and production work, occupations that take on the characteristics of clerical work, are predominantly female.
2. The higher the status and pay of the occupation, the more it is overrepresented by white men and the more it is underrepresented by minority men, and by women of all racial and ethnic groups.
3. Within several computer occupations (systems analyst, programmer, and operators), women's annual earnings were found to be less than those of men. Women are more likely to be employed in end-user industries than in the computer manufacturing industry itself. Evidence of gender segregation in the high tech industries and in highly technical occupations exists, indicating that women are relegated to less prestigious, low-paying, and higher-stress occupations.

Thus, computerization has increased rather than decreased the problems for employed women.

During the last 15 years a substantial body of evidence has emerged from studies in men to show that lack of control and high job demands at work are related to increased systolic and diastolic blood pressure, excretion of catecholamines, hypertension, cardiovascular disease, and mortality (Haynes, LaCroix, & Lippin, 1987). This chapter reviews studies that have examined the health effects of women's employment in occupations characterized by high demand/low control work. In addition, the effect of new computer technologies on the work and health of women in these occupations is highlighted.

EMPIRICAL SUPPORT FOR THE JOB STRAIN MODEL IN WOMEN

In a recent review Sorensen and Verbrugge (1987) presented several models of women's work and health that integrate research findings from studies of men with the unique concerns of women. Secretaries were recognized to be particularly vulnerable to adverse health consequences of work because they are often under considerable job pressure, a large proportion dislike the lack of advancement opportunities and are dissatisfied with their salaries, and their relationships on the job, particularly with their bosses, may cause distress.

In this chapter I use the job strain model presented by Karasek and others (Karasek, Russell, & Theorell, 1982; Cranor, Karasek, & Carlin, 1981) to review the women, work, and health literature. According to the Karasek model, low control over one's job ("low job control") is thought to be particularly stressful in combination with a highly demanding job ("high job demand"). The interaction of a substantial psychological work load with inadequate resources for exerting control results in a "high-strain" job situation. Several occupations for which women are frequently employed qualify as high-strain jobs: most clerical work, computer operator, saleswoman, telephone operator, waitress, assembler, and nursing aide (Cranor, Karasek, & Carlin, 1981).

Empirical support for the job strain model in women has been growing over the last 5 years. In 1985 investigators from Sweden reported incidence rates of hospitalization for several thousand women, ages 20–64, according to the job strain model (Alfredsson, Spetz, & Theorell, 1985). Significant elevations in hospitalization rates for myocardial infarction, presented as standardized mortality ratios, were seen for hectic, monotonous work (1.64), irregular working hours (1.52), low influence on holidays (1.45), low influence on work mates (1.33), lengthy working hours (1.31), and monotony (1.28) as compared to other working conditions (see also Chapter 10). Hectic, monotonous work and monotony were also associated with alcohol-related illnesses and gastrointestinal illness. Being tired during the day also led to a 2-fold elevated risk of myocardial infarction, a 1.5-fold risk of alcohol-related illness, and a 1.3-fold risk of gastrointestinal illness. Shift work was shown to be related to ischemic heart disease for both men and women (Åkerstedt, Knutsson, Alfredsson, & Theorell, 1984).

In a recent study of 571 women, ages 18–64, who were enrolled in Kaiser-Permanente in the northwestern United States, Hibbard and Pope (1987) reported significant associations of intrinsic work characteristics related to control (i.e., decision making, degree of challenge in the work, control over pace of work, variety in work, and extent to which worker can decide the way work is done) with self-reported health status and number of days hospitalized. In addition, the interaction of being an unmarried parent and reporting low control at work had an additional negative effect on health status.

In a 10-year prospective study of Finnish metal fabrication workers by Haan (1985), which included 600 men and 292 women, a two-fold risk for the incidence of cardiovascular disease was found among those exposed to high as compared to low levels of job strain. Controlling for sex as well as the standard coronary risk factors had no effect on the elevated risk. Thus, women as well as men were shown to have significant or higher coronary risk from working in high-strain jobs.

Finally, recent work from the Framingham Heart Study (Haynes, LaCroix, & Lippin, 1987; LaCroix, 1984; LaCroix & Haynes, 1987) showed a 2.9 relative risk for the development of coronary heart disease over 10 years among women employed in high-strain jobs as compared to other jobs. The evidence, then, for a health effect of high-strain employment in women is impressive. The remainder of this chapter concentrates on specific occupations that seem to be the job-strain model.

HEALTH EFFECTS OF CLERICAL EMPLOYMENT

Table 1 summarizes the results from eight large epidemiologic studies in the United States that examined the health effects of employment in women, with a focus on the data from clerical and sales workers. As can be seen, the majority of studies have been cross-sectional surveys. Two prospective cohorts (Framingham and Tecumseh) have followed women over time for the development of adverse health outcomes. Most of the studies of clerical workers, with the exception of the Health Interview Survey (Verbrugge, 1984), found elevated prevalence rates for acute symptoms and chronic health problems (including coronary heart disease) or elevated incidence rates of coronary heart disease (CHD) among clerical or salesworkers as compared to other workers. Mortality rates were elevated for some clerical and sales workers in the Wisconsin study (Passannate & Nathanson, 1985) whereas no significant associations were observed with mortality in the Tecumseh, Michigan cohort (House, Strecher, Metzner, & Robbins, 1986).

At least two of the studies examined the effect of job strain on health problems in the clerical work force. For example, further analysis of the clerical workers in the Framingham heart study by LaCroix (1984) showed a marked effect of high job demands and low job control on 10-year CHD incidence rates. Clerical and sales workers reporting these conditions had CHD incidence rates of 31.3%, compared to quite low rates of 2.4% among comparable workers reporting low job demands and high control (LaCroix, 1984). After controlling for the standard coronary risk factors, clerical workers with high demands and low control were 5.2 times as likely to develop CHD than the other groups combined. Likewise, Gregory (1984a) found the prevalence of self-reported acute symptoms to be two to three times greater among clerical women who reported their jobs to be stressful than among those who reported their jobs to be pleasant.

The somewhat discrepant results from the National Health Interview Survey (NHIS) have been explained by Verbrugge (1984) in several ways. First, the health indicators in NHIS are general measures of morbidity whereas other studies have concentrated on specific health problems (e.g., coronary heart disease, musculoskeletal or eye conditions). Secondly, many of the studies in Table 1 are community studies. By averaging data across the United States, the NHIS may disguise effects that are apparent in selected geographic locations. Thirdly, the NHIS definition of clerical worker does not include sales jobs, which are included in this category in many of the other studies. Finally, the NHIS only includes currently employed persons and does not report rates for retired clerical workers or for dropouts from the labor force due to poor health. Although one might also argue that cohort effects could be operational since the Framingham and Tecumseh cohorts worked in the 1940s to 1960s, the recent surveys of women suggest that more contemporary cohorts are also experiencing health problems.

HEALTH EFFECTS OF VDT WORK

Table 2 summarizes the results of seven cross-sectional studies in the United States that have examined the effect of video display terminal (VDT) work on a variety of health outcomes in women. Clerical workers and directory assistance operators have been the focal point for most investigations. The concentration on these high-strain occupations in the published studies to date is not surprising. At the outset it is important to note that most studies have assumed the *use* of the computer, rather than the computer per se, leads to job strain. In addition, the time spent on the computer per day varies across the studies.

All seven studies found significant elevations in symptoms of health problems among VDT users as compared to non-VDT users. Associations of VDT use with visual problems, musculoskeletal complaints, and tension/anxiety were found in all but one study (Starr, 1983), which was sponsored by the Bell laboratories. Four of the studies reported higher levels of job demands and/or lower levels of decision making among frequent users of VDTs (Baker, Delp, & Dellenbaugh, 1984; Haynes *et al.*, 1987; Rowland, 1984; Klitzman, Gordon, & Snow, 1986). For example, in the North Carolina office workers study, VDT users reported significantly higher job demands as compared to non-VDT users (55.7% vs. 33.8%,

Table 1. Studies on the Health Effects of Clerical/Sales Work

Principal investigator	Population studied	Type of study	Years of follow-up (if applicable)	Health outcomes assessed	Findings
Haynes & Feinleib (1980)	Framingham, MA, cohort; 387 ever-employed women; 142 clerical women, ages 45–64 yr; whites only	Prospective study starting in 1965	8	Incidence of coronary heart disease (CHD): angina, myocardial infarction (MI), coronary insufficiency, coronary death	CHD rates twice as high in clerical/sales jobs (10.6%) as compared to other occupational groups
Verbrugge (1984)	Detroit; representative sample; 202 currently employed working women; 76 clerical workers; age 18+; all races	Cross-sectional survey, 1978		Prevalence of chronic health problems (CHP), job limitations (JL), serious daily symptoms (SDS), prescription drug use (PDU)	Greater means in clerical vs. all currently employed: CHP: 4.3 vs. 3.9 JL: 1.17 vs. 1.14 SDS: 8.9 vs. 8.0 PDU: 17.3 vs. 15.4
Verbrugge (1984)	Health Interview Survey; all currently employed women age 17+; no sample sizes given for all employed or clerical women; all races	Cross-sectional survey, 1975–1976		Prevalence of acute conditions, activity limitations, short-term hospitalization, physician visits, restricted activity	No difference between clerical workers and all employed women
Gregory (1984a)	Office Worker Health and Safety survey; Cleveland and Boston; 960 clerical workers; mean age 29 yr; all races	Cross-sectional survey, 1980		Prevalence of eye strain (ES), headaches (H), muscle strain (MS), exhaustion (EX), stressful vs. pleasant job	Two to three times more symptoms in stressful vs. pleasant jobs: ES: 68.2% vs. 39.3 H: 67.7% vs. 30.6% MS: 57.7% vs. 30.6% EX: 64.9% vs. 20.6%

Study	Sample	Design	Ref.	Outcome	Findings
LaCroix (1984)	Framingham, MA, cohort; 350 currently employed women; 116 clerical and sales workers; ages 45–64; whites only	Prospective study starting in 1965	10	CHD incidence: angina, MI, coronary insufficiency, coronary death	Significant differences among clerical working women by job demands (JD) and supervision clarity (SC): high JD, low SC = 31.3%; low JD, low SC = 13.6%; high JD, high SC = 5.6%; low JD, high SC = 2.4%
Balshem (1984)	Major eastern university; 419 currently employed clerical workers; mean age 36.9; all races	Cross-sectional survey		Prevalence of psychosomatic complaints, hypertension, ulcers	Four top complaints were headaches (48.4%), eyestrain (46.1%), bad back (38.7%), and constant fatigue (25.1%); hypertension and ulcers significantly associated with subjective stress
Passannante & Nathanson (1985)	Wisconsin; 927,222 white civilian women in labor force; ages 16–64	Cross-sectional survey, 1974–1978		Age-specific death rates	Clerical workers (55–59 yr. and single, 60–64 yr. and divorced) had elevated death rate; sales workers, 60–64 years, had elevated rates of heart disease and cancer
House, Stretcher, Metzner, & Robbins (1986)	Tecumseh, MI, cohort, 963 employed women; ages 35–69; all races	Prospective study starting in 1967	9–12	Prevalence of CHD in 1967–1969; mortality over follow-up period	Clerical and sales workers had twice the prevalence of CHD than other women (11% vs. 3.6% for professionals, 5.8% for blue-collar, 7.0% for housewives). No association between occupation and mortality.

Table 2. Studies on the Health Effects of VDTs on Users

Principal investigator	Population studied	Type of study	Health outcomes assessed	Findings
Cohen, Smith, & Stammerjohn (1981a, b)	Four newspapers and one insurance company in San Francisco Bay area; 92 clerical VDT operators, 93 clerical controls; all races	Cross-sectional survey, 1979	Selected health complaints	Significantly more health complaints on 25 symptoms, including visual and musculoskeletal complaints, neck & shoulder pain, fatigue, anxiety, and irritability as compared to controls
Starr (1983)	Directory assistance operators using VDTs (145) vs. controls using paper directories (105)	Cross-sectional survey, 1980	Physical discomfort checklists	VDT operators experienced discomfort of the neck significantly more often than did operators who read paper (65% vs. 48%); several other discomforts showed numerically greater prevalence among VDT operators than phone operators, but not statistically significant (blurred vision, irritated eyes, sore eyes, sore shoulder, and upper or lower back pain)
Gregory (1984b)	National hotline; 873 VDT operators; 62% were clerical	Cross-sectional survey, 1983	Health symptoms	A large number of symptoms were reported among VDT users: 53.5% eyestrain 51.6% exhaustion 56.2% muscle pain 43.6% tension 48.6% vision problem

Study	Sample	Design	Measure	Results
Baker (1984)	1,055 Los Angeles clerical workers	Cross-sectional	Health symptoms	VDT users (25+ hrs. per week) reported significantly more ocular discomfort (3.6 vs. 2.6) (mean symptom score), musculoskeletal pain (6.4 vs. 4.3), and stress (6.4 vs, 4.9) than non-VDT users ($\leq$ 24 hr per week). Higher task demands modified the effect of VDT use in multivariate analyses.
Rowland (1984)	VDT telephone operators (145) and cordboard telephone operators not using VDTs (156); Ontario, Canada	Cross-sectional	General health symptoms	Significantly greater reports of VDT operators vs. cordboard operators for visual impairment: (40% vs. 22%) muscular postural problems (47% vs. 41%), psychosomatic symptoms (47% vs. 38%), headaches (53% vs. 44%) after controlling for confounders; job pressure associated with visual impairment, muscular/postural, & psychosomatic symptoms as well as in VDT operators.
Stellman (1986)	Clerical workers with and without VDTs (2,412)	Cross-sectional	Health symptoms	All-day VDT users reported significantly more eye symptoms and musculoskeletal strain than other clerks or part-time VDT operators. They also reported higher level of job demands and lower level of decision-making latitude.
Haynes et al. (1987)	297 clerical women using VDTs ($\geq$50% of time) vs. 230 clerical women not using VDTs frequently (<50% of time); employed in telecommunications industry in North Carolina	Cross-sectional	Symptom checklist, London school of hygiene cardiovascular questionnaire	VDT users were significantly more likely to report a number of symptoms as compared to non-VDT users: eyestrain (54% vs. 30%), headache (51% vs. 36%), fatigue (58% vs. 43%), tension (46% vs. 34%), angina (15% vs. 8%); in general, these differences were more pronounced in low-control work situations.

respectively) as well as lower job control (58.8% versus 42.8%, respectively) (Haynes *et al.*, 1987).

In two studies interaction of VDT work with job demands or job control resulted in even greater reports of health problems. In the Rowland (1984) study of Canadian workers, job pressure was significantly associated with visual impairment, muscular problems, and psychosomatic symptoms. In the North Carolina study (Haynes *et al.*, 1987) both high job demands and low control exacerbated the prevalence of eyestrain, headaches, tension, fatigue, and angina pectoris. In addition, the reported symptoms tended to increase with increased time spent on the VDT. Highest symptom reports were seen among those spending 75%–100% of their work time on the VDT, and least symptomatology was seen among those spending either less than 25% or 25%–49% of their times per day on the VDT.

Given future growth expectations for computer-related clerical jobs, noted earlier in this chapter, prospects for a healthy work force in the future are dim if changes are not made in the way VDTs are currently used. Levi (1987) has recently outlined a number of interventions that should be considered to improve the ways in which people can adapt to their working environment:

1. Increase the worker's control of the working arrangements.
2. Provide a mechanism for the worker to participate in decision making on the organization of her work.
3. Avoid imposing monotonous, machine-paced, short but frequent tasks on the worker.
4. Optimize automation.
5. Help the worker to view her specific task in relation to the total product.
6. Avoid quantitative work overload and underload.
7. Facilitate communication and support systems among workers.

In these ways, the new technologies can be used for the benefit rather than the detriment of both employee and employer.

HEALTH EFFECTS OF NURSING OCCUPATIONS

Three recent studies among nurses deserve attention, since some positions held by nurses and nurse's aides are considered high-strain occupations in the job strain model (Cranor *et al.*, 1981). Among 765 Canadian nurses studied by McLaney and Hurrell (1988), job control and job demands were significantly associated with job satisfaction, but not in an interactive fashion. The author showed that control appears to increase job satisfaction independent of the level of perceived job demands. In this regard increased task control, resource control, and control over the physical environment were more significant than decision control (assignment of tasks, deadlines, training others, and decisions about policies). Thus, for this occupational group, control over one's individual work pace, physical environment, and availability of supplies and equipment was enough to improve job satisfaction; control over policies or hiring was not necessary to improve satisfaction.

Two additional studies have shown that not all specialties in nursing experience health or psychological problems. In a study of 65 nurses in Sweden, Doncevic, Theorell, and Scalia-Tomba (1988) found that nurses working in a traditional role in a primary care center had greater objective work load and more physiological symptoms (elevated plasma catecholamines in the morning, high systolic blood pressure, and sleep disturbances) than traditional nurses working outside the primary health center or nontraditional nurses who were members of a primary health care team.

Of further interest was a study of 100 Dutch nurses that showed that nurses employed in short-stay psychiatry departments of a hospital had significantly more irritability, stress feelings, and lower scores on four job satisfaction scales (meaningfulness, growth satisfaction, supervisory satisfaction, and general work satisfaction) than nurses in a cardiac care unit in a general surgical department (Landeweerd & Boumans, 1988). These findings were contrary to expectation. The results were attributed to lack of clarity in the nurses' work in the short-stay departments along with few opportunities for training and new experiences. Thus, in conducting studies among nurses, the type of specialty and work within the nursing occupation must be taken into account.

FUTURE RESEARCH

One of the major limitations of the epidemiologic studies presented in this chapter is the preponderance of one-time cross-sectional studies, with few studies following women over time for adverse health outcomes. In cross-sectional studies there is always the possibility that women who drop out of work because of poor health are missed in the analysis. Thus, the first recommendation for future research is the implementation of prospective cohort studies of employed women, with particular focus on women employed in high-strain occupations.

Secondly, most of the studies summarized used self-reported questionnaire data to measure job strain and health outcomes. Future studies must combine self-reported data with valid medical tests or procedures that are indicative of disease. In this way, recall bias of health symptoms is avoided. Likewise, objective measures of the work environment should also be included.

REFERENCES

Åkerstedt, T., Knutsson, A., Alfredsson, L., & Theorell, T. (1984). Shift work and cardio-vascular disease. *Scandinavian Journal of Work, Environment, and Health, 10*, 409–414.

Alfredsson, L., Spetz, C. L., & Theorell, T. (1985). Type of occupation and near future hospitalization for myocardial infarction and some other diagnoses. *International Journal of Epidemiology, 14*, 378–388.

Baker, D., Delp, L., & Dellenbaugh, C. (1984). Health effects of video display terminals in relation to work environment and job task characteristics. *American Journal of Epidemiology, 120*, 479.

Balshem, M. (1984). *Job stress and health among women clerical workers: A case study* (preliminary results). Paper presented at the meeting of the American Anthropological Association, Denver.

Bianchi, S. M., & Spain, D. (1986). *American Women in Transition*, New York: Sage.

Cranor, L. A., Karasek, R. A., & Carlin, C. J. (1981). *Job characteristics and office work: Findings and health implications.* Paper presented at the National Institute for Occupational Safety and Health Conference on Occupational Health Issues Affecting Clerical/Secretarial Personnel, Cincinnati.

Doncevic, S., Theorell, T., & Scalia-Tomba, G. (1988). The psychosocial work environment of district nurses in Sweden. *Work and Stress, 2*, 341–351.

Gregory, J. (1984a). Results from working women's office worker health and safety survey. In B. G. F. Cohen (Ed), *Human aspects in office automation* (pp. 195–210). New York: Elsevier.

Gregory, J. (1984b). *Analysis of VDT operator questionnaire from 9 to 5 hotline.* Cleveland: 9 to 5, National Association of Working Women.

Haan, M. (1985). Job strain and cardiovascular disease: A ten-year prospective study. *American Journal of Epidemiology, 122*, 532.

Hartmann, H. I., Kraut, R. E., & Tilly, L. A. (Eds.). (1986). Effects of technological change: Employment levels and occupational shifts. *Computer chips and paper clips: Technology and women's employment* (Vol. I., pp. 62–126). Washington, DC: National Academy Press.

Haynes, S. G., & Feinleib, M. (1980). Women, work, and coronary heart disease: Prospective findings from the Framingham Study. *American Journal of Public Health, 70*, 113–141.

Haynes, S. G., LaCroix, A. Z., & Lippin, T. (1987). The effect of high job demands and low control on the health of employed women. In J. C. Quick, R. Rasbhagat, J. Dalton, & J. D. Quick (Eds.), *Work stress and health care* (pp. 93–110). New York: Praeger.

Hibbard, J. H., & Pope, C. R. (1987). Employment characteristics and health status among men and women. *Women and Health, 12*, 85–102.

House, J. S., Strecher, V., Metzner, H. L., & Robbins, C. A. (1986). Occupational stress and health among men and women in the Tecumseh community health study. *Journal of Health and Social Behavior, 27*, 62–77.

Hunt, H. A., & Hunt, T. L. (1987). The impact of technological change. In H. J. Hartmann (Ed.), Computer chips and paper clips. Technology and women's employment (Vol. II, pp. 223–267). Washington, DC: National Academy Press.

Levi, L. (1987). Future research. In R. Kalimo, M. A. El-Batawi, and C. L. Cooper (Eds.),

Psychosocial factors at work and their relation to health (pp. 239–245). Geneva: World Health Organization.

Karasek, R. A., Russell, R. S., & Theorell, T. (1982). Physiology of stress and regeneration in job-related cardiovascular illness. *Journal of Human Stress, 8* (March), 29–42.

LaCroix, A. Z. (1984). *Occupational exposure to high demand/low control work and coronary heart disease incidence in the Framingham cohort.* (Doctoral dissertation, University of North Carolina, 1985). *Dissertation Abstracts International, 45,* DA8425492.

LaCroix, A. Z., & Haynes, S. G. (1987). Gender differences in the health effects of workplace roles. In R. C. Barnett, L. Biener, & G. K. Baruch (Eds.), *Gender and stress* (pp. 96–121). New York: Free Press.

Landeweerd, J. A., & Boumans, N. P. G. (1988). Work satisfaction, health, and stress: A study of Dutch nurses. *Work and Stress, 2,* 17–26.

Mackay, C., & Cox, T. (1984). Occupational stress associated with visual display unit operation. In B. Pierce (Ed.), *Health hazards of VDTs* (pp. 137–144). New York: Wiley.

McLaney, M. A., & Hurrell, J. R. (1988). Control, stress, and job satisfaction in Canadian nurses. *Work and Stress, 3,* 217–224.

Passannante, M. R., & Nathanson, C. A. (1985). Female labor force participation and female mortality in Wisconsin 1974–1978. *Social Science and Medicine, 21,* 665–668.

Rowland, J. B. (1984). *Health effects of video display terminals: A comprehensive investigation of the economic, environmental, and psychosocial components of the work station.* Presentation made to the Office of Technology Assessment Workshop on Quality of Worksite Issues in Office Automation, Washington, DC.

Smith, M., Cohen, B. G. F., & Stammerjohn, L. W. (1981a). An investigation of health complaints and job stress in video display operations. *Human Factors, 23,* 387–400.

Smith, M. J., Cohen, B. G. F., Stammerjohn, L. W., & Happ, A. (1981b). Potential health hazards of video display terminals: Health complaints (DHHS - NCOSH Publication No. 81129). Cincinnati: DHHS.

Sorensen, G., & Verbugge, L. M. (1987). Women, work, and health. *Annual Review of Public Health, 8,* 235–251.

Spain, D. (1988). *Women's demographic past, present, future.* Paper presented at the Radcliffe Conferences on Women in the 21st Century. Defining the challenge: Emerging needs and constraints, Cambridge, MA.

Starr, S. J. (1983). Nonionizing radiations: Current issues and controversies. *Journal of Occupational Medicine, 25,* 95–97.

Stellman, J. M., Klitzman, S., Gordon, G. R., & Snow, B. (1987). Comparison of well-being among full-time, part-time VDT users, typists, and non-machine interactive display unit. In B. Knare (Ed.), *First International Scientific Conference on Work with Display Units* (pp. 303–306). Amsterdam: Elsevier.

Strober, M. H., & Arnold, C. L. (1987). Integrated circuits/segregated labor: Women in computer-related occupations and hightech industries. In H. I. Hartman (Ed.), *Computer chips and paper clips: Technology and women's employment* (Vol. II, pp. 211–237). Washington, DC: National Academy Press.

Verbrugge, L. M. (1984). Physical health of clerical workers. In B. G. F. Cohen (Ed.), *Human aspects in office automation* (pp. 211–237). New York: Elsevier.

9

Occupational Stress and Blood Pressure

Studies in Working Men and Women

**THOMAS G. PICKERING, GARY D. JAMES,
PETER L. SCHNALL, YVETTE R. SCHLUSSEL,
CARL F. PIEPER, WILLIAM GERIN,
AND ROBERT A. KARASEK**

The idea that stress may contribute to the development of high blood pressure and heart disease has been considered for many years, but convincing evidence for such an association has been difficult to find. One reason for this is that blood pressure is not a fixed entity but varies considerably from one moment to another. Furthermore, the conventional methods of measuring blood pressure, which typically involve a small number of readings taken in circumstances that are not representative of the normal daily environment, may result in distorted estimates of the true level.

In general, there are two ways of studying the effects of stress on the cardiovascular system. One is to measure the response to a standardized laboratory challenge (reactivity testing), the other to observe what happens in real life. Clearly, both approaches have their advantages and disadvantages; the former enables comparisons to be made between the

THOMAS G. PICKERING, GARY D. JAMES, PETER L. SCHNALL, YVETTE R. SCHLUSSEL, CARL F. PIEPER, AND WILLIAM GERIN • Cardiovascular Center, The New York Hospital, Cornell Medical Center, New York, New York 10021.   ROBERT A. KARASEK • Institute of Psychology, University of Aarhus, Risskov DK 8240, Denmark.

responses of different individuals or groups but suffers from doubtful generalizability to what goes on in real life (Pickering & Gerin, 1988). With the latter there is not so much concern about generalizability, but the less controlled environment makes comparisons between individuals harder to interpret; furthermore, there are technical limitations to what can be monitored in freely moving subjects.

For much of their lives women are at lower risk of developing high blood pressure and coronary heart disease than men, which cannot be accounted for by differences in the known risk factors for these conditions (Eaker, Packard, Wenger, Clarkson, & Tyroler, 1988). It is not known whether hereditary, hormonal, or environmental factors are responsible, but the fact that the incidence of both hypertension and coronary heart disease increases at the time of menopause is often interpreted as indicating a protective role for female hormones. However, it is also worth noting that while employment status per se did not increase the incidence of coronary heart disease in women in the Framingham Heart study, the only group of women whose incidence of this disease equaled that of the men consisted of mothers working in clerical jobs (Hayes & Feinlieb, 1980). Another popular idea is that the lower risk may be because women show less reactivity to behavioral challenges, manifested either by smaller increases of blood pressure and heart rate than men or by a lower rate of urinary catecholamine excretion. The biological relevance of such differences in reactivity between men and women is obscure, however, since women's reactivity is less than that of men mainly when women are exposed to traditionally "masculine" tasks and is at least as great as men's when exposed to more "feminine" tasks (Frankenhaeuser, 1983). Moreover, a direct causal role of reactivity in the development of cardiovascular disease has not been established (Pickering & Gerin, 1990).

USE OF AMBULATORY BLOOD PRESSURE MONITORING TO STUDY PSYCHOSOCIAL INFLUENCES ON BLOOD PRESSURE

In the last 10 years it has been possible to measure blood pressure during normal daily activities as a result of the introduction of noninvasive, ambulatory blood pressure monitors. Such devices are fully automatic and can take readings of blood pressure at regular intervals (typically every 15 minutes) over a 24-hour period (Pickering, Harshfield, Devereux, & Laragh, 1985). The subject can record in a diary his or her activity and location at the time of each reading; thus, it is possible to obtain a reliable profile of blood pressure over a full 24-hour period and to correlate changes of blood pressure with changes of activity and mood (Clark,

Denby, Pregibon, Harshfield, Pickering, Blank, & Laragh, 1987; James, Yee, Harshfield, Blank, & Pickering, 1986). The recorders do not perform well during vigorous physical activity or in noisy environments, however, so that some dampening of the true range of blood pressure variability is inevitable.

For most people the day can be divided into three periods of approximately 8 hours each, corresponding to time spent at work, at home, and asleep. When ambulatory blood pressure recordings are analyzed in this way, we have found that the pressure is, on average, about 5 mm Hg higher at work than at home, with a further fall during sleep (Pickering, Harshfield, Kleinert, Blank, & Laragh, 1982). Because our subjects were engaged mostly in sedentary jobs, the higher pressures are predominantly due, we believe, to psychosocial influences rather than to more vigorous physical activity during work.

The normal diurnal profile of blood pressure, described in a number of studies, shows a peak level of pressure in midmorning and a gradual decrease in the evening hours, reaching the lowest levels during sleep (Millar-Craig, Bishop, & Raftery, 1978). Two explanations for this pattern have been put forward: first, it may occur as a result of an intrinsic circadian rhythm of blood pressure; second, it may be determined by changing levels of activity at different times of day. We believe that the second explanation is the correct one for several reasons. When activity is restricted, as for example in patients with plaster casts in an orthopedic ward (Athanassiadis, Draper, Honour, & Cranston, 1969) or in subjects put on 24-hour bed rest (Van den Meiracker, Man In'tveld, Ritsema van Eck, Wenting, & Schalekamp, 1988), the profile of blood pressure is relatively flat during the day but still shows a decrease at night when the subjects go to sleep. Other subjects studied in the same setting but allowed to move about during the day show a greater diurnal variation of pressure.

We analyzed the recordings of 461 male patients with borderline hypertension by correlating the blood pressure readings with the corresponding activity recorded in the subjects' diaries (Clark et al., 1987), found that 16 commonly occurring activities accounted for the majority of the entries, and were able to assign a blood pressure level to each activity. In general, the activities that were associated with higher levels of blood pressure were those during which either physical or mental activity was increased (e.g., walking and talking on the telephone). In the analysis of the data, when pressure was adjusted for those activities (including sleeping), we did not find any residual diurnal variation of pressure; that is, time of day was a less significant determinant of blood pressure than activity. Perhaps the most conclusive evidence for the dominant effects of activity on diurnal blood pressure rhythms is provided by a study of shift workers. When these workers were studied on a normal daytime shift, the usual diurnal pattern of blood pressure was seen (Sundberg, Kohvakka, & Gordon, 1988). When the workers were studied a second time on the first occasion that they worked a night shift, there was an immediate reversal of the blood pressure pattern, with the highest level of pressure now occurring during the night. This pattern persisted for as long as they were working the night shift. In contrast, heart rate, which shows more of an intrinsic circadian rhythm, took longer to adapt to the new pattern.

USE OF ECHOCARDIOGRAPHY FOR STUDYING THE INFLUENCE OF PSYCHOSOCIAL FACTORS ON THE HEART

Ambulatory monitoring reveals the enormous variability of blood pressure. It also raises a question of major importance to those who are interested in the role of psychosocial influences on the development of hypertension and cardiovascular disease. Since it is much easier to demonstrate that stress can produce a transient increase of pressure rather than a sustained change, it becomes important to know whether the adverse effects of high blood pressure leading to coronary or cerebrovascular disease are determined solely by the average level of pressure over time or whether the transient surges of pressure that may occur in response to stress are also important. It would be extremely difficult to answer this question in prospective studies, however; it may be more practical to use cross-sectional studies in which the different modalities of blood pressure are related to measures of target organ damage, the most sensitive of these at the present time being left ventricular hypertrophy (LVH), which can be quantified on the echocardiogram (Devereux, 1987) and may show changes in patients who are still in the early stages of hypertension. Furthermore, the presence of LVH is an independent predictor of cardiovascular morbidity (Casale, Devereux, Milner, Zullo, Harshfield, Pickering, & Laragh, 1986).

A number of studies have shown that the correlation between blood pressure and LVH is closer for ambulatory blood pressure than for clinic pressure (pressures taken by a physician) (Rowlands, Glover, Leland, McLevy, Stallard, Watson, & Littler, 1982; Drayer, Weber, & De Young, 1983; Devereux, Pickering, Harshfield, Kleinert, Denby, Clark, Pregibon, Jason, Kleiner, Borer, & Laragh, 1983). In our own such study of 100 male patients the best correlations between LVH and blood pressure were with the blood pressure at work, which tended to be higher than the blood pressure at other times (Devereux *et al.*, 1983). In fact, not all subjects went to work on the day of the study although virtually all were employed; the reason for the better correlation with work blood pressure than with clinic blood pressure was that the correlation between ambulatory blood pressure and LVH was higher for the subjects who went to work on the day of the recording than for those who stayed at home. For those who did go to work the correlations were equally good whether the home or work blood pressures were taken. We interpreted these results as suggesting the possibility that the intermittent elevations of blood pressure associated with the regularly recurring stress of work might play a special role in contributing to the development of LVH. These results have since been confirmed by a Japanese group in a very different cultural setting (Baba, Ozawa, Nakamoto, Ueshima, & Omae, 1990). There can be no doubt that LVH can develop in this way because it readily occurs in athletes who exercise for only a few hours a day (Cohen, Gupta, Lichstein, & Chadda, 1980; Morganroth, Mason, Henry, & Epstein, 1975). Furthermore, Julius, Li, Brant, Krause, and Buda (1989) have shown that intermittent elevations of blood pressures produced for several hours a day by compression of the thighs can produce LVH, although in this experiment there was no tendency toward any sustained elevation of blood pressure.

THE ROLE OF OCCUPATIONAL STRESS IN RAISING BLOOD PRESSURE

One of the puzzling aspects of our study of LVH and ambulatory blood pressure was that although the correlation between the two was closest when studied on a workday, similar correlations were obtained whether the home or work pressures were used (Devereux *et al.*, 1983). We subsequently performed another study in which ambulatory blood pressures measured on a workday and a non-workday were compared in the same subjects (Pieper, Schnall, Warren, & Pickering, unpublished data). As expected, the blood pressure was significantly higher on the workday, but what was not anticipated was that the pressure was higher not only during the hours of work but also in the evening, when the subjects were at home. This finding indicates that there may be a carryover of the effects of the work environment to the home setting and might further explain why we found similar correlations between work and home pressures with LVH in subjects who were monitored on a workday (Devereux *et al.*, 1983).

The higher pressures on the workday were not due to an order effect, because in another study in which subjects were monitored on two workdays we found no difference between the ambulatory pressures measured on the two occasions and a very high degree of reproducibility (James, Pickering, Yee, Harshfield, Riva, & Laragh, 1988a).

Frankenhaeuser and associates (1989) have also compared blood pressures measured on a workday and a non-workday and found that for the majority of individuals the blood pressure was highest during the working hours and decreased by about 5 mm Hg on their returning home. Since the subjects measured their own pressures in the seated position, these differences cannot be explained by differences in physical activity. They did not find the same degree of carryover effect that we found, for home blood pressures in the evening were only minimally lower on the non-workday.

Our working hypothesis was that it was the psychosocial aspects of the work environment rather than the physical activity that was primarily responsible for the elevations of blood pressure at work. Since the elevation of blood pressure at work is variable from one individual to another, we sought an instrument for quantifying the effects of job stress. The one we chose was the job strain model (Job Content Survey) developed by Karasek and Theorell (Alfredsson, Karasek, & Theorell, 1982; Karasek, Theorell, Schwartz, Pieper, & Alfredsson, 1982; Karasek, Baker, Marxer, Ahlbohm, & Theorell, 1981). This has the advantage of having been shown to predict the prevalence of coronary heart disease, originally in a large Swedish study (Karasek *et al.*, 1981) but also subsequently in the United States (Karasek, Theorell, Schwartz, Schnall, Pieper, & Michela, 1988). However, previous studies using this model had not included measurements of blood pressure. We, therefore, sought to test the hypothesis that the association between job strain and coronary heart disease might be mediated by increased blood pressure.

In this model, job strain is defined by two orthogonal scales. The first is "psychological job demands," which is a measure of the work load. The second is "decision latitude," which is equivalent to the degree of control the subject perceives that he has over his job (the instrument was originally developed for men). Decision latitude is the combination of two subscales: "decision authority" and "skill discretion." These scales are evaluated by a 55-item questionnaire. Although the scores are based on the subject's perception of his job, it is possible to construct a "map" of different jobs with the two scales as the axes (Figure 1) based on the average scores of several individuals doing the same job. Most of the jobs in the high-strain quadrant (combining high demands with low control) are those that are traditionally regarded as blue-collar jobs whereas the professions (e.g., medicine, law, and accounting) are in the "active" quadrant, defined by high work load and high control. Since different individuals with similar job descriptions may have different perceptions of their level of job strain, the relationships shown in Figure 1 are only general approximations. It is worth noting that several studies have shown that cardiovascular (and

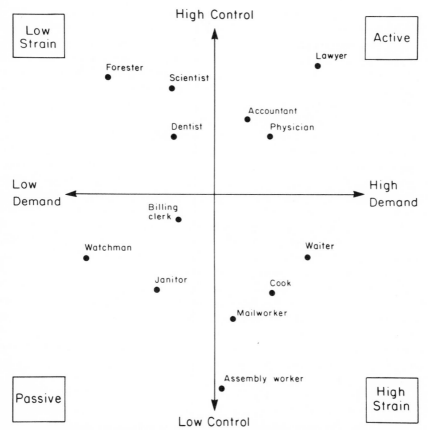

Figure 1. Karasek model of occupational stress, with average scores for various occupations. High and low levels of two components, Demand and Control, determine its four quadrants.

other) diseases are more prevalent in people with lower socioeconomic status, many of whom work in high strain jobs (Buring, Evans, Fiore, Rosner, & Henneberg, 1987; Rose & Marmot, 1981).

The Karasek model has much in common with the effort–distress model of Frankenhaeuser (1983), which also has two orthogonal axes of effort and control. Frankenhaeuser found that stress-provoking situations, both in the laboratory and in real life, elicit increases of both cortisol and catecholamine secretion.

In a study by our group, being conducted by Peter Schnall, of the association between job strain and blood pressure, a case-control design was used in which cases were defined as individuals who had an elevated diastolic pressure both on screening and at work (greater than 85 and 90 mm Hg, respectively) and controls had normal pressures in both situations (less than 85 mm Hg). Before doing the case-control study we screened 2,536 male and 1,653 female employees at seven work sites, which included a daily newspaper, a federal health agency, a brokerage firm, a beverage company, a hospital (nonprofessional employees), a sanitation department automotive repair center, and a retail store warehouse (Schlussel, Schnall, Zimbler, Warren, & Pickering, 1990). The prevalence of hypertension was, as expected, higher in men (16%) than women (5%) and higher in older and more obese subjects. Our survey also confirmed previous findings that married people have less hypertension than those who are single (Miall, 1987) and that the prevalence is higher in less well educated individuals (Hypertension Detection, 1987). Of greater interest was the finding of a significant variation in the prevalence of hypertension from one work site to another, ranging from 9% to 29% in the men and from 1% to 16% in the women. This last group consisted of warehouse workers, many of whom were packers, whose work was paced by machine and whose pay partly was dependent on their performance, which was monitored by coworkers.

The hypothesis for the case-control study was that exposure to job strain would increase the likelihood (odds ratio) of being a case. In seven work sites in New York we studied 87 cases and 128 controls. Not surprisingly, the cases tended to be older than the controls, but when the cases and controls were stratified by age, the odds ratio for the cases working in high-strain jobs was 3.1 (Schnall, Pieper, Schwartz, Karasek, Schlussel, Devereux, Ganav, Alderman, Warren, & Pickering, 1990). (High strain was defined by choosing cutoff points of job demand and decision latitude that would yield 20% of subjects in the high-demand low–decision control quadrant.) This association between job strain and high blood pressure could not be accounted for by any of the known factors influencing blood pressure, such as sodium intake, obesity, alcohol intake, education level, smoking, and level of physical activity. Neither of the two principal components of job strain—decision latitude and psychological demand—discriminated between cases and controls independently, indicating that the effects of job strain on blood pressure require the interaction of the two components. Furthermore, individuals in high-strain jobs had a greater left ventricular mass than the others.

These data thus strongly support our original hypothesis that subjects with great job strain have higher blood pressures and that this elevation of pressure may be sufficiently sustained to begin to lead to the development of LVH. Furthermore, since by definition there had to be at least a 5 mm Hg difference in ambulatory blood pressure between cases and controls, the effects on blood pressure of holding a high-strain job were of a clinically relevant magnitude. While it is difficult to draw definite conclusions about cause and effect from a cross-sectional study such as this, we can see no good reason why subjects with higher pressures should choose high-strain jobs, which would be the alternative explanation for our findings. One potential mechanism by which occupational stress might raise blood pressure, which was statistically controlled in this study, is through increased alcohol intake (McMahon, 1987), but this could not account for our findings.

ARE THERE GENDER DIFFERENCES IN THE ASSOCIATIONS BETWEEN STRESS AND BLOOD PRESSURE?

Our study of the associations between job strain and blood pressure has so far been confined to men, and it remains to be seen whether the findings can be extrapolated to women. Other work by our group, carried out by Gary James, suggests that there may be important gender differences in the interactions between psychosocial stress and blood pressure. In one study (James, Yee, Harshfield, & Pickering, 1988b) the ambulatory blood pressure recordings of 137 men and 67 women were analyzed to see whether factors such as changes of posture, location, and emotion, all of which were recorded by the subjects in their diaries, had similar effects on blood pressure in men and women. The blood pressure readings corresponding to each diary entry were transformed into Z scores to eliminate the influence of between-individual and between-sex differences in the average levels of blood pressure. Situation (at work, at home, or elsewhere) was a highly significant determinant of systolic pressure in both men and women but had less effect on diastolic pressure (Table 1). Posture (sitting, lying, or standing) had a highly significant effect on both systolic and diastolic blood pressure in women but, surprisingly, had no effect in men. Emotion (happiness, anger, and anxiety), self-reported in the AMBP diary, influenced both systolic and diastolic pressure in men, with the highest pressures occurring during anger, less high readings during anxiety, and the lowest during happiness. In women, the three emotional states were not a significant source of variation in the model, because all three tended to elevate systolic pressure by about the same amount. For diastolic pressure, men again showed the biggest changes during anger, whereas with women the biggest changes occurred with anxiety. As shown in Table 2, the absolute effects of anger on blood pressure while at work were twice as great in men as in women whereas at home there was little difference.

In another study James and colleagues (1989) analyzed data from

Table 1. Sources of Variation of Blood Pressure in Men and Women (Anova)

Situation	Men	Women
Posture		
Systolic	n.s.	0.0001[a]
Diastolic	n.s.	0.0005
Location		
Systolic	0.0001	0.0005
Diastolic	0.07	n.s.
Emotion		
Systolic	0.0001	n.s.
Diastolic	0.001	0.0001

Source: James, Yee, Harshfield, & Pickering (1988).
Note. S = systolic pressure, D = diastolic pressure
[a]p values from analysis of variance model showing relative contribution to explained variance.

ambulatory blood pressure recordings in 50 normotensive working women with technical and clerical jobs, who also kept diaries describing their activities, emotions, and perceptions of stress. The average pressures were 116/78 mm Hg at work, 113/74 mm Hg at home, and 102/63 mm Hg during sleep.

The most consistent behavioral predictor of systolic pressure was the perception that one's job is stressful, which was associated with higher pressures in all three situations—at work, at home, and during sleep (Table 3). The perception that there was more stress at work than at home on the day of the study and the perception that one's supervisor is supported were associated with higher systolic pressures at work, but not at home or during sleep. This last finding is paradoxical and as yet unexplained.

Potential sources of domestic stress were also related to blood pres-

**Table 2. Average Effects of Anger (in mm Hg)
Compared to Mean Blood Pressure[a] in Men and Women**

Group	Work	Home
Men		
Systolic	15.3	7.0
diastolic	13.1	8.4
Women		
Systolic	5.0	9.6
Diastolic	1.9	5.0

Source: James, Yee, Harshfield, & Pickering (1988).
[a]For men, 136/89; for women, 138/91.

Table 3. Psychosocial Factors Affecting Ambulatory Blood Pressure in Working Women

| | Systolic pressure | | | | | |
| | Work | | Home | | Sleep | |
	β^a	$p < t^2$	β	$p < t$	β	$p < t$
Job stressful	3.66	0.01	4.34	0.006	3.10	0.02
Stress difference	0.81	0.05	—	—	—	—
Boss unsupportive	−2.56	0.05	—	—	—	—
Children	—	—	2.58	0.05	—	—

| | Diastolic pressure | | | | | |
| | Work | | Home | | Sleep | |
	β^a	$p < t$	β	$p < t$	β	$p < t$
Stress difference	—	—	—	—	−1.19	0.001
Home stress	−0.72	0.05	—	—	—	—
Married	4.30	0.02	—	—	—	—
Children	—	—	3.09	0.005	2.58	0.01

Source: James, Cates, Pickering, & Laragh (1989).
^{a}Regression coefficient.

sure. Being married was associated with higher work diastolic pressure, while having children was associated with higher systolic and diastolic pressures at home. These data suggest that women have two full-time jobs, a finding analogous to the observation made in the Framingham Heart Study, that women employed in clerical jobs who also had children and were married to men with blue-collar jobs had the highest incidence of coronary heart disease (Haynes & Feinlieb, 1980).

Urine catecholamine excretion rates were also highest at work in the majority of subjects. The changes in urine norepinephrine and epinephrine were significantly correlated with the changes of systolic and diastolic blood pressure from sleep to work, but only among women who perceived greater stress at work on the day of the study (James, 1989). These results suggest that catecholamines have a more direct effect on blood pressure during periods of high stress.

CONCLUSIONS

Our results suggest that noninvasive ambulatory monitoring may provide a useful new technique for evaluating the effects of occupational and domestic stress on blood pressure. Blood pressure varies greatly throughout the course of the day and night, and there is increasing evidence that this variation is neither a constant, intrinsically determined circadian rhythm nor the result of random variability, but is determined to a large extent by what people are doing and feeling. While physical activity and posture are undoubtedly important determinants, emotional and psychosocial factors can have a surprisingly large influence.

There has been considerable interest in the role that emotions—particularly anger (and, to a lesser extent, anxiety)—may play in the development of cardiovascular disease. Hostility has been implicated in the development of coronary heart disease (Williams, 1984), and suppressed anger in hypertension (Julius, Schneider, & Egan, 1985). Our findings show that the experiences of both anger and anxiety during daily life are associated with significant increases of blood pressure, but that these patterns are different in men and women. Anger appears to have a greater effect on blood pressure in men, particularly while they are at work. In this context it is worth noting that most of the literature relating anger and hypertension has been based on studies of men (Esler, Julius, Zweifler, Randall, Harburg, Gardiner, & DeQuattro, 1977; Harburg, Erfurt, Havenstein, Cahpe, Schull, & Schork, 1973; Kahn, Medalie, Neufield, Riss, & Goldbourt, 1972).

We have also obtained evidence to indicate that the pattern of blood pressure change during the day is strongly influenced by perceived levels of stress both at work and at home. For the majority of working men, blood pressure falls on going home in the evening, and studies conducted in subjects on 24-hour bed rest or shift work demonstrate that this fall is situationally determined rather than being a function of the time of day. A similar pattern is seen in many women, with the notable exception of working mothers, who go home to face a different source of stress and whose blood pressure does not fall. Similar findings have been reported by Frankenhaeuser and associates (1989), who observed that male managers' blood pressure and urinary catecholamine excretion dropped sharply at 5:00 P.M. whereas female managers' blood pressure did not change and their catecholamine excretion actually increased. This was described as an "inability to unwind," and may parallel our findings of a carryover effect from work to home. These findings suggest that there may be limits on the extent to which it is possible to rigidly compartmentalize different sources of stress and relate them precisely to concomitant changes in physiological variables; when we go home in the evening, we do not necessarily leave our job-related stress behind us.

The ultimate effect of these stress-related influences on blood pressure remains to be established. Although the idea that intermittent elevations of blood pressure can eventually lead to sustained hypertension has been widely advocated, as well as the idea that subjects who show increased cardiovascular reactivity to stress-related stimuli are at increased risk of future hypertension, we have reviewed the evidence for this elsewhere and find little support for it (Pickering & Gerin, 1990). We do believe, however, that our finding of an increased prevalence of hypertension in men who report greater job strain may have the potential of providing some of the most convincing evidence for a primary role of psychosocial factors not only in the development of hypertension but also hypertensive heart disease. To demonstrate a direct causal relationship, however, these findings need to be replicated on a prospective basis, which we are currently attempting to do.

We are also impressed by the conceptual similarities between the job strain model of Karasek and Theorell and the effort–distress model of Frankenhaeuser. The former has been almost exclusively used in epidemiological studies of the chronic effects of occupational stress on health whereas the latter was developed to explain differing patterns of pituitary–adrenal and sympathetic nervous system arousal during short-term laboratory studies of the effects of different stressors. The two orthogonal components of the two models, which may be loosely interpreted as "work load" and "control," are strikingly similar. We believe that it would now be appropriate to attempt to synthesize the two models by verifying the job strain model in the laboratory, on the one hand, with measurements of cardiovascular variables as well as cortisol and catecholamine excretion and by attempting to extend the effort–distress model to long-term health consequences on the other.

ACKNOWLEDGMENTS

This work was supported in part by grants from the National Heart, Lung and Blood Institute of the National Institutes of Health, 2 HL-30605 and HL-37054.

REFERENCES

Alfredsson, L., Karasek, R., & Theorell, T. (1982). Myocardial infarction risk and psychosocial work environment: An analysis of the male Swedish working force. *Social Science and Medicine, 16*, 463–467.

Athanassiadis, D., Draper, G. J., Honour, A. J., & Cranston, W. I. (1969). Variability of automatic blood pressure measurements over 24-hour period. *Clinical Science, 36*, 147–156.

Baba, S., Ozawa, H., Nakamoto, Y., Ueshima, H., & Omae, T. (1990). Enhanced blood pressure response to regular daily stress in urban hypertensive men. *Journal of Hypertension, 8*, 647–655.

Buring, J. E., Evans, D. A., Fiore, M., Rosner, B., & Henneberg, C. H. (1987). Occupation and risk of death from coronary heart disease. *Journal of the American Medical Association, 258*, 791–792.

Casale, P. N., Devereux, R. B., Milner, M., Zullo, G., Harshfield, G. A., Pickering, T. G., & Laragh, J. H. (1986). Value of echocardiographic measurement of left ventricular mass in predicting cardiovascular morbid events in hypertensive men. *Annals of Internal Medicine, 105*, 173–178.

Clark, L. A., Denby, L., Pregibon, D., Harshfield, G. A., Pickering, T. G., Blank, S., & Laragh, J. H. (1987). A quantitative analysis of the effects of activity and time of day on the diurnal variations of blood pressure. *Journal of Chronic Diseases, 40*, 671–681.

Cohen, J. L., Gupta, P. K., Lichstein, E., & Chadda, K. D. (1980). The heart of a dancer: Noninvasive cardiac evaluation of professional ballet dancers. *American Journal of Cardiology, 45*, 959–965.

Devereux, R. B. (1987). Detection of left ventricular hypertrophy by M-mode echocardiography. Anatomic validation, standardization, and comparison to other methods. *Hypertension, 9* (Suppl. II), 19–26.

Devereux, R. B., Pickering, T. G., Harshfield, G. A., Kleinert, H. D., Denby, L., Clark, L., Pregibon, D., Jason, M. N., Kleiner, B., Borer, J. S., & Laragh, J. H. (1983). Left ventricular hypertrophy in patients with hypertension: Importance of blood pressure response to regularly recurring stress. *Circulation, 68*, 470–476.

Drayer, J. I. M., Weber, M. A., & DeYoung, J. L. (1983). BP as a determinant of cardiac left ventricular muscle mass. *Archives of Internal Medicine, 143*, 90–92.

Eaker, E. D., Packard, B., Wenger, N. K., Clarkson, T. B., & Tyroler, H. A. (1988). Coronary artery disease in women. *American Journal of Cardiology, 61*, 641–644.

Esler, M., Julius, S., Zweifler, A., Randall, O., Harburg, E., Gardiner, H., & DeQuattro, V. (1977). Mild high-renin essential hypertension: Neurogenic human hypertension? *New England Journal of Medicine, 296*, 405–411.

Frankenhaeuser, M. (1983). The sympathetic-adrenal and pituitary–adrenal response to challenge: Comparison between the sexes. In T. M. Dembroski, T. H. Schmidt, & G. Blumchen (Eds.), *Biobehavioral bases of coronary heart disease* (pp. 91–105). Basel: Karger.

Frankenhaeuser, M., Lundberg, U., Fredrikson, M., Melin, B., Toumisto, M., Mersten, A-L., Bergman-Losman, B., Hedman, M., & Wallin, L. (1989). Stress on and off the job as related to sex and occupational status in white-collar workers. *Journal of Organizational Behavior, 10*, 321–326.

Harburg, E., Erfurt, J. C., Hauenstein, L. S., Cahpe, C., Schull, W. J., & Schork, M. A. (1973). Socioecological stress, suppressed hostility, skin color, and black–white male blood pressure: Detroit. *Psychosomatic Medicine, 35*, 276–296.

Haynes, S. G., & Feinlieb, M. (1980). Women, work and coronary heart disease: Prospective findings from the Framingham Heart Study. *American Journal of Public Health, 70*, 133–141.

Hypertension Detection and Follow-up Program Cooperative Group. (1987). Educational level and 5-year all-cause mortality in the Hypertension Detection and Follow-up Program. *Hypertension, 9*, 641–646.

James, G. D. (1989). Perceived work stress increases daily blood pressure and catecholamine variation in young, healthy women. Presented at the Tenth Annual meeting of the Society of Behavioral Medicine.

James, G. D., Cates, E. M., Pickering, T. G., & Laragh, J. H. (1989). Parity and perceived job stress elevate blood pressure in young normotensive working women. *American Journal of Hypertension, 2*, 637–639.

James, G. D., Pickering, T. G., Yee, L. S., Harshfield, G. A., Riva, S., & Laragh, J. H. (1988). The reproducibility of average ambulatory, home, and clinic pressures. *Hypertension, 11*, 545–549.

James, G. D., Yee, L. S., Harshfield, G. A., Blank, S. G., & Pickering, T. G. (1986). The influence of happiness, anger, and anxiety on the blood pressure of borderline hypertensives. *Psychosomatic Medicine, 48*, 502–508.

James, G. D., Yee, L. S., Harshfield, G. A., & Pickering, T. G. (1988b). Sex differences in factors affecting the daily variation in blood pressures. *Social Science and Medicine, 26*, 1019–1023.

Julius, S., Li, L., Brant, D., Krause, L., & Buda, A. J. (1989). Neurogenic pressor episodes fail to cause hypertension, but do induce cardiac hypertrophy. *Journal of Hypertension, 13*, 422–429.

Julius, S., Schneider, R., & Egan, B. (1985). Suppressed anger in hypertension: Facts and problems. In M. A. Chesney & R. H. Rosenman (Eds.), *Anger and hostility in cardiovascular and behavioral disorders* (pp. 127–137). Washington, DC: McGraw-Hill.

Kahn, H. A., Medalie, J. H., Neufeld, N. J., Riss, E., & Goldbourt, U. (1972). The incidence of hypertension and associated factors: The Israeli Ischemic Heart Disease Study. *American Heart Journal, 84*, 171–182.

Karasek, R., Baker, D., Marxer, F., Ahlbohm, A., & Theorell, T. (1981). Job decision latitude, job demands, and cardiovascular disease: A prospective study of Swedish men. *American Journal of Public Health, 75*, 694–705.

Karasek, R. A., Theorell, T., Schwartz, J. E., Schnall, P. L., Pieper, C. F., & Michela, J. L. (1988). Job characteristics in relation to the prevalence of myocardial infarction in the U.S. Health Examination Survey (HES) and the Health and Nutrition Examination Survey (HANES). *American Journal of Public Health, 78*, 910–918.

Karasek, R. A., Theorell, T. G. T., Schwartz, J., Pieper, C., & Alfredsson, L. (1982). Job, psychological factors and coronary heart disease. *Advances in Cardiology, 29*, 62–67.

McMahon, S. (1987). Alcohol consumption and hypertension. *Hypertension, 9*, 111–121.

Miall, W. E. (1987). Some personal factors influencing arterial blood pressure. In J. Stamler, R. Stamler, & T. N. Pullman (Eds.), *The epidemiology of hypertension* (pp. 69–60). New York: Grune & Stratton.

Millar-Craig, M. W., Bishop, C. N., & Raftery, E. B. (1978). Circadian rhythm of blood pressure. *Lancet, 1*, 795.

Morganroth, J., Mason, B. J., Henry, W. L., & Epstein, S. E. (1975). Comparative left ventricular dimensions in trained athletes. *Annals of Internal Medicine, 82*, 521–524.

Pickering, T. G., & Gerin, W. (1988). Ambulatory blood pressure monitoring and cardiovascular reactivity testing for the evaluation of the role of psychosocial factors and prognosis in hypertensive patients. *American Heart Journal, 116*, 655–672.

Pickering, T. G., & Gerin, W. (1990). Cardiovascular reactivity in the laboratory and the role of behavioral factors in hypertension: A critical review. *Annals of Behavioral Medicine, 12*, 3–16.

Pickering, T. G., Harshfield, G. A., Devereux, R. B., & Laragh, J. H. (1985). What is the role of ambulatory blood pressure monitoring in the management of hypertensive patients? *Hypertension, 7*, 171–177.

Pickering, T. G., Harshfield, G. A., Kleinert, H. D., Blank, S., & Laragh, J. H. (1982). Blood pressure during normal daily activities, sleep and exercise. Comparison of values in normal and hypertensive subjects. *Journal of the American Medical Association, 247*, 992–996.

Rose, G., & Marmot, M. G. (1981). Social class and coronary heart disease. *British Heart Journal, 45*, 13–19.

Rowlands, D. B., Glover, D. R., Leland, M. A., McLevy, R. A. B., Stallard, T. H., Watson, R. D. S., & Littler, W. A. (1982). Assessment of left ventricular mass and its response to antihypertensive treatment. *Lancet, 1,* 467–470.

Schlussel, Y. R., Schnall, P. L., Zimbler, M., Warren, K., & Pickering, T. G. (1990). The effect of work environments on blood pressure. Evidence from seven New York organizations. *Journal of Hypertension, 8,* 679–685.

Schnall, P. L., Pieper, C., Schwartz, J. E., Karasek, R. A., Schlussel, Y., Devereux, R. B., Ganav, A., Alderman, M., Warren, K., & Pickering, T. G. (1990). The relationship between "job strain," workplace diastolic blood pressure, and left ventricular mass index. Results of a case-control study. *Journal of the American Medical Association, 263,* 1929–1935.

Sundberg, S., Kohvakka, A., & Gordon, A. (1988). Rapid reversal of circadian blood pressure rhythm in shift workers. *Journal of Hypertension, 6,* 393–396.

Van den Meiracker, A. H., Man In'tveld, A. J., Ritsema van Eck, H., Wenting, G. H., & Schalekamp, M. A. D. H. (1988). Determinants of short-term blood pressure variability: Effects of bed rest and sensory deprivation in essential hypertension. *American Journal of Hypertension, 1,* 22–26.

Williams, R. B., (1984). Type A behavior and coronary heart disease: Something old, something new. *Behavioral Medicine Update, 6,* 29–35.

10

On Cardiovascular Health in Women

Results from Epidemiological and Psychosocial Studies in Sweden

TÖRES THEORELL

INTRODUCTION

An increasing proportion of working men and women in Sweden regard their work as psychologically demanding. At the same time, most physical stressors are becoming less frequent (Statistics Sweden, 1982). Several studies in this field have indeed focused on psychosocial job factors that could be positively affected by interventions in work organization or social climate. Studies have shown that psychological job demands increase the risk of illness only when the workers have poor resources for "decision latitude" (possibility to influence decisions) and social support (see Johnson, 1986; Karasek, 1979; Karasek & Theorell, 1989; Theorell, 1989). Furthermore, recent studies (Johnson, 1986; Johnson, Hall, & Theorell, 1989) have shown that three environment dimensions—demands, decision latitude, and social support—probably interact in a multiplicative way in the promotion of illness processes. Theories (Karasek, Russell, & Theorell, 1982; Karasek & Theorell, 1989; Theorell, 1989) have been developed that propose or argue that job strain (a combination of high demands and low decision latitude) inhibits those mechanisms that protect the person

TÖRES THEORELL • National Swedish Institute of Psychosocial Factors and Health, S-104 01 Stockholm, Sweden.

against stress and at the same time increases the general arousal level. Such theories are close to those that have been developed using the individual's response to stressors as a basis for formulations (see, for instance, Chapter 3, in this volume; Kahn, 1974.)

Most of the studies on the significance of psychosocial job conditions for cardiovascular health have been performed on men. In recent years, however, several studies on women have been published, and most of them are reviewed in this volume by Haynes (Chapter 8). I shall focus on studies performed in Scandinavia.

INTERNATIONAL TRENDS IN CORONARY HEART DISEASE MORTALITY FOR MEN AND WOMEN

It was expected that the female incidence of coronary heart disease would increase as women entered the labor market in industrialized countries; however, there is no evidence so far of such an increase. Figure 1 shows life expectancy at birth for men and women in a number of industrialized countries (WHO, 1982). The diagram is organized in such a way that the number of countries with a given life expectancy is plotted on the y-axis. Separate data are given for men and women. The figure clearly shows the wide spread of both women's and men's life expectancy in the 1950s and the narrow one in the 1970s. It also shows that life expectancy increased considerably for both men and women between these decades and that the difference between men and women, contrary to expectations, became much more distinct than before. The two distributions are fairly narrow and distinctly separated in the 1970s but wider and intertwined in the 1950s. It is evident that during these years many changes have taken place in the countries studied. Major factors of importance for the longevity of women include the decreased number of pregnancies per woman and the more effective treatment of infections and other complications of childbirth. That is, the mortality risk associated with childbirth and pregnancy has decreased, and so has the possible long-term effect on health of many pregnancies. For men as well as women, nutritional state and health care services have improved dramatically, and physical risks at work have decreased.

Table 1, showing the age-adjusted percentage change in coronary heart disease mortality in European countries from 1972 to 1984 (Haukka, 1987), reflects more recent changes. Again, it is clear that the change is more favorable for women than for men. We may speculate about the causes—are they social or biological? And if social, what mechanisms are involved? Is it because women and men have different kinds of jobs? Is it

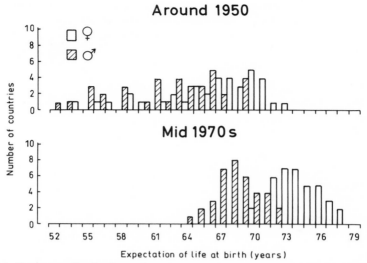

Figure 1. Frequency distributions of expectation of life at birth in 37 more developed countries, males and females, around 1950 and mid-1970s.

because the total life situation (including that of outside work) is different for men and women?

JOB CHARACTERISTICS OF DIFFERENT OCCUPATIONS: ASSOCIATIONS ON AN AGGREGATED LEVEL

In a study in Sweden, Alfredsson, Spetz, and Theorell (1985) related the occupations of all working people under 65 in five counties (approximately 600,000 men and 400,000 women) to the risk of becoming hospitalized for myocardial infarction or other diagnoses during a follow-up period of one year. The analysis was based on a classification of approximately 100 occupations. As part of the national surveys of level of living in Sweden, participants are asked how they regard their own jobs: Is the job hectic? Is it monotonous? Are there few possibilities of learning new things? Does the amount of overtime reach or exceed 10 hours a week? The participants are also asked about various subjective symptoms, such as fatigue and headache. In the analysis of the data the proportion of subjects in each occupation responding yes to each question was computed. Occupations were then divided at the median into hectic and nonhectic, monot-

**Table 1. Percentage Annual Change (Regression for the Years
1972–1984) in Coronary Heart Disease Mortality
in Various Countries**

	Men (%)	Women (%)
Belgium	−27	−29
Finland	−21	−25
Malta	−18	−22
Netherlands	−18	−19
Portugal	−13	−28
England and Wales	−11	− 7
Scotland	−11	− 8
France	−11	−23
Denmark	−11	−16
Federal Republic of Germany	−10	−10
Luxemburg	−10	− 1
Northern Ireland	−10	− 4
Norway	− 9	−15
Sweden	− 9	−21
Switzerland	− 6	.17
Austria	− 5	−14
Iceland	− 4	−23
Italy	− 2	−22
Ireland	0	−13
Czechoslovakia	+11	+ 6
Greece	+18	0
Bulgaria	+20	−11
Hungary	+38	+14
Yugoslavia	+39	+19
Spain	+52	+32
Romania	+60	+54

Note. Percentages are rounded off. Data was assembled from unpublished WHO tabulations, supplied through the courtesy of Dr. K. Uemura, WHO.

onous and nonmonotonous, and so forth. Furthermore, occupations above the median for both hectic and monotonous as well as those above the median for both hectic and nonlearning (i.e., a high percentage of subjects report few possibilities to learn new things) were identified. Age-standardized risks of hospitalization were computed for individuals working in occupations belonging to different psychosocial risk categories. "Monotonous" and "nonlearning" are important elements in low skill discretion, which is a basic component of low decision latitude, according to Karasek (1979). In this chapter occupations that are hectic and monotonous or hectic and have few opportunities for learning new things are hypothe-sized to be particularly dangerous combinations, since they are associated with "job strain," as initially defined by Karasek. Using standard meth-odologies for analyzing confounding variables, the following demographic factors were controlled for: full- versus part-time work, type of residence, type of community, number of children at home, and income. The results described in the following section of this chapter were subjected to analysis, and findings that were explained statistically by these factors have been excluded from the discussion.

Figure 2 shows the results of this analysis, using hospitalization for myocardial infarction as the dependent variable. The patterns for men and women are distinctly different, although there are also similarities. For both men and women, risk for myocardial infarction is higher in occupa-tions that a high proportion of workers describe as hectic and monotonous; this relationship is independent of age. We also observe that shift work is associated with increased risk in both genders. The differences patterns for men and women are as follows:

1. Women in occupations for which a high proportion of workers report subjective symptoms such as fatigue and headache have a higher

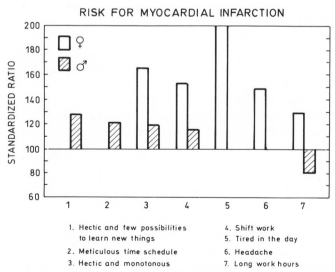

Figure 2. Some psychosocial occupational factors significantly associated in group analysis with risk of being hospitalized for myocardial infarction during one year of follow-up. Standardized morbidity ratios. Only findings that are significant after analysis of the effects of confounding have been included.

myocardial infarction hospitalization risk than other women. For men no such association is observed. The explanation of such a finding could be that women are more honest than men. The traditional male role is to be stoic and not admit any weaknesses—the John Wayne syndrome; that is, men may deny—or may be unaware of—bodily symptoms more than do women. A more pronounced denial tendency in men than in women was observed in one of our earlier studies of men and women hospitalized for a myocardial infarction (Billing, Lindell, Sederholm, & Theorell, 1980). Early recognition of bodily warning signs in general may be one of the factors that protects women from developing premature myocardial infarctions.

2. Women in occupations in which overtime (at least 10 hours/week) was reported to be common had a greater risk of becoming hospitalized for myocardial infarction than other women. For men the opposite phenomenon was observed: a moderate amount of male overtime was associated with "protection" against hospitalization for myocardial infarction, although we know from other studies that extreme amounts of overtime are associated with increased risk for men also (Hinkle, 1974). This difference between men and women can be seen from the perspective of traditional male and female social roles. In Swedish society women are much more prone than men to have responsibility for child care and domestic work, even in families where both wife and husband have jobs (Frankenhaeuser, Lundberg, Fredrikson, Melin, Tuomisto, Myrsten, Bergman-Losman, Hedman, & Wallin, 1989; Lundberg & Palm, in press). In practice this means that a woman who works overtime often encounters more frustrations than others after work. Child care, for instance, is not easily coordinated with overtime work.

Another factor that may be of great importance for explaining the male–female discrepancy in effect of overtime work is the fact that men in general enjoy more decision latitude and intellectual discretion in their jobs than women do. The results of an analysis by Cranor and associates (1981) of the male and female work force in the United States showed that men and women in general claim very similar psychological demands in their jobs but that women claim a much lower level of decision latitude on the job than do men. That is, there are many more female jobs in the job-strain category than there are male jobs. If one is forced to do overtime in a boring job where one has little say (i.e., low decision latitude), the effect is more likely to be harmful than when the decision latitude is high.

Although overtime may be more harmful for women, it should also be pointed out, however, that it is much less common among female than male workers. In order to cope with their dual roles, female workers frequently work part-time.

3. Men in occupations characterized as both nonlearning and hectic had a higher incidence of hospitalization for myocardial infarction than did other men. This predictor was the strongest of all psychosocial predictors for men, but it was not at all significant for women. This result is amplified by other findings relating various consequences to nonlearning occupations; these findings are presented in Table 2, which shows the relative age-adjusted risks of becoming hospitalized for other illnesses or conditions. The interpretation of these results is more difficult than it is for myocardial infarction alone, since cause–effect relationships for some of the other variables are more problematic. However, it is striking that working in a nonlearning occupation predicts hospitalization for many kinds of illnesses and conditions among men but has no predictive value for any diagnosis among women. This finding may reflect a difference either in how men and women define a nonlearning occupation or in the way in which they, with their different traditional social roles, handle the role of work in life. Development and learning at work may be more important to the traditional male role than it is to the traditional female role. Another interpretation of this finding is that women frequently do not realize that "silent" skills—those not acknowledged by society—are constantly developing in typical female caring occupations. This could be a female counterpart to the lack of association between psychological symptoms on one hand and risk of myocardial infarction in men on the other. However, the most important finding is that jobs that are characterized by a hectic tempo and lack the possibility of the worker's utilizing and developing knowledge ("monotony" and "nonlearning")—an important component of a low decision latitude—were associated with increased myocardial infarction risk for both genders.

The study by Alfredsson and associates (1985), relating occupation to hospitalization for myocardial infarction, was based on aggregated measures of work characteristics in more than 100 occupations. It involved only crude measurements of the working environment, since work sites in a particular occupation may vary considerably. However, this is not necessarily a disadvantage, because the technique allows the researcher to avoid individuals' personality-correlated distortions in describing the working environment. What can be predicted is the type of occupation that has unexpectedly high illness risks. The samples studied were very large, and the number of individuals lost in the follow-up very small (in the order of 1%). The study had a prospective design, with job characteristics identified one year and the follow-up performed the following year. One weakness is that persons who died outside a hospital were not included, but this is unlikely to have had any major effect on the types of observations Alfredsson and associates (1985) were making. Another weakness was that

Table 2. Significant Age-Adjusted Relative Risks of Hospitalization for Various Illnesses or Conditions in Relation to Psychosocial Job Characteristics

M = Men W = Women	Myocardial infarction			Suicide attempt		Alcohol related diseases		Psychiatric illness		Gastrointestinal illness		Traffic accident	
	M	M (<55 yr)	W	M	W	M	W	M	W	M	W	M	W
Not learning	1.1	1.4		2.4		2.6		2.3		1.7		1.5	
Monotony		1.4		2.0	1.5	2.3	1.9	2.1	1.5	0.6	1.6	1.5	
Hectic	1.3	1.6			1.4	0.5	1.2	0.6				0.7	
Hectic and not learning				2.2		1.4	1.3	1.4		1.5			
Monotonous	1.2	1.5	1.6		2.3		3.1		1.6		2.2		

Note. From Alfredsson, Spetz, & Theorell (1985).

although the researchers could adjust for known social risk factors, they did not have access to information on medical and biological risk factors. In general, other studies (see Karasek & Theorell, 1990) have shown that the association between serum lipoproteins and coronary heart disease does not cause spurious associations between psychosocial work conditions and heart disease risk. With regard to the other two major medical risk factors, cigarette smoking and hypertension, it is likely that some—but not all—of the association between psychosocial risk factors and heart disease risk are mediated by them (see Karasek & Theorell, 1989).

COMPARISON OF RISK FACTORS BETWEEN MEN AND WOMEN IN THE SAME OCCUPATIONS

The epidemiological five-county study in Sweden can provide only a crude association between working conditions (measured collectively) and illness risk. The results simply tell us that women in some kinds of occupations more frequently suffer from myocardial infarction than do women in other kinds of occupations. In order to obtain information on mechanisms on the individual level we have to follow persons during their working hours. Recently, a study (the "four occupations study") was performed at the National Swedish Institute of Psychosocial Factors and Health in which women and men in four occupations were compared with regard to mood states, biomedical cardiovascular risk factors and work conditions. The psychosocial dimensions at work were measured by the individuals themselves. Emotional states were recorded in diaries and repeated blood pressure measurements were made during working and leisure hours. Smoking habits were recorded by means of questionnaires, and serum lipids were assessed (Theorell, Ahlberg-Hultén, Berggren, Perski, Sigala, Svensson, & Wallin, 1987). Eighty-five men and 62 women, ages 25 to 60, were studied. The samples were selected from four widely different groups: physicians, waiters, symphony musicians, and air traffic controllers. The participation rate among women was higher than among men—81% versus 62%. Each subject was asked to participate in the study on four occasions during the year. Eighty percent participated at least twice, and a third on all four occasions. On each occasion, a self-administered questionnaire (according to Karasek and associates, 1988) was used for the measurement of psychological demands, possibility to use and develop intellectual skills (intellectual discretion), possibility to influence immediate decisions regarding what shall be done and how to do it (authority over decisions), and social support (positive climate) at work. Of particular interest from the perspective of long-term health is the relationship between psychosocial parameters at work on one hand and everyday emotional states and biological risk factors on the other.

The participants provided us with repeated assessments of mood states (as close to once an hour as possible) during 1–4 measurement days. For each day there was an average of 14 recordings per person (7 during working hours and 7 during leisure). At least three recordings were required for the calculation of an average blood pressure during working hours or during leisure. Mood states were calculated for the whole day (working hours and leisure) from a diary with a list of 23 mood adjectives. Thus, at least six measurements were required for a calculation of a mood state during a measurement day. For example, for "sadness" grade 2 or 3 (out of a range of 0–3), for one or both of the adjectives "blue" or "sad" was required. For each measurement day, the proportion of observations of mood that identified sadness was calculated, using the total number of observations as the denominator. In subjects with at least two measurement days, the subject's total mean was calculated. In subjects with only one measurement day, the proportion that day was used. Corresponding analyses were made for the following mood states: worry (feeling tense or nervous or worried), joy, and anger (feeling irritated or angry). Age standardization was not performed because the differences between the occupational groups were small, owing to the selection of subjects; the mean age for women was 38.3 and that for men 41.1.

None of the mood states varied significantly with age in women. Differences between reported emotional states in the women in the four occupational groups were nonsignificant. On the other hand, in several cases there were differences between men and women in the same occupation (the average for women falling outside the 95% confidence limits for men); in these cases the women reported more emotions in their diaries than did the men. Thus, female physicians more frequently reported sadness and anger than did their male colleagues. Female musicians more frequently reported sadness than did their male colleagues, and waitresses reported worry as well as joy more often than waiters. One interesting aspect of these findings is that while women, as expected, in general reported more emotions than men, different emotions were characteristically reported by women in different occupations. It could be that the moods of sadness and anger indicate a particularly bad frustration with the occupational role. This may be partly explained by the fact that female musicians who indicated they felt sad, as well as female physicians who described themselves as angry or sad work in occupations that have traditionally been dominated by men. Waitresses who reported feeling joyous or worried, on the other hand, work in an occupation that has traditionally been dominated by women.

The results of comparisons between women in the four occupations for psychosocial working conditions ("psychological demands," "intellectual discretion," "authority over decisions," and "positive climate") and the corresponding results for cardiovascular risk factors (smoking habits, blood pressure during activities at work and during leisure, serum triglycerides, and total serum cholesterol) are presented in Table 3. For each variable the differences between the female occupational groups have been tested by means of one-way analysis of variance. Furthermore, each occupational group has been compared with all other groups by means of a two-tailed t-test.

For intellectual discretion and authority over decisions, the differences between the groups were highly significant. Waitresses reported low intellectual discretion, and symphony musicians as well as air traffic controllers reported having little authority to make decisions. Female physicians, compared to women in the other three occupations, tended to report receiving little social support from coworkers whereas waitresses reported a more positive working climate than any other (male or female) group.

The medical–physiological results have been age adjusted separately for each gender. Low cardiovascular risk factor levels—for instance, low serum triglycerides, low cigarette consumption, and low diastolic blood pressure during working hours and leisure (average of several recordings; see Theorell et al., 1987)—were observed in female physicians whereas high levels were observed in waitresses and musicians. On a group level, job strain (when excessive psychological demands are being made) was associated with several cardiovascular risk factors.

Gender Differences

Among waiters and symphony musicians, women reported lower job demand levels than men. Male waiters reported a higher skill discretion level than their female colleagues, and male physicians also reported a higher level of authority over decisions than their female colleagues. Male air traffic controllers tended to report more authority over decisions than their female colleagues. The overall picture is consistent with the American data for men and women reported earlier, although the details in the Swedish study are different in different occupations. Men tended to report slightly higher demand levels and a higher decision latitude than women. Women tended to report higher levels of social support than men, and this was particularly true for waitresses and symphony musicians.

The most pronounced gender differences in working conditions were found among waiters; male waiters reported an adverse psychosocial work environment (high level of job strain and low level of support). Again, this

Table 3. Results of Comparisons between Female Occupational Groups in the Study of Four Occupations

Risk factor	Analysis of variance		t-tests
Cigarette smoking	*	Physicians ($n = 17$) < waitresses ($n = 18$)	**
		Physicians < symphony musicians ($n = 9$)	*
Total serum cholesterol	n.s.	n.s.	—
Serum triglicerides	*	Physicians < waitresses	*
Systolic blood pressure work	n.s.	n.s.	
Diastolic blood pressure at work	*	Physicians < symphony musicians and waitresses	**
		Physicians < air traffic controllers ($n = 8$)	*
Systolic blood pressure at leisure	n.s.	n.s.	—
Diastolic blood pressure at leisure	0.06	Physicians < symphony musicians and waitresses	*
Psychological demands	n.s.	Physicians > symphony musicians	*
Intellectual discretion	***	Air traffic controllers, physicians, and symphony musicians > waitresses	***
Authority over decisions	***	Physicians, waitresses, and air traffic controllers > symphony musicians	***
		Physicians and waitresses > air traffic controllers	**
Positive climate[a]	0.06	Waitresses > physicians	*

*p <0.05 (two-tailed tests). **p <0.01. ***p < 0.0001.
[a]Approximately, support at work.

may have something to do with the dominant gender in the occupation: there are more waitresses than waiters. It should be pointed out that women and men do actually have slightly different work tasks even when they work in the same occupation, and the reported differences in psychosocial job factors between genders may therefore reflect "true" differences.

Arousal

With regard to the difference between systolic blood pressure during work and during leisure—an index of "arousal" at work—no significant differences were found between the female groups, but one striking observation was that female physicians had significantly smaller differences between work and leisure hours when compared to all other women and men in the study (0.35 mm Hg with a standard error of mean of 1.53, whereas corresponding averages in other groups ranged from 2.05 mm Hg with a standard error of mean of 1.16 in male physicians to 6.92 mm Hg with a standard error of mean of 1.03 in male air traffic controllers). This result is consistent with observations of Frankenhaeuser and colleagues (1989; Chapter 3, this volume) on female managers in the Volvo company; these women were shown to have marked blood pressure elevations on returning home from work. It is possible that the difficulty of combining household and work responsibilities may cause unusual arousal in female physicians.

Other Observations

Although differences between groups were not significant, female physicians tended to have higher sleep disturbance scores than any other male or female group in the study. Female physicians have been observed to have a high suicide rate (Arnetz, Hörte, Hedberg, Theorell, Allander, & Malker, 1987a) and high burnout scores (Arnetz, Andrasson, Strandberg, Eneroth, & Kallner, 1987b), and it is possible that the findings in the four occupations study illustrate emotional tensions due in part to the dual role of these women and in part to the caring role itself; that is, there may be higher expectations of female than of male physicians from their surroundings and from themselves for emotional responses to their encounters with human suffering. The finding that female physicians report a lower decision latitude than their male colleagues is consistent with the female double-role hypothesis. On the other hand, compared to other women, female physicians have a favorable work situation compared to most other occupations, one with a high decision latitude; the low coronary risk is consistent with this finding. Physicians do not have a high coronary heart disease incidence in epidemiological studies (Arnetz et al., 1987a).

In conclusion, the study of men and women in the four occupations indicated that women reported more emotional reactions and more job strain than did men. Waitresses described a high level of job strain but good social support. Physicians reported an active job situation (high demands and high decision latitude) with poor social support. The findings in the four occupations study on cardiovascular risk factors supported the job strain hypothesis for coronary heart disease. Female physicians, with their poor social support, showed evidence of emotional tension. The mechanisms underlying coronary heart disease are not the same as those underlying burnout and depression (see Karasek & Theorell, 1990).

Social Support

The study indicates that social support may operate differently in men and women. The question is whether the interactions of the three main job dimensions—demand, control, and support—are gender-specific. Johnson (1986) addressed this problem directly in a cross-sectional study of the prevalence of cardiovascular illness symptoms in a randomly selected sample of the Swedish working population. The cardiovascular illness symptoms were identified in two steps: first of all, a number of questions regarding past illness episodes and current symptoms and medications were asked; then, an expert panel judged the presence or absence of cardiovascular illness. Measurements based on interview data that had been factor analyzed were computed for psychological demands, lack of control, and lack of social support on the job felt by each person in the study.

In general, stronger associations between social support at work and cardiovascular symptoms were found for women than for men. In particular, the combination of high demands and lack of support was very important for women. Another striking observation is the marked social class difference for men but not for women; among blue-collar men the classical Karasek model, using the combination of high demand and lack of control of work as predictors, very strongly predicts the prevalence of cardiovascular symptoms, but this is not true among white-collar men. In that group the combination of demand and lack of support and the combination of lack of control and lack of support were more important predictors of heart disease symptoms than the combination of demand and lack of control (see Table 4).

Findings in the Swedish studies described earlier thus illustrate that the associations between work environment factors and cardiovascular health show similarities as well as dissimilarities between women and men. This speaks in favor of more gender-specific research in the future, as suggested by Waldron (1976).

PERSONALITY CHARACTERISTICS
AND CORONARY HEART DISEASE IN WOMEN

What about individual psychological traits? Could they explain part of the specific "female" association between work environment and coronary heart disease (CHD) risk? One of the most extensive published studies on women, personality, and risk of CHD development is the one by Hällström and associates (1985) on a randomly selected sample of women

Table 4. Individual and Combined Effects of Psychological Job Demands, Work Control, and Work Social Support by Sex and Class on Age-Adjusted Relative Risk of Coronary Heart Disease in Randomly Selected Working Swedes

Factor	Blue-collar men	White-collar men	Blue-collar women	White-collar women
Job demands	1.36*	1.32	1.21	1.14
Work control	1.42**	1.03	1.12	1.07
Social support at work	1.13	1.16	1.27*	1.33
Job demands and work control	3.55****	1.03	1.43	1.13
Job demands and social support at work	1.82***	1.81**	1.68***	2.06**
Work control and social support at work	1.97**	1.86*	1.86*	1.44
Job demands and work control and social support at work	7.22****	2.44**	2.19	1.95

Note. Prevalence data based upon randomly selected working Swedes (Survey of Level of Living). From Johnson (1986).
*p < .10. **p < .05. ***p < .025. ****p < .01.

in Göteborg. Personality factors and subjective experience of strain were assessed by means of several of the currently used self-administered personality questionnaires, and psychiatric interviews provided information on psychosocial stressors and mental disorder. The results indicated that high ratings of passive dependency, neuroticism, experience of strain, grade of mental disorder, and severity of depression were predictive of angina pectoris. A low rating of aggression was predictive of future development of electrocardiographic changes indicating ischemic heart disease. Low ratings of guilt feelings and neurotic self-assertiveness were predictive of increased risk of developing a clinically overt myocardial infarction. The authors state that dimensions related to Type A behavior, such as aggression, were not predictive of ischemic heart disease. In the Framingham study (Haynes, Feinleib, & Kannel, 1980) Type A behavior as such did not seem to predict increased incidence of coronary heart disease in women, although in that study Type A behavior interacted with a high strain job in producing increased CHD risk (La Croix, 1984).

The findings in the study by Hällström and associates (1986) and the findings in the Framingham study (Haynes, Feinleib, & Kannel, 1980) diverge from findings in other studies of men's CHD personalities in which hostility and striving for achievement are typical findings (Matthews & Haynes, 1986). Thus, it is quite possible that the individual traits predictive of CHD in women are different from those in men. It is also possible that these differences in some way reflect social gender roles; that is, hostility and striving for achievement that are associated with high CHD risk in men are traditional male social traits and submissiveness a traditional female trait. When these traits collide with family and work roles, psychophysiological tensions may arise that could increase the risk of coronary heart disease. In Westernized countries, however, there has been a decreasing emphasis on the female roles; the number of children has decreased and there is a slight relaxation of the demand on women to provide services at home. On the other hand, women very often have to fulfill dual roles in the family and at work, and this may frequently result in psychological problems. Part of the reason why women are more able to avoid the serious manifestations of coronary heart disease than men could be that they—together or as individuals—identify their own psychological symptoms in difficult situations and actively try to deal with them.

It should be pointed out that the situation could change drastically in the future. In particular, the changing smoking habits of women as well as the drastic changes in their degree of involvement at work could decrease their advantage in longevity. For instance, waitresses in the study of four occupations reported high levels of job strain and good social support from their workmates; their excessive smoking habits may represent a destructive common collective coping strategy. The fact that women have enjoyed longer life expectancies than men despite more psychosocially adverse working conditions may not continue to hold true.

ACKNOWLEDGMENTS

This work is a result of collaboration by many researchers. Contributions to the theoretical models underlying the research have been made by sociologists Robert A. Karasek and Jeff V. Johnson. Maud Söderholm has provided constructive criticism of the manuscript. Other members of the research group in this work are Gunnel Ahlberg-Hultén, Lars Alfredsson, Aleksander Perski, Filis Sigala, Jan Konarski-Svensson, and Britt-Marie Wallin.

REFERENCES

Alfredsson, L., Spetz, C-L., & Theorell, T. (1985). Type of occupation and near-future hospitalization for myocardial infarction and some other diagnoses. *International Journal of Epidemiology, 14*, 378–388.

Arnetz, B. B., Andrasson, S., Strandberg, M., Eneroth P., & Kallner, A. (1987b). Läkares psykosociala arbetsmiljö: Stress, hälsorisker, trivsel. *Läkartidningen, 84*, 816–824.

Arnetz, B. B., Hörte, L-G., Hedberg, A., Theorell, T., Allander, E., & Malker, H. (1987a). Suicide patterns among physicians related to other academics as well as to the general population. *Acta Psychiatrica Scandinavica, 75*, 139–145.

Billing, E., Lindell, B., Sederholm, M., & Theorell, T. (1980). Denial, anxiety and depression following myocardial infarction. *Psychosomatics, 21*, 639–645.

Cranor, C., Karasek, R. A., & Carlin, C. (1981, July). Job characteristics and office work: Findings and health implications. Paper presented at National Institute of Occupational Safety and Health conference on occupational health issues affecting clerical/secretarial personnel, Cincinnati.

Frankenhaeuser, M., Lundberg, U., Fredrikson, M., Melin, B., Tuomisto, M., Myrsten, A-L., Bergman-Losman, B., Hedman, M., & Wallin, L. (1989). Stress on and off the job as related to sex and occupational status in white-collar workers. *Journal of Organizational Behavior, 10*, 321–346.

Hällström, T., Lapidus, L., Bengtsson, C., & Edström, K., (1986). Psychosocial factors and risk of ischemic heart disease and death in women: A twelve-year follow-up of participants in the study of women in Gothenburg, Sweden. *Journal of Psychosomatic Research, 30*, 451–460.

Haukka, S. (1987). Activities for the prevention of coronary heart disease (CHD) in Finland. *Heart Beat, 4*, 1–3.

Haynes, S., Feinleib, M., & Kannel, W. B. (1980). The relationship of psychosocial factors to coronary heart disease in the Framingham study: III. Eight-year incidence of coronary heart disease. *American Journal of Epidemiology, 111*, 37–58.

Hinkle, L., Jr. (1974). The effect of exposure to culture change, social change and changes in interpersonal relationships on health. In B. P. Dohrenwend & B. S. Dohrenwend (Eds.), *Stressful life events, their nature and effects* (pp. 9–44). New York: Wiley.

Johnson, J. V. (1986). The impact of workplace social support, job demands and work control upon cardiovascular disease in Sweden (Report No. 1). Division of the Social Psychology of Work, Department of Psychology, University of Stockholm.

Johnson, J. V., Hall, E., & Theorell, T. (1989). The combined effects of job strain and social isolation on the prevalence of cardiovascular disease and death in a random sample of the Swedish working male. *Scandinavian Journal of Work, Environment, and Health, 15,* 271–279.

Kahn, R. (1974). Conflict, ambiguity and overload: Three elements in job stress. In A. MacLean (Ed.), *Occupational stress* (pp. 47–61). Springfield, IL: Thomas.

Karasek, R. A. (1979). Job demands, job decision latitude and mental strain: Implications for job redesign. *Administrative Science Quarterly, 24,* 285–307.

Karasek, R., Russell, S. R., & Theorell, T. (1982). Physiology of stress and regeneration in job-related cardiovascular illness. *Journal of Human Stress, 3,* 29–42.

Karasek, R. A., & Theorell, T. (1990). *Healthy work.* New York: Basic Books.

Karasek, R. A., Theorell, T., Schwartz, J. E., Schnall, P. L., Pieper, C. F., & Michela, J. L. (1988). Job characteristics in relation to the prevalence of myocardial infarction in the US Health Examination Survey and Health and Nutrition Examination Survey. *American Journal of Public Health, 78,* 910–918.

La Croix, A. Z. (1984). *Occupational exposure to high demand/low control work and coronary heart disease incidence in the Framingham cohort.* Unpublished doctoral dissertation, University of North Carolina, Chapel Hill.

Lundberg, U., & Palm, K. (in press). Total workload and catecholamine excretion in families with preschool children. *Work and Stress.*

Matthews, K. A., & Haynes, S. G. (1986). Type A behavior pattern and coronary disease risk: Update and critical evaluation. *American Journal of Epidemiology, 123,* 923–960.

Statistics Sweden. (1982). Sveriges Statistiska Centralbyrå. Arbetsmiljö. Levnadsförhållanden 1979: Sveriges officiella statistik Rep. nr 32, Stockholm.

Theorell, T. (1989). Personal control at work and health. In A. Steptoe & A. Apples (Eds.), *Stress, personal control and health.* New York: Wiley.

Theorell, T., Ahlberg-Hultn, G., Berggren, T., Perski, A., Sigala, F., Svensson, J., & Wallin, B-M. (1987). Arbetsmiljö, levnadsvanor och risk för hjärt-kärlsjukdom. Stress Research Reports Nr 195, National Institute of Psychosocial Factors and Health.

Waldron, I. (1976). Why do women live longer than men? Part I. *Journal of Human Stress, 2,* 2–11.

World Health Organization. (1982). Levels and trends of mortality since 1950. New York: United Nations Publications.

IV

Interaction between Women's Work and Reproductive Issues

11

Reproductive Technologies, Women's Health, and Career Choices

KERSTIN HAGENFELDT

Reproductive technologies are used both to control and to promote fertility. Recent developments in both these fields were unforeseen a generation ago. Today, women in most Western countries expect to be able to plan pregnancies in relation to education and career choices. This planning, however, mainly concerns the issue of not having children and is accomplished with modern contraceptives and access to safe abortion. The other goal, having children as planned, is not as easily attained by all women. By postponing the first child, a growing population of women will find they are unable to conceive and will require assistance from medical technology.

In other parts of the world women have fewer choices. In many third-world countries their educational level is low. Early marriage, early childbirth, and many children too often and too late in life compromise women's reproductive health and diminish their chances of contributing to society.

CONTROL OF FERTILITY

Family Planning Services

In principle, contraceptives and advice about their use are available today to most married couples in Europe and North America. In countries

KERSTIN HAGENFELDT • Department of Obstetrics and Gynecology, Karolinska Hospital, S-104 01 Stockholm, Sweden.

with a national health service, family planning is available through mother and child care centers, government clinics, hospitals, general practitioners, and gynecologists. In other countries the costs are often covered by health insurance or subsidized by government funds to voluntary organizations or private physicians. The quality of the services and access to them vary greatly between and within countries. In many countries women prefer private medical services to clinics for practical reasons: the difficulty in making appointments, long waiting lists, inconvenient hours, lack of continuity of care, predominance of male physicians, and ignorance of counselors about women's changing needs for family planning at different stages of life.

Adolescents are everywhere at a disadvantage. The predominant attitude is a refusal to accept the fact that this group needs special consideration. Even where clinics are open to adolescents, the young persons are often reluctant to visit the same place that neighbors, relatives, or other acquaintances do. Opening hours are important, as is the possibility of a consultation without an appointment. Clinic staff need to be familiar with the problems of this age group, which call for a different approach from that with adults. Many family planning programs in Europe and the United States have set up special facilities for adolescents. An example is the youth clinics in Sweden, developed over the past 15 years and run by specially trained midwives who take an active part in sex education in schools in their area and thereby establish good contacts with their potential clients.

Fertility Trends

In Europe and North America the past century has seen a substantial reduction in total fertility, that is, the average number of children born per woman during her fertile years. This fall in fertility began in the 1870s. By the mid-1930s the crude birthrate (live births/1,000 of population)—14.4 in Sweden, 15.3 in England and Wales (Coale, 1969)—and other indices of fertility had reached a low in most of Western Europe. The decline in Europe was paralleled in the United States, where it had begun even earlier and from a higher level. Between 1830 and 1930 the crude birthrate for white Americans fell from 50 less than 18 (Population Reference Bureau, 1982).

The full explanation for the decline in fertility is not known. In the late 19th and early 20th century it was no doubt mainly a consequence of the "European pattern" of delayed marriage and high celibacy. Other factors have also contributed: (1) the decline in mortality (with more children surviving, fewer births are needed to achieve a given family size); (2) rising costs and diminished economic advantage of children in an urbanized, industrial society; (3) higher status of women and the extension of education and employment of women (since the burden of pregnancy, parturition, and child care are all women's tasks, a woman's occupation outside the home will of necessity be an important factor restricting family size); (4) the economic depression and its accompanying mass unemployment between World War I and II; and (5) religious changes and the development of a secular attitude toward life (van de Walle & Kuodel, 1980).

World War II was followed by an economic upswing in Western Europe and North America. Unemployment was low and birthrates began to rise, particularly in the United States. Western and Eastern Europe also had a "baby boom," but it was shorter than in the United States. The rise in birthrate in Western Europe was attributed to earlier age at marriage and a higher marriage rate. The subsequent fall is coinciding with the changing role of women, the growing proportion of women with college education and in the labor force, the development of new contraceptive technology (the pill and IUDs), increasing use of sterilization of men and women, and liberalization of abortion laws (Baldwin & Winquist-Nord, 1984).

Fertility and Its Relation to Women's Educational Status

Even in a country such as Sweden, with a very low fertility rate, fertility varies in relation to women's social background and education. Daughters of farmers and unskilled workers are having more children than are those of professional parents. For women born between 1941 and 1945, the mean number of children at age 35 was 1.9, 2.1 and 1.6 for these three categories, respectively. The social background also influences the age of the woman at her first birth, being lowest among the daughters of unskilled workers. Official statistics (SOU, 1982) show that at the age of 35, women with a college education had fewer children (1.7) than those with a high school education (1.9) and those who had not completed high school (2.2).

The same trend was seen in the United States, where 80% to 87% of women born between 1940 and 1944 who had not completed high school were mothers at the age of 25, compared with 52% to 60% of women with a college education. In 1973 the average number of children born to ever-married women was 3.0 among women with 0 to 11 years of education and 1.7 among those with more than 13 years of schooling (Pratt, Mosher, Bachrack, & Horn, 1984).

CONTRACEPTIVE PRACTICE

Adolescents

Of the world population in the year 2000, 20% (or some 1.2 billion people) will be 11 to 19 years of age. Premarital sexual activity is high in this age group in the Western world, and in many developing countries marriage usually occurs during late adolescence. A survey among Swedish teenagers in 1983 indicated that almost 50% of both boys and girls had had coital experience by the age of 16 (Lewin & Helmius, 1983). The corresponding figures for Denmark in 1987 were 30% to 40% (Rasmussen & Munck, 1987) and for the United States in 1982, 20% and 40% for white and black women, respectively (Pratt *et al.*, 1984). The use of contraceptives at first intercourse among adolescents varies between 25% and 50%, the lowest seen among the youngest teenagers. The condom is the preferred method, followed by the pill and coitus interruptus.

The incidence of teenage pregnancy (abortion and delivery) is an important indicator of the quality of contraceptive counseling in a developed country. Teenage pregnancy rates differ among European countries and the United States. While some of the differences have to do with cultural variations, the teenage abortion rate does constitute a measure of our competence in sex education and counseling.

Adolescent pregnancy carries specific risks. There is an increased maternal mortality and morbidity as well as an increased perinatal mortality. Where abortion is legal, teenagers often seek medical advice at a later stage of pregnancy than do adult women, when there is an increased risk of medical complications and psychological sequelae. In all cultures early pregnancy inhibits the girl's education and future economic possibilities. Teenage abortions amount to 25% of all abortions performed in Canada, England and Wales, Finland, Norway, and the United States (Henshaw, 1987). Since the liberalization of the Swedish abortion law teenage abortion has decreased year by year, from 30/1000 in 1975 to 18/1000 in 1987, constituting 16.1% of all legal abortions in the latter year (see Figure 1).

Adults

The main contraceptive methods used in Europe and the United States in the first half of this century were withdrawal, or coitus interruptus, and the condom. Developments in contraceptive technology have changed the contraception pattern from moderately effective, coitus-related, male-dominated, nonmedical methods to highly effective, non–coital-related, female-dominated methods that need the involvement of medical authorities.

The contraceptive pill (OC) is available in all countries, mostly through prescription by physicians or midwives. The use of the pill outweighs all other methods in Belgium, Canada, France, Hungary, the Netherlands, Sweden, the United Kingdom, West Germany, and the United States. It is particularly popular among younger women, and this

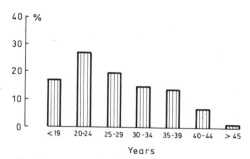

Figure 1. Age distribution of legal abortions in Sweden, 1987 (N = 34,486).

has prompted a discussion among lay people about the risks of promiscuity and within the medical community about an increased incidence of sexually transmitted diseases, as well as about cervical dysplasia and cancer of the cervix and the breast. On the other hand, use of the pill has been found to decrease pelvic inflammatory disease in women under the age of 25. In the older age group (women > 35 years old) the risk of cardiovascular disease, mainly myocardial infarction particularly in smokers, has been stressed. The specific concern for these two age groups, the very young and older women, has led to rules for prescription of the pill that sometimes encroach on the autonomy of women and their ability to choose the method they find most attractive.

The intrauterine device (IUD) is most popular in the Scandinavian countries, where it accounts for 26% to 39% of all contraceptive use in women ages 20 to 44 years (SOU, 1982; Berent, 1984). The method gained ground after the introduction of copper IUDs in the early 1970s and is used by both parous and nulliparous women. The debate on a possible relation between the use of the IUD and pelvic inflammatory disease (PID) has influenced clinical practice in most countries. Owing to the prevalence of sexually transmitted diseases in the younger age group with an increased risk of PID, counselors generally do not recommend the method to young women except in relations that are strictly monogamous, where the male partner is obliged to share the decision about the contraceptive method.

In the past 2 years pharmaceutical companies have withdrawn all IUDs except Alzas Progestasert from the U.S. market, not for safety reasons but because of the risks of legal damages and high insurance costs. Several U.S. medical and family planning organizations as well as women's groups have publicly expressed their concern about this and called for immediate measures to bring back the FDA-approved copper IUDs. One device was recently reintroduced on the U.S. market. Owing to the added costs for insurance, which have to be carried by each woman using the device, the IUD has become extremely expensive.

The condom is and probably will remain for many years the only reversible male contraceptive. Together with coitus interruptus and spermicides, it has been the leading form of contraception in Europe from the late 19th century. It is still widely used and has grown in importance as a means of preventing sexually transmitted diseases, including the Acquired Immune Deficiency Syndrome (AIDS) infection. At present, with those infections as a serious threat to health, it is essential that family planning counselors inform all their clients about and encourage the use of the condom. It should be used together with other methods, particularly in new relations. Access to condoms needs to be easier as a means to combat the AIDS threat.

Voluntary sterilization as a family planning method has increased in importance during the last two decades. It is less popular in Scandinavia, but in the United Kingdom and in the United States it accounts for 21% and 26% of all contraception, respectively. The method was more popular among males than females, but with the introduction of the simpler laparoscopic procedure female sterilization has gained ground (Ross, Huber, & Houg, 1986). Sterilization raises specific ethical questions because it requires surgery and is irreversible. The individual who is going to decide on the method needs qualified information, perhaps education to understand the procedure and its implications. It has been shown, by investigating reasons for regret and requests for refertilization, that the procedure is particularly hazardous in subjects who are under the age of 30, who are operated on in the immediate postpartum or postabortion period, or who are living in an unstable relationship.

Legal abortion constitutes an important method of family planning. All European and North American countries except Belgium, Ireland, and Malta have legalized abortion. Among developed countries the USSR has the highest known abortion rate—68% of all pregnancies; the lowest is the Netherlands—9.7% (Henshaw, 1987). Levels of contraceptive practice and types of methods affect a country's abortion rate. When widespread publicity was given to the potential hazards of the pill, abortion rates rose in several countries in Western Europe. Induced abortion has been the most controversial issue in medical ethics, politics, and health law during the last century. The initial argument for legalizing abortion was that it would improve maternal health by reducing illegal abortions and allow the termination of pregnancy in women whose medical condition warranted it. Clearly, legalization of abortion has reduced maternal mortality in most countries. In Czechoslovakia, where abortion laws were made less restrictive in the 1950s, abortion-related mortality fell by 56% and 38% in the periods 1953–1957 and 1958–1962, respectively. No country in Europe or North America experienced a decline of this size without legalizing abortion. The impact of abortion laws on mortality is illustrated by Romania, where the enactment of a restrictive abortion law in 1966 was followed by a sevenfold increase in death from abortion (Henshaw, 1987).

One issue in the abortion debate has been the right of women to decide on the fate of a pregnancy. This right is a foundation of the laws in several countries in Europe and North America; in most, the woman can exercise her right during the first 10 to 12 weeks of pregnancy, a sign of the growing significance accorded to the fetus as pregnancy advances. If a choice has to be made between the woman's wish to interrupt the pregnancy and the right of the fetus to continued development, the woman's claim has to be increasingly weighty as pregnancy advances in order for the woman's wish to prevail. As regards the woman's health, the risk of the abortion procedure also increases with advanced pregnancy.

Safety of Contraceptive Methods

When a person decides on the use of a specific method for fertility control, consideration has to be paid to its theoretical and practical effectiveness and the medical risks of side effects. In a country with access to safe, early legal abortion, there is a case to be made for the use of a less effective method with fewer side effects. On the other hand, in a country with no back-up abortion when a method fails and with high maternal mortality, the method of choice is the most effective contraceptive method that will provide the maximal health benefit for the woman.

Contraceptive Technology and Health Issues in Third-World Countries

The World Health Organization estimates that half a million women die in pregnancy and childbirth every year; the vast majority of these deaths—about 99%—occur in developing countries. In Africa a woman's lifetime chance of maternal death is 1:25; the figure for northern Europe is 1:9,850. The causes of death include 25% to 50% from illegal abortions of unwanted pregnancies. Other causes are pregnancies in women too young or too old and too frequent births, with the increased likelihood of obstetric complications. For the thousands of women who die in pregnancy and childbirth, millions more are permanently disabled as a result of complications both from unsafe abortion procedures and complications during delivery. For every death, it is estimated that 10 to 15 women are handicapped in one way or another (Starrs, 1987). Dr. H. Singh, India, said at the International Safe Motherhood Conference in Nairobi in 1987: "Mothers are not dropped from heaven. They are born as undervalued, neglected girls and grow as exploited, uneducated children. The mother-to-be must become self-confident and self-reliant, and for this she needs nutrition, education and employment" (Starrs, 1987).

The importance of women's education in terms of health for themselves and their families has been repeatedly stressed in recent years. Data from the World Fertility Survey, carried out in 38 developing countries have been analyzed (Weinbergen, 1987) and indicated that from 2% to 98% of married women of fertile age have had no schooling, while the proportion with 10 or more years of education ranges from 0% to 24%. The survey shows an overall pattern of decreasing fertility with increasing education, except in sub-Saharan Africa, where differences are small. The total marital fertility rate (the average number of births a woman would have by 25 years after her first marriage) in the WFS material from 38 developing countries decreased from 6.7 in women with no schooling to 4.6 in women with 7 or more years of education. In countries at a higher level of development, like Colombia or Mexico, the decrease was even more significant, from 6.8 to 3.2 for Colombia and from 7.9 to 4.1 for Mexico.

Examination of the proximate determinants of fertility, age at marriage and contraceptive practice, reveals the ways in which educational levels affect these intermediates. The age of marriage is a significant determinant of fertility, since it affects the period of exposure to pregnancy. The mean age at marriage rises with years of education, from 19.2 in women with no schooling to 23.0 in women with 7 or more years of education. In the least developed countries, such as Bangladesh, the increase is 4.5 years, from 15.0 years to 19.5 years for a woman's age at marriage. The use of contraceptives also correlates with education. Overall, the proportion of married women practicing contraception at the time of the survey was 24% higher among those with 7 or more years of education than it was among those with no education, when controlled for age differences between educational groups. Even a few years of schooling had a marked effect on contraceptive prevalence. Within each development level, countries were divided into those having "weaker" and "stronger" family planning programs. In the middle- to low-development group, the countries with stronger programs had substantially higher than average levels of contraceptive use in all educational groups.

The conclusion from the data of the World Fertility Survey is that the higher status of women, based on better education, will benefit her reproductive health by increasing age at marriage and thereby decreasing early pregnancies. Furthermore, a more widespread use of contraceptives will lead to fewer pregnancies, more optimal spacing between childbirths, and avoidance of pregnancies too late in life, thereby increasing the health of both the mother and her children (see Figure 2).

Breast-Feeding

Lactation is part of the reproductive cycle, and before the use of modern forms of contraception it was the major method of ensuring adequate intervals between births. Until the end of the last century in the Western world breast-feeding, often for a long period, was extremely widespread, and it still is in most third-world countries. The delay in the return of postpartum fertility in lactating women varies with the pattern of breast-feeding, nutrition, and cultural factors. Many studies in developing countries have shown that long birth intervals are associated with improved health, both for the woman and the nursing child as well as for subsequent children (IPPF [International Planned Parenthood Federation], 1988). It is therefore necessary to uphold breast-feeding patterns even in circumstances where woman have joined or want to join the labor force after childbirth. It is also necessary that modern contraceptives used in the postpartum period not compromise lactation.

INFERTILITY

Epidemiology of Infertility

It is calculated that some 10% to 15% of couples in the Western world are involuntarily infertile. It is not known whether this figure is rising, but more and more couples are seeking medical advice for their problems.

Fecundity—that is, the reproductive potential in women—is highest between the ages of 20 and 25 and then gradually declines. It is not clear to what extent this decline may reflect the influence of other factors such as male fecundity and coital frequency. Also, because these data are based on fertility rates for mostly parous women, they do not indicate the risk of infertility for women who postpone their first child until a later age (Hendershot, Mosher, & Pratt, 1982). A French study was able to eliminate the influence of many of these extraneous factors by studying conception rates after artificial insemination with donor sperm in more than 2,000 nulliparous women whose husbands were azoospermic. The study showed that the probability of conceiving declined noticeably around the age of 30

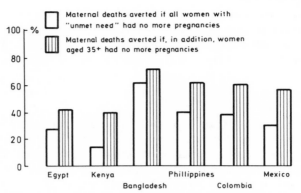

Figure 2. Percentage of maternal deaths resulting from abortions, spontaneous, legal, and illegal, and all other pregnancy and delivery complications potentially preventable through family planning, in selected countries, in married fecund women who want no more children but are not using an effective contraceptive method (= unmet needs) (compiled from Starrs, 1987).

(Schwartz & Mayaux, 1982). A population survey from the USA has confirmed that the risk of infertility increases steadily with maternal age, particularly after the age of 30 (Population Information Program, 1983). The reason for this could be that the aging process affects ovulatory function or the viability of the ovum; cumulative environmental exposures may also contribute. In addition, pelvic endometriosis and the increasing risk of pelvic inflammatory disease with sexual exposure will undoubtedly contribute to the overall increase in infertility with age. The decline in fertility with the age of the woman may also partially reflect an increase in early, unrecognized pregnancy loss rather than a decrease in conceptions. Chromosomal abnormalities, which account for a substantial proportion of spontaneous abortions, particularly at early gestational ages, are known to rise with age (Hay & Barbano, 1972). Spontaneous abortion of clinically diagnosed pregnancies also rises with increased maternal age. Some 25% of pregnancies in women over the age of 40 will end in a miscarriage, compared with 11% in women between 20 and 25 years of age (Jansen, 1982). With rising maternal age there is also an increase in chromosomal abnormalities, mainly that involved in Down's syndrome, and in other forms of malformation such as anencephaly, spina bifida, and other major defects (Hook, 1981).

The present situation, with delayed birth of the first child, tends to increase the age of couples consulting for infertility. The mean age among 500 consecutively evaluated couples at the Infertility Clinic, Department of Obstetrics and Gynecology, Karolinska sjukhuset, Stockholm, was 33.2 years for the women and 34.3 years for the men. The main reason for infertility was tubal disease in the woman (30%), followed by anovulation (23%). Of the husbands, 5% had azoospermia or severe defects in the ejaculate as a reason for the couple's inability to conceive. In 10% of the couples no explanation was found (so-called unexplained infertility).

Treatment of Infertility

Article 16.1 of the United Nations Declaration of Human Rights states that "men and women of full age, without any limitation due to race, nationality or religion, have the right to marry and to found a family." The "right to found a family" is indisputable when it relates to the normal freedom to reproduce and the assistance of society with control of fertility, but it is questionable if it refers to "positive rights." Does a childless couple have the right to be assisted by society in terms of medical care, expensive drugs, and high technology treatment for the woman to conceive? A society that intends to follow this interpretation would be morally obliged to provide, directly or indirectly, access to health services for the treatment of infertility. The problem in every society is deciding at what level of assistance society should aim. What is adequate in treatment of infertility? The question was simple in the 1940s and 1950s, when few methods were available. The debate began with the introduction, in the 1960s, of new and expensive drugs to induce ovulation and, in the 1970s, of microsurgical correction of tubal disease. During the past decade, with possibilities for noncoital reproduction such as artificial insemination by husband (AIH), artificial insemination by donor (AID), in vitro fertilization (IVF), gamete-intra-fallopian-tube-transfer (GIFT), and surrogate motherhood, the questions have become overwhelming.

In principle, infertility investigation and treatment are available everywhere in Europe and North America and at relatively little cost to the couples in countries with national health services. In practice, however, the situation is far from ideal. National health service hospitals have to deal with the whole spectrum of female pathology—gynecological cancers, complicated deliveries, and so forth—and infertility has low priority in the demand for a bed or surgery. Costly treatment, such as AID or IVF, is subjected to regulations and rules that tend to discourage a couple from choosing the treatment they want. There are also long waiting lists; in Sweden today there is a 1- to 2-year wait for AID and a 4- to 5-year wait for IVF in most public hospitals. Where the procedure is performed privately the wait is shorter, but the cost to the couple is very high and therefore, in practice, prohibitive for the less well-off.

Adverse Pregnancy Outcome, Occupational Exposures, and Environmental Pollutants

The growing participation of women in the labor force and increasing exposure to chemical pollutants in the environment have led to considerable concern about possible hazards to reproduction. Depending on the time and duration of exposure, such pollutants can result in an inability to conceive (infertility), early or late miscarriage, late intrauterine death, neonatal death, low birth weight, or malformations. It has been suggested that "time to conceive" might be used in the study of environmental pollutants (Baird, Wilcox, & Weinberg, 1986), in addition to following a pregnancy to outcome.

Many of the substances suspected of lowering fertility are also thought to be involved in pregnancy loss. For more then a century, lead has been known to have an adverse effect on reproduction (Rome, 1976); as early as 1949, in the Swedish Work Environment Act, women of all ages and men under 18 were excluded from work with lead paints. In a study from Sweden excessive rates of pregnancy loss were found among women working in and living in the vicinity of a smelter (Nordström, Beckman, & Nordensson, 1978). The emission of toxic products other than lead from the smelter, such as copper, arsenic, mercury, cadmium, and sulfur dioxide, made it difficult to determine whether lead was the only reason for the adverse pregnancy outcome.

Textile workers exposed to high levels of carbon disulfide have been reported to have an increased incidence of menstrual disturbances, infertility, and pregnancy loss (Sullivan & Barlow, 1979). Among chemical pollutants, the use of dioxin in herbicides has raised concern over possible adverse effects on female reproduction, but the data are not conclusive (Council on Scientific Affairs, 1982). In the early 1970s a lot of attention was paid to reports of increased rates of adverse pregnancy outcome among female hospital workers employed in operating rooms; the risk was attributed to anesthetic gases (Cohen, Bellville, & Brown, 1971). Other investigators argued that the increased rates could be due to other factors, such as distress and the emotional and physical work load (Axelsson & Rylander, 1982; Vessey, 1978). The study by Axelsson and Rylander addresses a problem that is inherent in all published research on environmental factors and adverse reproductive outcome, namely, the recall bias in retrospective data; a woman who has not conceived or has had an adverse pregnancy outcome may overestimate the amount of exposure to a possibly hazardous agent.

This issue is also a problem in published studies on the possible effects on fertility and pregnancy outcome in women working with video display terminals (VDT). Work with VDTs is now a sine qua non in almost all occupational fields. In many activities in which women employees are numerous (education, medical care, financing, insurance, restaurants, hotels, and retail trade), employees use VDTs for 20% to 90% of their working time (Westlander & Magnusson, 1988). The widespread use of VDTs in the home and at work has raised concern regarding the effect of low-frequency electromagnetic fields from the terminals. Clusters of spontaneous abortions have indeed been reported among female workers using VDTs, but they are thought to represent random statistical events (Bergquist, 1984).

If VDT use does prove to have an adverse effect on reproductive events, women of fertile age would have to be excluded from a large part of the labor market. This is therefore a highly important issue and several studies have addressed the problem in recent years (Eriksson & Källen, 1986a,b; Goldhaber, Polen, & Hiatt, 1988; Kurppa, Holmberg, Rantala, Nurminen, & Saksen, 1985; McDonald, Cherrey, Delorme, & McDonald, 1986). The risk of miscarriage and a possible increase in congenital malformations have been studied in those reports. The studies are all of a retrospective nature and are therefore subject to the problem mentioned earlier, that is, recall bias. In the Montreal study (McDonald *et al.*, 1986) more than 60,000 pregnancies were analyzed. The risk of spontaneous abortion did not differ with the amount of VDT work. Two Swedish studies (Eriksson & Källen, 1986a,b) found no statistically significant increase in the risk of miscarriage after stratification for occupational stress and cigarette smoking.

In a recent case control study by Goldhaber and associates (1988) among 1,500 pregnant women, a significantly elevated risk of miscarriage was found for those who reported using VDTs more than 20 hours a week during the first trimester of pregnancy, compared to other working women who reported not using VDTs. When VDT use was examined within occupational groups, a dose–response trend for miscarriage was observed among administrative-support–clerical workers but not among workers in other occupational groups. Also in this study the findings could reflect recall bias, with women who suffered adverse outcomes overreporting the number of hours they spent each week on VDTs. Other theories about VDT links with adverse pregnancy outcome hypothesize an effect of radiation, a negative ergonomic environment, and stress. None of the studies mentioned above indicate an increased risk of congenital malformations (Eriksson & Källen, 1986a,b; Eriksson, Källen, & Westerholm, 1985; Goldhaber *et al.*, 1988; Kurppa *et al.*, 1985; McDonald *et al.*, 1986).

Still, the question of an adverse reproductive outcome of occupational or environmental exposure is not fully resolved. In the absence of convincing results from experimental studies, more epidemiological work is needed. The results to date underscore the need for large cohort studies of women in the fertile age group in order to provide objective measurements of exposures to both occupational and environmental pollution, ergonomic factors, and stress. These types of studies should preferably be performed in a society where a high frequency of women of fertile age are working outside the home and where careful supervision is performed during pregnancy. In Sweden all women attend the antenatal clinics from early pregnancy, and these clinics and the delivery wards use the same records and the same reporting system for the outcome of pregnancy. A more in-depth report of factors at work and in the community should be added to the records and evaluated continuously in a prospective way to give early warning signals on occupational and/or environmental factors that may influence the reproductive outcome.

Infertility in Third-World Countries

Concern about population growth and reproductive health has prompted many countries to adopt family planning policies. Some 85 countries, representing 95% of the population of the developing world, now provide public support for family planning services in order to make contraceptives accessible to their populations. However, asking couples to voluntarily restrict their fertility must be accompanied by measures enabling them to regulate all aspects of fertility, including services for the diagnosis and treatment of infertility.

The prevalence of infertility has been studied by WHO in several developing countries. The primary infertility rate, that is, the proportion of women who have never conceived, was found to be 1.6% to 3.6% in Asian and Latin American countries. All sources of information indicate that infertility is most common in sub-Saharan Africa, up to 12% in Cameroon (Frank, 1983). The secondary infertility rate, that is, the proportion of women who are unable to conceive again after a first pregnancy, is difficult to determine with any degree of accuracy but is certainly higher than primary infertility, particularly in the developing world.

The etiology of infertility has also been investigated by WHO in both developed and developing countries. From 1980 to 1986 a study was carried out at 33 WHO centers in 25 countries throughout the world using a standardized protocol and involving more than 8,500 couples, 53% from the developing world (World Health Organization, 1988). The major reason for infertility among women was identified as infection, and infection-related infertility varied between 28% and 65% in third-world centers. The rate of tubal occlusion in sub-Saharan Africa was over three times greater than in other areas. Likewise, 8% to 12% of the male partners of infertile couples have a preventable infection-related cause of infertility. In many societies the inability to conceive and give birth to a healthy child is considered to be the woman's fault, rather than a problem for the couple, when in fact either or both may have an identifiable factor associated with infection. The stigma of infertility often leads to marital disharmony and divorce as well as social ostracism. The cost of infertility— investigation and high technology treatment—can usually not be carried by the health budget in countries in the developing world.

The findings of the WHO studies highlight the importance of genital tract infections as a cause of infertility; most of these infections are potentially preventable. Introducing simple techniques for the diagnosis of sexually transmitted diseases and improved methods for treatment is one matter of the utmost importance for the reproductive health of women and will decrease the future demand for high-cost technology treatment of infertility.

CONCLUSIONS

Avoidance of adolescent pregnancy will increase women's educational possibilities and improve their career choices. Childbirth too early in life involves an increased risk to the health of the woman. A higher legal marriage age will decrease the number of adolescent pregnancies in many developing countries. A high frequency of premarital sexual activity calls for sex education and family planning counseling in order to avoid unwanted pregnancies that end in an abortion, legal or illegal, depending on the laws of the country in which the woman is living. Contraceptives must be selected while bearing in mind both their use-effectiveness and the positive and negative effects on health at different stages of the woman's life.

Breast-feeding is one of the most important methods for family planning and benefits women's and children's health. As such, it should be encouraged, and obstacles against it should be resolved; that is, women's working conditions should allow the continuation of breast-feeding.

The growing participation of women in the labor force, new techno-logical inventions, and the increased exposure of women to chemical pollutants in the environment necessitate continuous supervision of women's reproductive health and reproductive outcome.

Postponing childbearing to the fourth decade in life will increase the risk of infertility because of lower fecundity and will increase the demand for medical treatment. Common causes of infertility, that is, sexually transmitted diseases, should be prevented through mass programs, including education, screening programs, and treatment.

High technology procedures to relieve infertility that used to be regarded as incurable have been developed and should be available, but it must be realized that the existence of the methods can put pressure on childless couples and unwittingly force them into a parenthood that, deep down, was not wanted.

REFERENCES

Axelsson, G., & Rylander, R. (1982). Exposure to anesthetic gases and spontaneous abortion: Response bias in a postal questionnaire study. *International Journal of Epidemiology, 11*, 250–256.

Baird, D., Wilcox, A., & Weinberg, C. (1986). Use of time to pregnancy to study environmental exposures. *American Journal of Epidemiology, 124*, 470–480.

Baldwin, W. H., & Winquist-Nord, C. (1984). Delayed childbearing in the US: Facts and fiction. *Population Bulletin, 39*(4), 1–42.

Berent, J. (1984). Family planning in Europe and the USA in the 1970s. World Fertility Survey. Comparative studies. International Statistical Institute, Voorburg, the Netherlands.

Bergqvist, U. H. (1984). Video display terminals and health. *Scandinavian Journal of Work, Environment, and Health, 10*(Suppl. 2), 1–88.

Coale, A. J. (1969). The decline of fertility in Europe from the French revolution to World War II. In S. Behrman, L. Corsa, & R. Freedman (Eds.), *Fertility and family planning*. Ann Arbor: University of Michigan Press.

Cohen, E. N., Bellville, J. W., & Brown, B. W. (1971). Anesthesia, pregnancy and miscarriage: A study of operating room nurses and anesthetists. *Anesthesiology, 35*, 343–347.

Council on Scientific Affairs. (1982). Health effects of Agent Orange and dioxin contaminants. *Journal of the American Medical Association, 248*, 1895–1896.

Eriksson, A., & Källen, B. (1986a). An epidemiology study of work with video screens and pregnancy outcome: I. A register study. *American Journal of Industrial Medicine, 9*, 447–458.

Eriksson, A., & Källen, B. (1986b). An epidemiology study of work with video screens and pregnancy outcome: II. A case control study. *American Journal of Industrial Medicine, 9*, 459–475.

Eriksson, A., Källen, B., & Westerholm, P. (1985). Ingen ökad risk för fosterskador hos kvinnor med bildskärmsarbete. *Läkartidningen, 82*, 2180–2184.

Frank, O. (1983). Infertility in sub-Saharan Africa: Estimates and implications. *Population and Development Review, 9*, 137–142.

Goldhaber, M. K., Polen, M. R., & Hiatt, R. A. (1988). The risk of miscarriage and birth defects among women who use visual display terminals during pregnancy. *American Journal of Industrial Medicine, 13*, 695–706.

Hay, S., & Barbano, H. (1972). Independent effects of maternal age and birth order on the incidence of selected congenital malformations. *Teratology, 6*, 271–279.

Hendershot, G. E., Mosher, W. D., & Pratt, W. F. (1982). Infertility and age: An unresolved issue. *Family Planning Perspectives, 14*, 287–289.

Henshaw, S. K. (1987). Induced abortion: A worldwide perspective. *Family Planning Perspectives, 13*, 12–16.

Hook, E. B. (1981). Rates of different chromosomal abnormalities at different maternal ages. *Obstetrics and Gynecology, 58,* 282–285.

Kleinman, R. L. (Ed.). (1988). *Family planning handbook for doctors.* London: International Planned Parenthood Federation.

Jansen, R. P. S. (1982). Spontaneous abortion incidence in the treatment of infertility. *American Journal of Obstetrics and Gynecology, 143,* 451–473.

Kurppa, K., Holmberg, P. C., Rantala, K., Nurminen, T., & Saksen, L. (1985). Birth defects and exposure to video display terminals during pregnancy. *Scandinavian Journal of Work, Environment, and Health, 11,* 353–356.

Lewin, S., & Helmius, G. (1983). *Ungdom och sexualitet.* Department of Sociology, Uppsala University, Uppsala, Sweden.

McDonald, A. D., Cherrey, N., Delorme, C., & McDonald, J. C. (1986). Visual display units in pregnancy: Evidence from the Montreal survey. *Journal of Occupational Medicine, 28,* 1226–1231.

Nordström, S., Beckman, L., & Nordensson, I. (1978). Occupational and environmental risks in and around a smelter in Northern Sweden III. Frequencies of spontaneous abortion. *Hereditas, 88,* 51–54.

Population Information Program. (1983). Infertility and sexually transmitted diseases: A public health challenge. *Population Reports. Series L: Issues in World Health,* No. 4.

Population Reference Bureau. (1982). U.S. Population: Where we are, where we are going. *Population Bulletin, 37*(2), 1–50.

Pratt, W. F., Mosher, W., Bachrach, C., & Horn, M. (1984). Understanding U.S. fertility. *Population Bulletin, 39*(5), 1–42.

Rasmussen, K., & Munck, M. (1987). Sexual activity and contraceptive habits among young people. *Ugeskrift Laeger, 149,* 46–47.

Rome, W. N. (1976). Effects of lead on the female and reproduction: A review. *Mt. Sinai Journal of Medicine, 43,* 542–552.

Ross, J. A., Huber, D. H., & Hong, S. (1986). Worldwide trends in voluntary sterilization. *International Family Planning Perspective, 12,* 34.

Schwartz, D., & Mayaux, M. J. (1982). Female fecundity as a function of age: Results of artificial insemination in 2,193 nulliparous women with azoospermic husbands. *New England Journal of Medicine, 306,* 404–406.

SOU. (1982). Women and children: Official statistics of the Swedish National Central Bureau of Statistics. Stockholm.

Starrs, A. (1987). Preventing the tragedy of maternal deaths: A report on the International Safe Motherhood Conference. Nairobi, Kenya.

Sullivan, F. M., & Barlow, S. M. (1979). Congenital malformations and other reproductive hazards from environmental chemicals. *Proceedings of the Royal Society of London. Series B: Biological Sciences, 205,* 91–110.

Van de Walle, E., & Kuodel, J. (1980). Europe's fertility transition: New evidence and lessons for today's developing world. *Population Bulletin, 34*(6), 1–42.

Vessey, M. P. (1978). Epidemiological studies of the occupational hazards of anesthesia: A review. *Anaesthesia, 33,* 430–438.

Weinberger, M. B. (1987). The relationship between women's education and fertility: Selected findings from the World Fertility Survey. *Family Planning Perspective, 13,* 35–46.

Westlander, G., & Magnusson, B. (1988). Swedish women and new technology. In G. Westlander & J. M. Stellman (Eds.), *Women and health* (Vol. 13). New York: Hawort Press.

World Health Organization Special Programme of Research, Development and Research Training in Human Reproduction. (1988). *Research in human reproduction: Biennial report 1986–1987.* Geneva: Author.

12

Women, Work, and Menopause

PHILIP M. SARREL

INTRODUCTION

Menopause occurs in American women at an average age of 51. At this time in their lives a majority of today's women work outside the home for pay at least part-time, if not full-time (McKinlay, 1988). There is considerable evidence that women who are working experience fewer symptoms at menopause and are better able to cope with the stresses of family and relationships. On the other hand, there are almost no studies of work performance and the effects of menopausal symptoms or related disease conditions; yet there is reason to believe that many women are negatively affected.

At age 51 life expectancy is more than 30 years, of which a considerable part could be spent in meaningful and satisfying work. Indeed, for many women mid-life and the later years are the most creative. This was true of, for example, Kathe Kollwitz, who wrote in her diary, "For the last third of life there remains only work. It alone is always stimulating, rejuvenating, exciting and satisfying" (Kollwitz, quoted in Heilbrun, 1988, p. 127). And true of Isak Dinesen, one of whose characters proclaims, "Women when they are old enough to have done with the business of being women, and can let loose their strength, must be the most powerful creatures in the world" (Dinesen, quoted in Heilburn, 1988, p. 128). And yet for many millions of women menopause does not mark the beginning of their best and most creative years but, rather, the onset of decline in health and the quality of their lives.

PHILIP M. SARREL • Obstetrics and Gynecology and Psychiatry, Yale University School of Medicine, New Haven, Connecticut 06510.

Menopause is the time of the last menstrual flow. Menstruation ceases when there is insufficient ovarian hormone production to maintain the uterine lining, the endometrium. After menopause the endometrium becomes atrophic, that is, endometrial cells and vasculature shrink and disappear. The primary hormonal change is a marked decrease in ovarian estradiol-17β production. Postmenopausal levels of this hormone are about one-tenth the premenopausal levels. After menopause there is also a marked decline in ovarian progesterone production as ovulation all but ceases. Estradiol-17β and progesterone are released directly into the bloodstream, flow throughout the body, and diffuse into many different cells. There are specific cells in the body that contain nuclear proteins that are receptors for these hormones. When receptor–hormone complexes are formed, the potential exists for these complexes to attach to DNA at a variety of gene sites, promoting RNA formation and subsequently influencing cellular growth and metabolism. As a result, the functioning of many different organ systems can be stimulated or modified. These are called "target organ systems" and include the bone, cardiovascular, nervous, skin, genitourinary, and gastrointestinal systems.

When a decrease in ovarian steroids occurs at any time in the life cycle, not only with menopause, a variety of symptoms can develop, signaling altered system function. For example, low estradiol-17β often triggers a reaction in the nervous and cardiovascular systems, manifested as a hot flash or warm flush. About 80% of women who have been studied in menopause research programs develop this symptom in the years immediately before and after the menopause, and almost as many develop problems of sleep disturbance. Because so many organ systems are influenced by ovarian steroids, many different symptoms have been attributed to the menopausal decline in hormone production. At the same time, however, symptoms could be due to other factors in a woman's life, including other biological changes as well as psychological and environmental forces. It is also important to recognize that women in the general population may not suffer the same incidence or severity of symptoms as women studied in menopause programs. Whatever the cause or the frequency, it is characteristic for millions of women to develop symptoms at menopause that interfere with their capacity to function at home and in the workplace.

In addition to the signs and symptoms of the "menopause syndrome," there is a further and more ominous meaning to the effects of the hormone changes. As women live longer, disease conditions begin to develop that have been related to the absence of the ovarian steroids. For example, about one-third of women develop osteoporosis. By age 60, 10% of American women have sustained a wrist fracture, and as women move into their 60s and 70s they face an ever-increasing incidence of vertebral and hip fractures. While the latter fractures don't occur until today's woman has left the workplace, that is, until after age 65, it is quite possible that tomorrow's woman, who could and would work for another decade or more, may find she cannot because of osteoporosis. Far more important is the problem of cardiovascular disease, rare in women before menopause and common afterward; female mortality is primarily due to cardiovascular disease. Although coronary heart disease and cerebrovascular disease are killers of predominantly elderly women, the signs and symptoms of coronary artery disease and cerebral disease are manifest in women in their 50s and do become significant factors in women who become unable to maintain work functions. Also, it is known that nerve cells are hormone sensitive, and it is possible that ovarian hormone insufficiency alters neurological functions, such as sensory perception and cognition.

MEANINGS OF THE MENOPAUSE

In a recent article Professor Diczfalusy has calculated that by the year 2000, 12% of the world's population will be women over the age of 45. Within the first quarter of the twenty-first century global life expectancy at birth will be 70 years (Diczfalusy, 1987). How different that is from the beginning of our present century, when life expectancy at birth in the Western developed nations was but 38 years and only 6.1% of American women were beyond the menopause age. Today there are 40 million women in America who are postmenopausal, representing more than 30% of the female population. With a life expectancy into their 80s, the vast majority of women will live through their menopause and long enough to die of diseases affected by the hormonal changes of the menopause.

During the past 20 years a great deal of information has become available concerning hormone actions, changes at menopause, and the effects of hormone replacement therapy. We have learned about the cancer-inducing effects of estrogens and of the protective effects of progestins. At the same time, we have learned that estrogen can alleviate symptoms and prevent disease. As a result, it now appears probable that a safe and effective regimen can be offered to those women suffering from menopause symptoms and/or those facing an increased risk of disease. In this chapter, I would like to briefly review what I believe are the most important of these findings with respect to women's health and women's capacity to function in the workplace. Because a number of researchers have conducted studies to understand the impact of work and social class on menopausal symptoms and subsequent disease development, I will summarize these findings. At the present time there is an ongoing study at Yale University, the Yale Mid-Life Study, in which a wide variety of biological and psychosocial measures are being taken before and during hormone replacement. Among these measures are several that determine the effects of menopause symptoms on work capacity in and out of the home. In this chapter I report preliminary results of these studies.

THE SIGNIFICANCE OF OVARIAN HORMONES

Deficiency of estradiol-17β leads to a variety of signs and symptoms of altered function. As already mentioned, the most common are sleep disturbance and vasomotor instability (i.e., hot flashes). But many different target organs are affected, and consequently many other signs and symptoms may develop. Numbness, small-joint pain, urinary urgency and incontinence, vaginal dryness and dyspareunia, palpitations, headache, anxiety attacks, depression, and altered memory function are all potential effects of such deficiency. These signs and symptoms are not peculiar to the menopausal woman, since they also occur in response to other causes of estradiol-17β deficiency.

Table 1 indicates the incidence in the ongoing Yale Mid-Life Study of menopausal symptoms at a level that interferes with capacity to function either at home or in the workplace. A 1973 Swedish study (Bengtsson, 1973) indicates that symptoms such as hot flashes, depression, and sexual dysfunction continue in 30% or more of postmenopausal women for at least 5 years and in over 25% of women for more than 10 years. Every tenth woman had symptoms 17 years after menopause (Hammar *et al.*, 1988). The effects on sexual function are seen in a study of women attending a menopause clinic in London (Sarrel & Whitehead, 1985). Over 80% of the women suffered one or more sexual dysfunctions, with 4 out of 5 of these women developing the problems at menopause. Although sleep disturbance, hot flashes, anxiety attacks, and depression are the symptoms that most often affect capacity to function at work outside the home, the fact that so many women have an unsatisfactory sexual relationship in their marriage should also be considered as a stress factor impairing work function.

The immediate signs and symptoms of estradiol-17β deficiency are certainly upsetting and warrant attention, but they are not usually life-threatening. As the life span lengthens, however, and the period of time of hormonal deficiency increases, the consequences become more serious. Conditions such as urogenital atrophy, osteoporosis, atherosclerosis, and peripheral nerve degeneration reflect the long-term effects of loss of the

Table 1. Yale Mid-Life Study: Menopause Symptoms
Described at Initial Study Visit According to
Percentage at Severity and Frequency Level
Affecting Daily Function

Symptom	Percentage
Sleep disturbance	65
Vasomotor instability	56
Sexual dysfuction/self	60
Sexual dysfuction/partner	57
Memory loss	51
Depression/anxiety	49
Urinary difficulties	40
Impaired sense of touch	29
Numbness in fingers/toes	18

cell growth and anabolic activity generated by estradiol-17β. Hormone replacement appears to modify or prevent these conditions.

An illustration of the many different effects of estrogens and progestins is seen in cardiovascular research on the role of estrogens in preventing arteriosclerotic disease. This subject has received a great deal of attention in the medical literature since 1986 (Henderson, Paganni-Hill, & Ross, 1988). Although conflicting findings have been reported, there is considerable data indicating that women treated with estrogen replacement therapy appear to have a significantly reduced risk of heart attack and stroke when compared with untreated women (Bush, Barrett-Connor, & Cowan, 1987; Henderson, Paganni-Hill, & Ross, 1988). Several mechanisms have been proposed to explain the preventive effect of estradiol-17β on cardiovascular disease. Studies indicate that estradiol-17β generates an increase in high-density lipoprotein (HDL), which is believed to be a protective factor against arteriosclerosis (Fahraeus, Larsson-Cohn, & Wallentier, 1982). Other reported effects of estradiol-17β include control over the release of epinephrine and norepinephrine (Hamlet, Rorie, & Tyce, 1980), vasodilation leading to increased blood flow (Sarrel, 1988), and retardation of aortic atherogenesis (Hough & Zilversmit, 1986). Estradiol-17β receptors have been localized in the smooth muscle layer of canine arteries, including the coronary and carotid vessels (Horwitz & Horwitz, 1982). The effects of ovarian steroids on arterial flow appear significant. Decreased blood flow and instability of vasomotor function develop when estradiol-17β is deficient; estrogen replacement enhances and stabilizes blood flow.

Cardiovascular disease is rare in women before menopause. For example, in a Mayo Clinic series only 27 out of 95,000 women under the age of 40 admitted to the hospital were diagnosed with coronary artery disease (Underdahl & Smith, 1947). There are no deaths due to cardiovascular disease in the premenopausal women among 1,600 women followed in the Framingham Heart Study (Dawber, 1980). After menopause, however, the situation changes. The incidence of cardiovascular disease rises rapidly and eventually matches that of men (Colditz, Willett, & Stampfer, 1987). For example, Bengtsson reports findings among 578 Swedish women, ages 50 to 54. By this age 13% had a history of either myocardial infarction or angina. An additional 14 women had died of heart attack by age 54. After menopause, cardiovascular disease becomes the leading cause of mortality in women in the United States, equaling three to four times the annual number of deaths from lung, breast, endometrial, and ovarian cancers combined (National Center for Health Statistics, 1988). It would appear that biological and psychosocial factors combine to cause cardiovascular morbidity and mortality after menopause. For example, in the Framingham Heart Study, clerical workers with children were identified to have an increased incidence of coronary heart disease. In a number of other studies, similar groups of working women have the most severe menopause symptoms. Among these mid-life workers with heart disease the most important predictors were suppressed hostility, a nonsupportive boss, and decreased job mobility. The significance of social class is revealed in the finding that there is an added risk of heart disease in being married to a blue-collar worker (Haynes & Feinlieb, 1982).

In a recent literature review LaRosa (1988) concludes, "It is not the stressfulness of the job alone that is a risk factor for coronary heart disease but the perception of the degree of control on the job that contributes to the risk." In exploring the relationship between underlying personality variables in postmenopausal women and associated psychological and psychosomatic complaints, Collins, Hanson and Eneroth (1983) found correlations with anxiety-proneness and with "the feeling that external factors determined one's life" (Coleman & Antonucci, 1983). It seems that neither menopause nor certain kinds of work are very healthful for women, and when the two combine the results can be disastrous.

WORK, SOCIAL LOSS, AND MENOPAUSE SYMPTOMS

Many women pass through menopause with minimal if any symptoms and appear to be examples of the Kathe Kollwitz and Isak Dinesen models. To fully understand the variables that determine symptomatology calls for a biopsychosocial paradigm. Koeske (1982) has argued convincingly for an integrated approach that recognizes the need to understand the combined impact on health of hormonal change and environmental stress at mid-life. Most studies do not, unfortunately, adhere to such standards. Nevertheless, for the moment, let me review those studies that have been published regarding the impact of work on menopause symptoms. At least 10 different studies have sought to determine the effects of work and social class on frequency and intensity of menopause symptoms; these are summarized in Table 2, which indicates a variety of confirmatory as well as conflicting findings.

Hallström's analysis of the Göteborg cohort did not find any significant association between symptom reports and social class or employment status (Hallström, 1973). This study was done in the late 1960s and early 1970s. Van Keep and Kellerhals (1974) studied data from 448 Swiss women living in Zurich in 1972; these authors eliminated from their study those women who worked for pay and classified their subjects according to the social class of their husbands. They determined that upper-class women had more symptoms at menopause but for a shorter time than lower-class women, many of whom failed to "recover" from the impact of menopausal changes. In 1973 Jaszmann reported that working-class women, compared with middle-class women, were found to report more psychological and somatic symptoms. Often cited is Severne's (1979) study of over 800 Belgian women, which found that lower-class women with a job experienced additional stress and tension during the menopause. McKinlay and Jefferys (1974) in Britain, however, failed to find any association between symptoms and employment status, social class, domestic work load, or

Table 2. Studies on the Effects of Work and Social Class on Menopause Symptoms

Author	Year	Country	Work effect	on symptoms Social class effect on symptoms
Hallström	1973	Sweden	No	No
Van Keep & Kellerhals	1974	Switzerland		Yes
Jaszmann	1973	Netherlands		Yes
Severne	1979	Belgium	Yes	Yes
McKinlay & Jefferys	1974	Great Britain	No	No
Coleman & Antonucci	1983	United States	Yes	Yes
Powell	1977	United States	Yes	
Nolan	1986	United States	Yes	
Hunter, Battersby, & Whitehead	1986	Great Britain	Yes	Yes
McKinlay	1988	United States	Yes	

marital status. In contrast are the findings of Coleman and Antonucci (1983), who examined data from the University of Michigan's Survey of Modern Living. In this study were 389 women, ages 40 to 59, of whom 206 worked outside the home and 183 were homemakers. These authors found the women who worked outside the home to have a higher self-esteem, less psychological anxiety and depression, and better physical health than the homemakers. Among the workers, they found that women with high incomes had more psychological anxiety than those with less incomes. In a smaller study of 40 working women Powell (1977) reported significantly lower psychiatric symptom scores among those employed full-time than among those employed part-time.

Nolan (1986) wisely points out that most behavioral science studies have examined the relationship between environmental events, for example, work and health, without taking into consideration the women's menopausal status; that is, most studies fail to distinguish between a 48- to 52-year-old having regular menses and an age-matched counterpart who is perimenopausal or postmenopausal. In her study of 47 women Nolan (1986) reported that working women in the perimenopause had hot flashes that became less frequent or absent in their postmenopausal years whereas unemployed women suffered more from hot flashes for a longer time through both the perimenopause and postmenopausal years.

Two recent studies should be mentioned. In 1986 Hunter, Battersby, and Whitehead reported results from 682 British women (66% of the women were employed; 29% full-time and 37.8% part-time) attending a menopause clinic in London. From data gathered as part of a general health survey, psychosocial factors were compared to the incidence and severity of menopause symptoms. Social class correlated with psychiatric and cognitive difficulties as well as with sleep disturbance and somatic complaints. Women who were employed had the least symptoms, women who were unemployed had the highest incidence of somatic complaints and anxiety disorders. The last of the studies I wish to cite is an ongoing study, preliminary results of which were presented in April 1988 at a conference sponsored by the National Institutes of Health/American Fertility Society. At that meeting Sonja McKinlay reported on a study of 2,300 Massachusetts women randomly selected from the general population (three-fourths of the women were employed). McKinlay (1988) concluded that work appears to play a protective role in health and that menopause symptoms are fewer among working women.

None of the studies cited reported whether or not menopause symptoms or medically related conditions impaired women's work functions or played a role leading to their leaving the work force. It is widely written that the unemployed are not as healthy as employed persons either physically or mentally. To what extent were the women unemployed because of physical and/or mental conditions secondary to menopause effects? This and other questions regarding the effect of menopause on work are addressed in the Yale Mid-Life Study.

YALE MID-LIFE STUDY FINDINGS REGARDING MENOPAUSE SYMPTOMS AND WORK

The Yale Mid-Life Study is a multidisciplinary approach to understanding the significance of menopause changes and hormone replacement therapy with regard to several different body systems and everyday functions. Biological investigations include studies of peripheral nerve function, peripheral blood flow, and skin structure. Psychological measures include the SCL-90, a 90 question review of psychological symptoms, the mini-mental status, and memory tests. A menopause symptom index, called the Mensi, registers and scores menopause symptoms before and during hormone replacement. The subjects are women who are postmenopausal, have not received prior hormone replacement therapy, and have estradiol and FSH levels meeting recognized criteria for menopausal status. Each woman is seen for 6 months, during which her biological, psychological, and social functioning is evaluated in seven individual interviews. A double-blind, placebo/drug randomized protocol is used as well as an open treatment program for women unwilling to participate in a placebo study.

At the time of initial evaluation and during treatment, determination is made of the women's work function. Unfortunately, it is too soon to compare the placebo with the treated groups. At this time, I can share the initial visit findings and preliminary results after hormone treatment.

Initial visit findings from 130 women show 20% are homemakers and 80% (104) are employed outside the home. Their average age is 52.65 years, with an age range from 31 to 65. The age distribution 30–39, 40–44, 45–49, 50–54, 55–59 and 60–69 is 8%, 5%, 16%, 40%, 16% and 15%, respectively. The racial distribution is 125 Caucasian, 4 black, and 1 Oriental. Among the 104 women working outside the home, 74 are professional, 11 work at secretarial jobs, 10 are semiskilled, and 9 hold a variety of jobs including travel agent, factory inspector, and waitress.

Two-thirds of the women working outside the home stated at their initial interview that menopause symptoms had a moderate to severe effect on their capacity to function at work (Figure 1). Seven of the 104 women

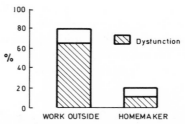

Figure 1. Proportion of postmenopausal women reporting work dysfunction at initial interview in Yale Mid-Life Study (N=130).

working outside the home (7%) had quit work because of symptoms developing at the time of menopause. (This group included two bankers, a hairdresser, two factory workers, a teacher, and a dress designer.) Fifteen of the 26 homemakers (58%) felt their capacity to function at home had been adversely affected.

The most common symptom affecting work outside the home was sleep disturbance, which was a complaint of 69/104 women (66%). Also frequently described were the effects of hot flashes, anxiety attacks, depression, and memory loss (Figure 2). Headaches, palpitations, and extreme fatigue were less common complaints.

Thirty women have had an interview evaluation, using the Mensi, of menopause symptoms and effects on work performance at each of seven visits over a 6-month period. All of these women were known to be treated with estradiol and progestin replacement during this time. Eighteen of the 30 women (60%) noted the negative impact of menopause symptoms on work performance at a moderate to severe level at the time of the initial visit. After 6 months of treatment only 5 of the women (16.7%) gave similar ratings of their work performance, and 2 of the 5 were found to have been inadequately treated (i.e., they had not absorbed the hormones they were given, and their various blood and physiological studies showed no change).

We have recently begun to use the Social Adjustment Scale (Holmes & Rahe, 1967), a test designed to evaluate work function. The test is being administered to all new patients attending our clinics, including women in our double-blind placebo study. Before- and after-treatment findings are only available for 10 women although baseline scoring has been done for over 40. None of the placebo data is available, since the code has not yet been broken for those women. We are finding however, that the Social Adjustment Scale is most useful in our type of clinical research, and

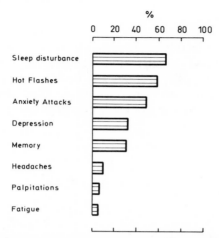

Figure 2. Proportion of postmenopausal women reporting various symptoms affecting work outside the home. Yale Mid-Life Study (*N*=104).

preliminary findings indicate a high level of effect of menopause symptoms on work function, confirming the findings of our previous evaluations.

The Yale Mid-Life Study is limited in size, compared to other studies of menopausal women and work function, and is also limited by the fact that it examines issues among women who already have problems rather than among women in the general population. Nevertheless, the study serves to raise awareness of the fact that there are women whose ability to function is compromised by menopausal changes and that hormone replacement appears to have a role in restoring function for such women.

CONCLUSIONS

As it becomes clear that women, whose representation in the work force continues to grow, can benefit physically, psychologically, and socially by continuing to work after menopause, it is necessary to understand the ways in which work affects menopausal symptoms and the ways in which menopausal symptoms and subsequent ill health affect the capacity to work and create during the part of adulthood that begins at mid-life. The right to proper health care should not be denied a woman, whatever her age.

ACKNOWLEDGMENTS

The work reported in this presentation is in part derived from a larger study of hormones and women at mid-life funded by the National Institute of Aging, Grant No. AG06201-02. Dr. William Glazer and Dr. Carolyn Mazure helped in the study design. Mary Ellen Rousseau, C. N. M., assisted in interviewing the women and collecting these data, as did Ms. Valerie Abbott.

REFERENCES

Bengtsson, C. (1973). Ischaemic heart disease in women. A study based on a randomized population sample of women and women with myocardial infarction in Goteborg, Sweden. *Acta Medica Scandinavica, 5*, 1–128.

Bush, T. L., Barrett-Conner, E., Cowan, L. D., Rosner, B., Speizer, F. E., & Hennekeos, C. H. (1987). Cardiovascular mortality and non-contraceptive use of estrogen in women. *Circulation, 75*, 1102–1109.

Colditz, G. A., Willett, W. C., & Stampfer, M. J. (1987). Menopause and the risk of coronary heart disease in women. *New England Journal of Medicine, 316*, 1105–1110.

Coleman, L., & Antonucci, T. (1983). Impact of work on women at midlife. *Developmental Psychology, 19*, 290–295.

Collins, A., Hanson, V., & Eneroth, P. (1983). Post-menopausal symptoms and response to hormone replacement therapy: Influence of psychological factors. *Journal of Psychosomatic Obstetrics and Gynecology, 2*, 227–233.

Dawber, T. R. (1980). *The Framingham Study: The epidemiology of atherosclerotic disease*. Cambridge, MA: Harvard University Press.

Diczfalusy, E. (1987). Introduction: Menopause, developing countries, and the 21st century. In D. Mishell (Ed.), *Menopause: Physiology and pharmacology* (pp. 1–19). Chicago: Year Book.

Fahraeus, L., Larsson-Cohn, U., & Wallentier, L. (1982). Lipoproteins during oral and cutaneous administration of 17β-estradiol to menopausal women. *Acta Endocrinologica, 101*, 597–602.

Hallström, T. (1973). *Mental disorder and sexuality in the climacteric*. Copenhagen: Scandinavian University Books.

Hamlet, M. A., Rorie, D. K., & Tyce, G. M. (1980). Effects of estradiol on release and disposition of norepinephrine from nerve endings. *American Journal of Physiology, 239*(Heart Circ Physiol 8), H450–H456.

Hammar, M., Berg, G., Gottvall, T., & Lindgren, R. (1988). Every tenth woman vegetative and vaginal discomfort 17 years after menopause. *Lakantidningen, 85*(23), 2073–75.

Haynes, S. G., & Feinlieb, M. (1982). Women, work and coronary heart disease: Prospective findings from the Framingham Heart Study. *American Journal of Public Health, 70* (2), 133–141.

Heilbrun, C. G. (1988). *Writing a woman's life*. New York: Norton.

Henderson, B. E., Paganni-Hill, A., & Ross, R. K. (1988). Estrogen replacement therapy and protection from acute myocardial infarction. *American Journal of Obstetrics and Gynecology, 159*, 312–317.

Holmes, T. H., & Rahe, R. H. (1967). The social adjustment rating scale. *Journal of Psychosomatic Research, 11*, 213–224.

Horwitz, K. B., & Horwitz, L. D. (1982). Canine vascular tissue are targets for androgens, estrogens, progestins, and glucorticoids. *Journal of Clinical Investigation, 69*, 750–758.

Hough, J. L., & Zilversmit, D. B. (1986). Effect of 17β-estradiol on aortic cholesterol content and metabolism in cholesterol-fed rabbits. *Arteriosclerosis, 6*, 57–63.

Hunter, M., Battersby, R., & Whitehead, M. I. (1986). Relationships between psychological symptoms, somatic complaints and menopausal status. *Maturitas, 8*, 217–228.

Jaszmann, L. (1973). Epidemiology of the climacteric and post-climacteric complaints. In P. A. Van Keep & C. Lauritzen (Eds.), *Ageing and oestrogens* (pp. 22–25). Basel: Karger.

Koeske, R. (1982). Toward a biosocial paradigm for menopause research: Lessons and contributions from the behavioral sciences. In A. Voda, M. Dinnerstein, & S. O'Donnel (Eds.), *Changing perspectives on menopause*. Austin: University of Texas Press.

LaRosa, J. H. (1988). Women, work and health: Employment as a risk factor for coronary heart disease. *American Journal of Obstetrics and Gynecology, 158*, 1597–1602.

McKinlay, S. (1988, April). Social Factors and Responses to Menopause. Conference on the Menopause. Bethesda, MD: National Institutes of Health.

McKinlay, S. M., & Jefferys, M. (1974). The menopausal syndrome. *British Journal of Preventive Social Medicine, 28*, 108–115.

National Center for Health Statistics. (1988). Vital Statistics of the United States, 1986, Vol. II, Mortality, Parts A and B (DHHS Publication Nos. 88-1122 and 88-1114). Public Health Service, Washington, U.S. Government Printing Office, Washington, D.C.

Neugarten, B., & Kraines, R., (1965). Menopausal symptoms in women of various ages. *Psychosomatic Medicine, 27*, 263–266.

Nolan, J. W. (1986). Developmental concerns and the health of midlife women. *Nursing Clinics of North America, 21*(1), 151–159.

Powell, B. (1977). The empty nest, employment and psychiatric symptoms in college-educated women. *Psychology of Women Quarterly, 2*, 35–43.

Sarrel, P. M. (1988). Effects of ovarian hormones on the cardiovascular system. In J. Ginsburg (Ed.), *The circulation in the female* (pp. 117–141). Canisforth, England: Parthenon.

Sarrel, P. M., & Whitehead, M. I. (1985). Sex and menopause: Defining the issues. *Maturitas, 7*, 217–224.

Severne, L. (1979). Psychosocial aspects of the menopause. In A. A. Haspels & H. Musaph (Eds.), *Psychosomatics in perimenopause* (pp. 101–120). Baltimore: University Park Press.

Underdahl, L. O., & Smith, H. L. (1947). Coronary artery disease in women under the age of 40. *Proceedings of Staff Meetings at the Mayo Clinic, 22*, 479.

Van Keep, P. A., & Kellerhals, J. M. (1974). The impact of sociocultural factors on symptom formation: Some results of a study on ageing women in Switzerland. *Psychotherapy and Psychosomatics, 23*, 251–263.

13

Premenstrual Distress

Implications for Women's Working Capacity and Quality of Life

AILA COLLINS

The premenstrual syndrome (PMS) is characterized by a number of somatic, affective, cognitive, and behavioral disturbances that arise in the luteal phase of the menstrual cycle and that are accentuated premenstrually. What is decisive for the diagnosis of PMS is the timing of symptoms: a sudden onset in the luteal phase and disappearance with full menstrual flow. Dalton (1977, 1984) has defined PMS as "the recurrence of symptoms in the premenstrual phase with absence of symptoms in the postmenstruum" (p. 3). The most frequently reported symptoms include irritability, depression, loss of energy, food cravings, loss of sexual interest, bloatedness, and breast tenderness. This chapter includes a brief review of the literature on PMS and a report of the results of a study on psychological characteristics and occupational stress in women who suffer from PMS.

Although physical symptoms, such as swelling, breast discomfort, and perceived weight gain, frequently occur simultaneously with the mood and behavioral changes of the premenstrual phase, they are usually better tolerated and are generally not responsible for the disruption of lifestyle that often accompanies PMS. Instead, it is the cyclical and often unanticipated loss of control over emotional reactions to everyday events that are most distressing to women who suffer from PMS (Stout & Steege, 1985). Women suffering from PMS report having emotional outbursts over every-

AILA COLLINS • Psychology Division, Department of Psychiatry and Psychology, Karolinska Institute, S-104 01 Stockholm, Sweden.

day trivial matters. The dimension of irritability can cover a whole range of behaviors, from a cross word or remark to violent quarrels, slamming doors, or throwing things (Dalton, 1984). A characteristic feature of PMS is the loss of control in individuals who would not normally even raise their voice. Women suffering from PMS describe themselves as impatient, intolerant, spiteful, vindictive, fault-finding, quarrelsome, and quick-tempered (Dalton, 1984). Often the incident that provokes the anger—and it can be a relatively minor matter—has been present for some time, but suddenly the woman explodes with anger. Afterward, she is often over-whelmed by guilt feelings. Some women may become completely with-drawn and isolate themselves from family and friends. Social commitments are canceled, and feelings of depression and passivity may dominate. Hallman (1986) reported depression to be a central dimension of PMS.

Premenstrual insomnia or sleep disturbance may leave the woman exhausted at work the following day. Many women describe difficulties in concentrating or impairment of memory and judgment. Others feel that they are less creative in their work. Objective studies of intellectual perfor-mance during different phases of the menstrual cycle have yielded very little evidence of lowered capacity in the premenstruum. Clare (1985), in a review of the etiology of PMS, concludes that there is no evidence that women perform differently during the premenstrual days compared to other parts of the cycle; a similar conclusion was reached by Sommer (1982).

The long-term consequences of the cyclic recurrence of this distress-ing combination of mood and behavioral change are often a deterioration of interpersonal relationships, perceived inefficiency at work, and feelings of inadequacy, hopelessness, and guilt. That is, two important areas of the woman's life are seriously affected: perceived work efficiency and interper-sonal relationships.

The prevalence of PMS varies in different reports. In two prospective Swedish studies of relatively large populations (Andersch, 1980; Hallman & Goergiev, 1986), the incidence of a mild to moderate PMS was about 70%. About 10% of women are estimated to be in need of some form of medical attention for premenstrual problems (Andersch, 1980). These women are also absent from work more often and for longer periods of time than are women who do not suffer from PMS (Hallman, 1986), although none of the women gave premenstrual symptoms as a cause of their absence from work. PMS occurs at all ages during women's fertile lives, but women between 30 and 45 report a markedly higher frequency of symptoms. Young women do not usually associate their changes in mood with different phases of the menstrual cycle. Increased awareness and, perhaps, knowledge of one's own bodily functions are associated with age. It is common for a woman to discover that she suffers from PMS at around the age of 30. Both physiological and social factors may contribute to this:

greater demands are usually placed on women of this age. They often occupy multiple roles, being housewives with preschool children at home and working women with full-time jobs outside the home. Hallman (1987), reporting an association between parity and frequency of premenstrual symptoms, speculated that going through the stages of pregnancy and looking after young children may in themselves create stress factors that may intensify premenstrual problems. Wendestam (1980) and Wood and associates (1979) found no association between parity and premenstrual symptomatology.

Many theories have been proposed to explain the causes of PMS, which range from purely biochemical to social and psychological factors. However, there is no one theory that adequately explains this syndrome. Findings to date suggest that multiple and interacting social, psychological, and biological factors are involved in the etiology of PMS.

METHODOLOGICAL PROBLEMS

The highly conflicting results from different studies may in part reflect some major methodological problems associated with research on PMS. One critical problem is subject selection. Most earlier studies relied on selection based on a history of premenstrual complaints. It is well known among researchers that an invitation to participate in studies on PMS results in numerous positive replies. Some studies have demonstrated that women who present themselves as suffering from PMS have not always made the correct self-diagnosis. Bäckström and Hammarbäck (1986) and Rubinow, Hoban, Grover, Galloway, Roy-Byrne, Andersen, & Merriam, (1988) stress that a considerable percentage of women with a history of PMS do not actually show evidence of cyclical mood changes or menstrual-cycle-related symptoms when studied longitudinally, using daily ratings of mood and somatic symptoms. It seems clear that careful prospective ratings of mood and symptoms over at least one menstrual cycle are necessary for diagnosing PMS.

PSYCHOLOGICAL CORRELATES
OF PREMENSTRUAL SYNDROME

The lack of a verifiable biological theory explaining PMS has directed attention to the possibility that women who complain of PMS differ from women who are symptom-free on a number of personality traits.

Many researchers have hypothesized an association between PMS and psychological factors such as personality traits, psychiatric disturbances, and life events. Certain psychological factors may predispose women to develop cyclical mood changes. Social learning and negative attitudes toward menstruation are seen as possible explanations for negative menstrual experiences. Paulson (1961) found that women with premenstrual symptoms were more likely than others to have mothers who suffered from PMS. A much-quoted study is the one by Ruble (1977), in which she convinced a group of women that they were in their premenstrual phase and found that they reported a higher incidence of premenstrual symptoms than did women who believed themselves to be in the middle of their cycle. This study demonstrates the effects of expectation on symptoms. However, the differences between the groups were fairly small, especially for symptoms such as tension, irritability, and mood swings, symptoms that are reported most frequently by women suffering from PMS. It is also possible that the responses observed in Ruble's study were influenced by demand characteristics.

In one of the earlier studies Rees (1953) found an association between intensity of PMS and a neurotic disposition. Similar results from a study of 500 randomly sampled women were obtained by Coppen and Kessel (1963), who reported positive correlations between neuroticism, as measured by Eysenck's Personality Inventory, and premenstrual symptomatology. Gough (1975) found that women who were described as shy, self-doubting, help-seeking, and self-defeating were more likely to suffer from PMS than other women. On the other hand, Wendestam (1980) did not find any relationship between premenstrual symptoms and neuroticism or extraversion in a Swedish study. Watts, Dennerstein, and de Lattorne (1980) reported that women complaining of PMS had significantly higher levels of trait anxiety and neuroticism and held more negative attitudes about their bodies than did women without PMS. Clare (1983), in a study of British women who consulted general practitioners, found a highly significant relationship between psychiatric disturbance, marital unhappiness, and premenstrual complaint.

More recent studies by Collins, Lundström, Nordström, Nilsson, Hamfelt, & Eneroth (1986) and Hallman (1987) showed that PMS sufferers scored higher than symptom-free control subjects on somatic anxiety, muscular tension, and indirect aggression and lower on socialization as measured by the Karolinska Scales of Personality (Schalling, 1978).

These results indicate that "premenstrual complainers" have certain personality characteristics that distinguish them from other women. Clare (1983) concluded that they seem to be a vulnerable group of women who have difficulties coping with stressful life events. Clare has suggested that psychological disturbances and adverse social factors may serve to heighten the woman's sensitivity to aspects of her menstrual functioning and, indirectly, to focus her attention on changes occurring during her menstrual cycle that she would otherwise ignore. Hammarbäck and associates

(1989) have pointed out that women seeking help for PMS are a heterogeneous group and that women with underlying affective or neurotic disorders may experience premenstrual aggravation of their psychiatric condition. However, there are women who have none of these traits and who experience severe premenstrual mood changes.

Is it true that women who complain of premenstrual symptoms are less capable of coping with environmental stress? Not many studies have examined the relationship between stress factors and the exacerbation of premenstrual symptoms. Siegal and associates (1979), studying the association between life events and menstrual symptoms, found that undesirable life events were related to an increase in menstrual distress. The authors suggest that a woman's ability to cope with menstruation, psychologically as well as physically, is compromised by stressful life experiences. A woman's ability to cope with stressful events and internal biological changes may be modulated by a number of factors, such as life events, the absence or presence of social support, and degree of satisfaction with work and home life.

BIOCHEMICAL FACTORS

From the outset Frank (1931), in his initial description of premenstrual tension, assumed that the cyclical nature of the symptoms was due to alterations in hormonal levels. Figure 1 shows the pattern of hormonal variation during the menstrual cycle. A whole range of later studies focused on the role of progesterone, and decreasing levels of this hormone have been related to emotional symptoms (Dalton, 1977; Dennerstein, Spencer-Gardner, Gotts, Brown, Smith, & Burrows, 1985). However, more recent and methodologically careful studies have failed to find progesterone deficiency in women with premenstrual symptoms (Andersch, 1980; Rubinow et al., 1988).

An alternative theory implicates excess estrogen production; estrogen withdrawal has been associated with menstrual migraine (Magos, Zilkha, & Studd, 1983). Failure to find consistent evidence to support this theory has focused attention on the ratio between estrogen and progesterone. Studies of the effects of oral contraceptives have suggested that women with premenstrual irritability might be particularly susceptible to endogenous estrogen dominance in the luteal phase of the cycle (Cullberg, 1972). To date, these hypotheses remain unproven; no study reporting specific hormonal abnormalities consistently linked to premenstrual symptoms has been published.

In recent years interest in the complex interaction of sex hormones and neurotransmitter systems in the brain has directed attention to the

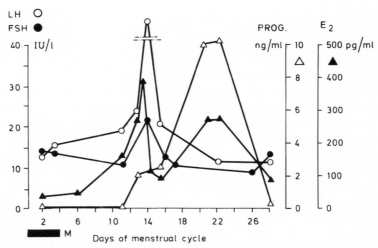

Figure 1. Hormonal fluctuation during the menstrual cycle; mean levels of progesterone, estradiol, LH, and FSH during a 28-day cycle.

possible role of serotonin, noradrenaline, and dopamine in premenstrual affective symptoms (Taylor, Matthew, Ho, & Weinman, 1984; Williams, Harris, & Dean, 1985). A popular treatment for premenstrual symptoms has been pyridoxine, which is a coenzyme in the biosynthesis of serotonin. The effects of pyridoxine (vitamin B_6) were examined in a double-blind crossover study of women with premenstrual symptoms (Collins, 1987); no significant effect over placebo was found. In the same study, platelet serotonin uptake kinetics were examined in women with premenstrual symptoms and control subjects and found no significant differences (Malmgren, Collins, & Nilsson, 1987).

It should also be noted that British and Canadian studies have suggested that women who suffer from PMS have a defective essential fatty acid metabolism and that treatment with dietary supplementation with essential fatty acids will alleviate symptoms (Brush, Watson, Horrobin, & Manku, 1984).

DOES PMS AFFECT WOMEN'S WORKING CAPACITY AND QUALITY OF LIFE?

Unhappiness with the work situation was found to be related to premenstrual symptoms (Wood *et al.*, 1979). Although clinical studies of

PMS are numerous, virtually none have investigated how women's reproductive health, including premenstrual problems, are related to different aspects of the work situation. There have been no systematic studies on the effects of job strain or overload on women's reproductive health, yet women are often exposed to work environments characterized by high demands and low control. Studies of general aspects of women's health show that women in high strain jobs, defined as high demand combined with low control, have more complaints such as chest pain (LaCroix & Haynes, 1987; Chapter 8, this volume).

The majority of Swedish women of fertile age are employed and thus spend a great deal of their time in the workplace. Most of them have multiple roles to fulfill, and because they are busy women with many engagements and commitments, they experience some degree of role strain. To date there are no studies of the relations between menstrual cycle changes and the way women cope with the stresses of everyday life, multiple role involvement, and work stress. There is an urgent need to study this neglected area and to begin to analyze the relationships between menstrual cycle changes, symptoms experienced, and characteristics of women's work. There is growing evidence that employment per se has a positive effect on women's psychological well-being and is associated with fewer symptoms of illness in general (La Rosa, 1988; Verbrugge, 1983; Chapter 2, this volume). There has been some debate as to whether multiple roles affect women's mental and physical health negatively or positively. Recent studies by Barnett and Baruch (1987) indicate that multiple role involvement is beneficial for women (see also Chapter 6, this volume). However, the situation for women suffering from PMS may differ from that of other women. The demands from conflicting roles, together with various stresses in the workplace, may be particularly difficult to cope with during the phase of acute premenstrual symptoms. We need to identify specific characteristics of the work environment as well as demands of conflicting roles that may be particularly negative for women suffering from premenstrual symptoms.

A STUDY OF WOMEN WITH PREMENSTRUAL SYMPTOMS: PSYCHOLOGICAL CHARACTERISTICS AND OCCUPATIONAL STRESS

The main aim of the present study was to examine the clinical effects of treatment of premenstrual symptoms with dietary supplementation of essential fatty acids (Collins & Landgren, 1991); in addition, a psychological assessment of women with premenstrual symptoms was made. The results reported here concern the psychological assessment of how PMS affects women's working capacity and quality of life.

The subjects were recruited through the population register by random sampling. Letters were sent to 8,000 women, ages 30–45, in the Stockholm County districts of Solna and Sundbyberg, inviting them to participate in the study. About 300 women replied that they suffered from PMS and were interested in taking part. After a careful diagnostic screening procedure, 59 women with premenstrual symptoms and 30 control subjects entered the study, which covered ten menstrual cycles for the women with PMS and one menstrual cycle for the control subjects; 38 women with PMS and 27 control subjects completed the study. The ages of the women with PMS ranged from 30 to 45 years with a mean of 37.6, and those of the control subjects had the same range with a mean of 38.2 years. All the women had a history of regular cycles, and none had taken oral contraceptives for at least 6 months prior to entering the study.

All subjects filled out two personality scales: the Karolinska Scales of Personality, designed by Schalling and measuring different aspects of Anxiety-Proneness, Aggression–Hostility, Detachment, Impulsivity, and Socialization (Schalling, 1978). The women with PMS scored significantly higher on somatic anxiety, psychic anxiety, and muscular tension compared to women who did not suffer from PMS. The results, which are in agreement with earlier findings, suggest that women suffering from PMS have higher anxiety levels than nonsufferers.

Also, the Swedish version of Rotter's Locus of Control Scale showed some interesting differences between the two groups. The women with premenstrual symptoms scored significantly higher on all but one of the locus of control subscales as compared to the symptom-free control subjects. In other words, women who suffer from PMS tend to feel, to a greater extent than do women who do not complain of PMS, that they cannot control important events in their lives. Whether the external locus of control contributes to premenstrual symptomatology, rather than being an effect of suffering from PMS, cannot be assessed on the basis of these data. However, women suffering from PMS sometimes state that the symptoms "control" them and that they feel "trapped."

In a semistructured interview the women suffering from PMS were asked questions concerning the extent to which their symptoms affected their daily lives, including their working capacity. They also completed a questionnaire designed to measure different aspects of their domestic and working lives as well as the effects of PMS on these dimensions. Ratings were made on a 10-point scale, where zero denotes a minimum degree and ten a maximum degree of each dimension studied.

The women were employed in various occupations, such as child care, nursing, clerical and secretarial work, and teaching. They were cate-gorized according to occupation: Group 1 was a fairly heterogeneous group of women holding intermediary service jobs including nursing, child care, sales and clerical work, and Group 2 comprised women in professional and managerial jobs, all having supervisory functions with relatively greater decision authority than the women in Group 1. There was no significant difference in level of education or age between the two groups. The women in Group 1 reported having been employed 18.2 years, on average, with a mean of 11.7 years in the current job. Subjects in Group 2 had been employed 16.6 years, on average, with a mean of 11.3 years in the current position.

Of the women in Group 1, 71% worked full-time; compared to 83% of the women in Group 2. The remaining women worked part-time, ranging from 50% to 80% of full-time. Three students and one housewife without employment outside the home were excluded from this group comparison. Of the women in Group 1 80% were married, compared to 66% in Group 2; 58% of the women in Group 1 and 66% of those in Group 2 had children.

Work Conditions

Premenstrual symptoms in the workplace constitute a problem that many women hide. This attitude was revealed in the interviews: many of the women stated that they do not talk about their problems and that they try to conceal the fact that they suffer from PMS in the workplace. A few women expressed fears that if it became known in their workplace that they suffer from PMS, this might be held against them for promotion.

Women in both groups rated their jobs as requiring a relatively high degree of the following dimensions: concentration, attention, perse-verance, speed, social ability, ability to solve conflicts, and responsibility. When asked to rate the degree to which each of these dimensions was most affected by their premenstrual symptoms, the results showed that women in managerial jobs rated their ability to concentrate as significantly more affected by PMS than did women in service jobs (Figure 2). In the interview women in both groups reported that the abilities to concentrate and to interact with other people were those most affected during their premenstrual phase. They felt that their mood swings, uneven temper, and feeling of being "on edge" seriously affected their ability to interact smoothly with others in the workplace. It is evident that the degree to which PMS interferes with work requirements varies with the nature of the work. The present data do not, however, allow a detailed analysis of such an interaction.

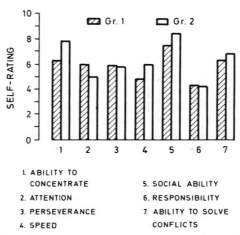

Figure 2. Mean ratings of two groups of women (Group 1 in service jobs, Group 2 in managerial jobs) on the effect of PMS on various work requirements.

Is it possible to schedule work routines to make it easier for women? The women were asked to rate to what extent they were able to take PMS into account when scheduling and carrying out their work routines. Both groups of women experienced a relatively low degree of freedom to do this. The results were confirmed in the interviews, during which the women stated that due to time pressure or other job demands it was usually not possible to consider premenstrual symptoms in their work (see Table 1).

Social Support and Functioning

Do other people empathize with women who have premenstrual symptoms? The women were asked to rate the degree of social support and understanding they received from their coworkers, their superiors, and from their families. Table 1 shows that the women in service jobs received a fair amount of social support from coworkers; 75% in Group 1 (service workers) and 50% of the women in Group 2 (managers) reported that they were able to talk openly with coworkers about their symptoms, particularly with female coworkers. The greatest difference between the two groups was found in social support from superiors: women in managerial jobs did not experience receiving social support from their superiors whereas the women in service jobs experienced receiving relatively strong social support ($p < .001$). These results are in agreement with recent

Table 1. Self-Ratings of Two Groups of Women (Group 1 in Service Jobs, Group 2 in Managerial Jobs) on a Questionnaire Measuring Aspects of Work and Domestic Life

	Group 1		Group 2	
Dimension measured	Mean	SE	Mean	SE
Degree to which PMS can be considered				
Scheduling work	2.08	0.43	3.00	1.61
Carrying out work	2.80	0.52	3.50	1.52
Social support				
Coworker	4.17	0.75	2.33	1.49
Superior	3.59	0.18	0.00	0.00
Spouse	6.60	0.70	1.00	0.44
Children	3.78	0.82	2.75	1.32
Role conflict				
Work vs. partner role	3.28	0.62	5.17	1.66
Work vs. parental role	4.54	0.86	5.80	2.37
Effect of PMS on role conflict				
Work vs. partner role	5.64	0.75	6.83	1.51
Work vs. parental role	7.06	0.70	8.75	0.94
Different functioning with PMS				
At work	5.63	0.55	7.00	0.92
At home	7.13	0.53	7.66	0.92
Effect of PMS on social activities				
Meeting friends	6.00	0.52	7.50	0.95
Going to parties	6.45	0.52	4.83	1.14
Arranging parties	7.66	0.46	8.33	1.28
Other activities	5.52	0.56	7.00	1.03

Note. The scale was an 11-point scale, with endpoints at 0 and 10, where 0 denotes "not at all" and 10 denotes "extremely."

findings by Frankenhaeuser and associates (1989); see also Chapter 3, this volume. The lack of social support for women in managerial jobs is probably due in part to the fact that they do not interact with either other women or superiors on a daily basis.

Does the family serve as a buffering network for women with PMS? The majority of women in Group 1 (service workers) rated their spouses to be supportive and understanding whereas the women in Group 2 (managers) rated their spouses to be significantly less supportive ($p < .001$).

It appears that the women make a great effort to carry out their work in a normal way and inhibit the expression of symptoms at work. Then they take home pent-up angry feelings and have emotional outbursts over everyday matters or chores. It seems clear that this is very much a family drama, involving all members of the family. Many of the women reported recurrent quarrels and incidents of punitive action directed at the children and indicated that when their premenstrual phase is over, they experience strong feelings of guilt and regret and make every effort to make up for their negative behavior.

The women considered the division of labor at home, that is, equality between their partners and themselves as far as domestic duties are concerned, to be fairly reasonable. These duties included cleaning, shopping, cooking, looking after the children, gardening, being responsible for managing family finances, and caring for elderly parents. When asked whether they felt that their premenstrual symptoms in any way affected the division of labor at home, the women indicated that this was not the case. They stated that they usually continued to do all the chores but tended to complain and were able to see inequalities more clearly. The women in Group 1 (service workers) felt that PMS affected the sharing of the upbringing of children more than did the women in Group 2 (managers) ($p < .05$).

We asked the women to rate the degree of role conflict they experienced between being employed versus being a parent and being employed versus being a partner. Both groups of women indicated experiencing a fair amount of role conflict, more so with regard to being employed versus being a parent. The role conflicts tended to be more pronounced in Group 2. The self-ratings also showed that premenstrual tension symptoms serve to accentuate these role strains, somewhat more so for Group 2 (see Table 1). When asked to rate the degree of satisfaction they felt with how they allocate their time between work, home, and leisure time, the women in Group 2 were significantly less satisfied ($p < .05$) than those in Group 1 (cf. Chapters 3 and 6).

In the interviews the women stated that they felt less satisfied with themselves as parents and wives, as well as in their professional roles, during the premenstrual phase. They often had strong feelings of inadequacy and self-blame, which they did not experience during other parts of their menstrual cycle.

The women were asked to rate the extent to which they felt that they functioned differently at work and at home during their premenstrual phase as compared to other parts of the cycle. Both groups of women rated their functioning to be considerably different both at work and at home (see Table 1). When asked whether they considered PMS to be an acceptable reason for absence from work due to illness, 63% in Group 1 and 66% in Group 2 stated that they did not consider it to be acceptable, because "it is not an illness." Interestingly, 43% of the women in service jobs and 33%

of the women in managerial jobs reported that they had, in fact, stayed at home because of premenstrual symptoms an average of 3 to 4 days during the preceding 12 months; none of them had given premenstrual symptoms as the reason for their absence.

The women also rated the extent to which their social activities (meeting friends, going to parties, arranging parties at home, going to a movie, and so forth) were influenced by their symptoms; these activities were considerably affected in both groups. In the interview the women reported that their social life, as well as vacations, was often planned with the intention of avoiding the premenstrual phase of their cycle.

CONCLUSIONS

Women who suffer from PMS are affected by their symptoms in many ways. The symptoms have negative consequences for their work as well as for their family life. The data from the present study show that PMS affects women's different roles and the way women experience their work efficiency and social relationships both at home and at work. Ability to concentrate and interaction with other people were the dimensions most affected. Many of the jobs that women typically occupy are jobs in the service sector, where smooth interaction with others and flexibility are demanded. Patience in dealing with difficult customers or clients is often a prerequisite in these jobs, a quality that women who suffer from PMS have difficulty sustaining. In order to identify dimensions that are particularly critical for women who suffer from PMS, we need to look more closely at different aspects of the work environment to which women are exposed. Women with PMS feel that they cannot control important events in their lives. The dimension of control may be important not only in their personal lives but also in the workplace. Autonomy both in terms of tempo and work content may be particularly important for women who suffer from PMS. Thus, women occupying different positions with differing degrees of control at work may experience job-related reproductive issues, including premenstrual symptoms, differently. We need to examine the role of job strain and the authority to make decisions at work on how women cope with PMS. Future research should be designed to examine the relationships between different work environments, including those requiring heavy physical labor, different organizational settings, and different work demands on the one hand and reproductive health on the other.

Social support seems particularly important for women who suffer from PMS. The women in more traditionally female jobs received more social support from coworkers, superiors, and their husbands than did the women in managerial positions. It seems that women in these positions have a more difficult situation, since they do not receive much understanding or sympathy from others for their symptoms. On the other hand, they should have a greater chance of scheduling their work to avoid the most acute phase of premenstrual symptoms. However, such a difference was not obtained in our data.

We did not find much evidence of dissatisfaction in the ratings of the women over equality between the sexes in the division of household duties. However, this issue was frequently brought up in the interviews. It is well documented that women who are employed continue to carry most of the responsibility for the home and children (Frankenhaeuser, Lundberg, Fredrikson, Melin, Tuomisto, Myrsten, Hedman, Bergman-Losman, & Wallin, 1989; Haw, 1982; Hofferth & Moore, 1979; see also Chapter 3, this volume). The women perceived inequalities more clearly during the premenstrual phase but were unable to change the situation. This could mean that the women's perception of the sharing of household duties changes over the menstrual cycle or that they are better able to tolerate perceived inequality at other times but not during the premenstrual phase. It would be interesting to involve husbands of women suffering from PMS in a study to get their perspective on these issues and their attitudes toward their wives' premenstrual problems.

Although we are still to a large extent ignorant of the true nature, etiology, and effective treatment of PMS, this does not mean that we cannot do anything for women who suffer from premenstrual symptoms. Efforts should be made to help women with PMS to recognize and gain more control of their cyclical mood changes. Women can learn to derive strength from the positive mood changes that occur in the follicular phase and at midcycle and utilize these periods to be productive and creative. Women with PMS can also learn better coping skills, such as planning ahead and avoiding particularly stressful demands at times when premenstrual symptoms are likely to occur. Management in organizations should be made more aware of the fact that many women suffer from premenstrual symptoms, and work routines should be designed to allow for planning and self-scheduling to a much greater extent than exists at present.

ACKNOWLEDGMENTS

This work was supported in part by grants from the John D. and Catherine T. MacArthur Foundation Network on Health and Behavior. I am grateful to Lena Andersson Svensson for assistance in the data collection and analysis and for many thoughtful comments.

REFERENCES

Andersch, B. (1980). *Epidemiological, hormonal and water balance studies in premenstrual tension.* Unpublished doctoral dissertation, University of Gothenburg.

Barnett, R. C., & Baruch, G. K. (1987). Social roles, gender and psychological distress. In R. C. Barnett, L. Biener, & G. K. Baruch (Eds.), *Gender and stress* (pp. 176–190). New York: Free Press.

Brush, M., Watson, S., Horrobin, D., & Manku, M. (1984). Abnormal fatty acid levels in women with premenstrual syndrome. *American Journal of Obstetrics and Gynecology, 150,* 363–366.

Bäckström, T., & Hammarbäck, S. (1986). Definition and determinants of the premenstrual syndrome. In L. Dennerstein & I. Frazer (Eds.), *Hormones and behavior* (pp. 130–136). Amsterdam: Elsevier.

Clare, A. W. (1983). Psychiatric and social aspects of premenstrual complaint. *Psychological Medicine Monograph* (Supplement 4). Cambridge: Cambridge University Press.

Clare, A. W. (1985). Hormones, behaviour and the menstrual cycle. *Journal of Psychosomatic Research, 29,* 225–233.

Collins, A. (1987). The psychobiology of premenstrual tension. In G. Burrows, O. Petruccio, & D. Llewellyn-Jones (Eds.), *Psychosomatic aspects of reproductive medicine* (pp. 23–33). Victoria, Australia: York Press.

Collins, A., & Landgren, B. M. (1991). *A double-blind crossover study of treatment of women suffering from PMS with essential fatty acids.* Unpublished manuscript.

Collins, A., Lundström, W., Nordström, L., Nilsson, C. G., Hamfelt, A., & Eneroth, P. (1986). Psychoneuroendocrinological characteristics of premenstrual tension: Effects of treatment with vitamin B_6. In L. Dennerstein & I. Frazer (Eds.), *Hormones and behavior* (pp. 183–196). Amsterdam: Elsevier.

Coppen, A., & Kessel, N. (1963). Menstruation and personality. *British Journal of Psychiatry, 109,* 711–721.

Cullberg, J. (1972). Mood changes and menstrual symptoms with different gestagen/estrogen combinations. *Acta Psychiatrica Scandinavica, 236,* 1–86.

Dalton, K. (1977). *The premenstrual syndrome.* London: W. Heineman.

Dalton, K. (1984). *The premenstrual syndrome and progesterone therapy.* London: W. Heineman.

Dennerstein, L., Spencer-Gardner, C., Gotts, G., Brown, J., Smith, M., & Burrows, G. (1985). Progesterone and the premenstrual syndrome: A double-blind crossover trial. *British Medical Journal, 290,* 1617–1621.

Frank, R. T. (1931). The hormonal causes of premenstrual tension. *Archives of Neurology and Psychiatry, 26,* 2053–2057.

Frankenhaeuser, M., Lundberg, U., Fredrikson, M., Melin, B., Tuomisto, M., Myrsten, A-L., Hedman, M., Bergman-Losman, B., & Wallin, L. (1989). Stress on and off the job as related to sex and occupational status in white-collar workers. *Journal of Organizational Behavior, 10,* 321–346.

Gough, H. (1975). Personality factors related to reported severity of menstrual distress. *Journal of Abnormal Psychology, 84,* 59–65.

Hallman, J. (1986). The premenstrual syndrome: An equivalent of depression? *Acta Psychiatrica Scandinavica, 73,* 403–411.

Hallman, J. (1987). *Premenstrual tension.* Unpublished doctoral dissertation, University of Uppsala.

Hallman, J., & Georgiev, N. (1986). The premenstrual syndrome and absence from work due to illness: *Journal of Psychosomatic Obstetrics and Gynecology, 14,* 1–9.

Hammarbäck, S., Johansson, U-B., & Bäckström, T. (1989). Diagnostic aspects of menstrual linked mood changes. In E. V. van Hall & W. Everaerd (Eds.), *The free woman* (pp. 638–645). Carnforth, England: Parthenon.

Haw, M. A. (1982). Women, work and stress: A review and agenda for the future. *Journal of Health and Social Behavior, 23*, 132–144.

Hofferth, S. L., & Moore, K. A. (1979). Women's employment and marriage. In R. E. Smith (Ed.), *The subtle revolution* (pp. 99–124). Washington, DC: The Urban Institute.

LaCroix, A. Z., & Haynes, S. G. (1987). Gender differences in the health effects of workplace roles. In R. C. Barnett, L. Biener, & G. K. Baruch (Eds.), *Gender and stress,* (pp. 96–121). New York: Free Press.

La Rosa, J. H. (1988). Women, work and health: Employment as a risk for coronary heart disease. *American Journal of Obstetrics and Gynecology, 158*, 1597–1602.

Magos, A., Zilkha, K., & Studd, J. (1983). Treatment of menstrual migraine by estradiol implants. *Journal of Neurology, Neurosurgery and Psychiatry, 46*, 1044–1046.

Malmgren, R., Collins, A., & Nilsson, C. G. (1987). Platelet serotonin uptake and effects of vitamin B_6 treatment in premenstrual tension. *Neuropsychobiology, 18*, 83–88.

Paulson, M. (1961). Psychological concomitants of premenstrual tension. *American Journal of Obstetrics and Gynecology, 81*, 733–738.

Rees, L. (1953). The premenstrual tension syndrome and its treatment. *British Medical Journal, 1*, 1014–1016.

Rubinow, D., Hoban, C., Grover, G., Galloway, S., Roy-Byrne, P., Andersen, R., & Merriam, G. (1988). Changes in plasma hormones across the menstrual cycle in patients with menstrually related mood disorder and control subjects. *American Journal of Obstetrics and Gynecology, 158*, 5–11.

Ruble, D. (1977). Premenstrual symptoms: A reinterpretation. *Science, 197*, 291–292.

Schalling, D. (1978). Psychopathy related personality variables and psychophysiology of socialization. In R. Hare & D. Schalling (Eds.), *Psychopathic behavior: Approaches to research* (pp. 85–106). London: Academic Press.

Siegal, J., Johnson, J., & Sarason, I. (1979). Life changes and menstrual discomfort. *Journal of Human Stress, 5*, 41–46.

Sommer, B. (1982). Cognitive behavior and the menstrual cycle. In R. C. Friedman (Ed.), *Behavior and the menstrual cycle,* (pp. 101–128). Basel: Marcel Dekker.

Stout, A., & Steege, J. (1985). Psychological assessment of women seeking treatment for premenstrual syndrome. *Journal of Psychosomatic Research, 29*(6), 621–629.

Taylor, D., Matthew, R., Ho, W., & Weinman, M. (1984). Serotonin levels and platelet uptake during premenstrual tension. *Neuropsychobiology, 12*, 16–18.

Watts, S., Dennerstein, L., & de Lattorne, J. D. (1980). The premenstrual syndrome: A psychological evaluation. *Journal of Affective Disorders, 2*, 257–266.

Wendestam, C. (1980). *Mental changes in the premenstrual phase.* Unpublished doctoral dissertation, University of Gothenburg.

Verbrugge, L. M. (1983). Multiple roles and physical health of women and men. *Journal of Health and Social Behavior, 24*, 16–30.

Williams, M., Harris, R., & Dean, B. (1985). Controlled trial of pyridoxin in premenstrual tension. *Journal of International Medical Research, 13*, 174–179.

Wood, C., Larsen, L., & Williams, R. (1979). Social and psychological factors in relation to premenstrual tension and menstrual pain. *Australian and New Zealand Journal of Obstetrics and Gynaecology, 19*, 111–115.

V

Conclusion

14

Summary and Implications for Future Research

CARY L. COOPER

Oh, lift me as a wave, a leaf, a cloud?
I fall upon the thorns of life? I bleed?
Shelley

A United Nation's report in 1980 stated that "women constitute half the world's population, perform nearly two-thirds of its work hours, receive one-tenth of the world's income and own less than one-hundredth of the world's property." Today the situation is even more intense, with women in the developing countries entering the work force at a higher rate, working longer hours, and striving for better career opportunities (Davidson & Cooper, 1984; Lewis & Cooper, 1989). It is extremely timely, therefore, that a book exploring the interrelationships between women's work and their health and stress should be published at this time. This book represents a major advance in our knowledge in the field by bringing together in one volume leading international researchers, who review their own work and significant studies in the area and highlight some of the newest research methodologies.

This book is organized into four main themes: sex differences (facts and myths); the interface between work and the family (multiple roles); work load and cardiovascular health; and the interaction between women's work and reproductive issues. In the first section the chapters explore a range of issues of great importance to research in and understanding of gender and workplace issues. First, Eleanor Maccoby examines what expe-

CARY L. COOPER • Manchester School of Management, University of Manchester, Institute of Science and Technology, Manchester M60 1QD, England.

riences individuals bring with them into the workplace: participation in same-sex and mixed-sex groups in childhood and adolescence. Research in this field is important in understanding how both men and women are likely to behave in adult work groups, what training experiences are likely to be the most effective for women at work, how the education process might be organized to minimize potential future problem areas, and how dual-career couples might cope with their changing roles. Ingrid Waldron picks up on the sex differences theme and explores the widespread concern that employment may have a damaging effect on women's health. She reviews the literature in the field, carefully examining important methodological issues. Her conclusions suggest that many of the longitudinal studies show that women's participation in the workplace has had less detrimental effects than expected, at least for unmarried women; the effects of married women's participation in the workplace have been mixed.

From some perspectives, raising the question of health effects of women's multiple roles presents an unpleasant dilemma. If it is shown that women who perform multiple roles are adversely affected by employment, there are those (usually senior male executives) who might argue that the women are "ineffective copers" and should concentrate on their domestic role. If, on the other hand, the evidence suggests that these women have less ill health effects from work, there will be others who, to minimize women's effective coping skills, rationalize the results by suggesting that they are only part-time workers or that they are less committed at work than men, and so on. What we need to do is to distance ourselves from this organizational political discourse on whether employed women are more or less healthy than men as a result of work and concentrate on the issues and problem areas in the workplace that put undue and unnecessary strain on working women (as well as men) so that we can organize working environments in a way that helps to nurture and develop both. This is what Marianne Frankenhaeuser attempts to highlight in her chapter on the psychophysiology of sex differences in terms of occupational status. Indeed, she has found that men and women who are similar in employment status show similar behavioral characteristics, and that personal control and social support have roughly the same buffering effects on both. These similarities, however, disappear when the men and women return to their home environment. Utilizing the biopsychosocial model as a framework, Frankenhaeuser has provided a vehicle for an early diagnosis, as well as a platform for identifying, stressors for both men and women, which should help enormously in any approach to minimizing stress at work.

The second section of this volume explores the issues of multiple roles, the interface between work and the family. Robert Kahn examines the concept of productive activity as an alternative to conventional definitions of work, comparing men and women throughout the life course, considers causes and effects of these patterns; and discusses the implications of this for policy on a national level. For Kahn, productive activity involves paid employment, unpaid work in the home, work done in voluntary organizations, and direct help provided to relatives and friends. He rightly draws our attention to the differential way in which gender plays its part in each of these activities and how national statistics and policies ought to be geared to these activities. Camille Wortman, Monica Biernat, and Eric Lang concentrate specifically on the impact of multiple roles on married women professionals. In their longitudinal investigations they highlight the experiences of role conflict so often alluded to in qualitative and cross-sectional research. They also explore data that increasingly indicate that "women's job stress is associated with decreased marital functioning and satisfaction," and the implications of this for both research and practice. They draw attention to what is needed in future research—to more fully assess "the antecedents and consequences of the inequities in household responsibilities and child care," issues that are at the heart of many multiple-role problems.

The concept of multiple roles is explored further in Rosalind Barnett and Nancy Marshall's study of the effect of work and family roles among two groups of health care professionals on mental well-being. The authors found that mental well-being and psychological distress are related to concerns about overload at work, to the presence or absence of rewards from helping others, and to their locus of control in decision making. They also found that women who have partners report higher well-being than single women, and that the quality of their experience in each of their roles as worker, partner, and parent has a differential and independent contribution to their mental well-being. One of the important contributions of this research is the authors' conclusion that "to understand the contribution of workplace rewards and concerns to women's mental health, we must include simultaneous study of family-role occupancy and family-role quality." After all, women (and men) function in the worlds of work and family, and their mental health reflects their experiences in both arenas. Thus, the authors draw our attention to the positive benefits of work as a second arena for enhanced mental well-being. This kind of research focus, particularly with an added longitudinal feature, should be of enormous practical importance in exploring the link between dual-career lifestyles and health.

The next section of the book raises issues regarding the link between work stress and cardiovascular health, or its associated risk factors. The first chapter in this section concentrates on a model that proposes that workplace stress (time pressure, difficulty unwinding and job strain) creates a negative mood (depression, tension, and suppressed anger) that can manifest itself in a negative coping strategy (e.g., smoking). Chesney is concerned about the implications in terms of cardiovascular and other diseases of increased levels of smoking among women workers. She feels that cigarette smoking is the most significant "public health threat for women." Her model of workplace stress and smoking provides a useful framework for understanding how to introduce and promote smoking cessation programs in the workplace. While Chesney is concentrating on one of the stress outcomes or coping responses (i.e., smoking), Haynes, in her chapter, reviews the literature to see if the variables of high job demand and low control (Karasek, 1979) are associated with significant adverse health among women as well as among men. She explores the literature for data on clerical workers, sales personnel, and nurses, and contends that many of the jobs women tend to occupy are, by their very nature, high-demand–low-control jobs. In addition, women have been progressively introduced to new technology, particularly the VDT, adding another risk factor to their already long list of stressors.

Pickering and his colleagues focus more on the link between blood pressure and occupational stress, highlighting the research evidence that blood pressure is generally higher at work than at home and that this cannot be explained away by physical activity. The stress of work, they suggest, is strongly implicated in this equation. Furthermore, blood pressure seems to be higher for women both at home and at work, particularly for women with children. For men, blood pressure tends to fall when they return home from work, which does not seem to be true for women. This raises a number of issues about the role of men in the home and the carryover effects of stress at work for women. Pickering and his colleagues also discuss the nature of different occupations as they relate to the models of stress proposed by Karasek (1979) and Frankenhaeuser in her chapter. There are research implications here for exploring the predictive validity of these models in terms of gender differences. And finally in this section Theorell explores specifically the relationship between psychosocial work stressors and cardiovascular illness risk in women. In his study, Professor Theorell has found some similarities to the studies of Pickering and associates but also some dissimilarities. The fact that women who reported moderate amounts of overtime were more likely to be at risk of myocardial infarction than men highlights the pressures on women of bearing domestic responsibilities on top of the paid-employment stresses.

In the final section of the book, the authors explore the interaction between women's work and reproductive issues. Hagenfeldt outlines the importance of family planning in terms of women's career choices and health. The issues of pregnancy and its relation to women's education and contraceptive practice, as well as a host of other important issues directly affecting women at work (avoidance of adolescent pregnancy, importance of contraception, breast-feeding), are raised. Sarrel, on the other hand, examines the changes of the menopause, its signs and symptoms, and the disease processes that develop as a result of hormone deficiency. In addition, he focuses on how menopause affects women at work and at home. Issues surrounding menopause, heart disease, and working women over the age of 50 are highlighted. These issues are further developed in the chapter by Aila Collins, which focuses on a particular study indicating how premenstrual tension syndrome (PMS) directly affects women's work routines and family life. This attention to women's health concerns and their work is fundamental to understanding the demands of work and the family in an increasingly dual career culture in Western society.

The chapters in this distinguished collection make a significant contribution to the debate about women, work, and stress. They raise important issues, provide the necessary intellectual food for thought, and highlight, either directly or indirectly, the methodological foundation stones for future research. To build on this work, we must attempt in future research to do the following: (1) introduce more longitudinal studies so that we can more securely draw cause-and-effect conclusions from our investigations; (2) use community-wide studies so that we can have confidence in generalizing our results to a large segment of the population as well as make differentiated comparisons in a single investigation; (3) use as many objective health measures as is practical (e.g., measures that provide ambulatory monitoring of the impact of stress on the job on a day-by-day basis), in conjunction with more subjective psychosocial ones; (4) as far as is possible, use subjects as their own controls, collect data from subjects at home as well as work, and consider innovative control and comparison groups; (5) more fully develop our theories about women, work, and stress so that our research efforts relate more specifically to the testing, adapting, and developing of our conceptual frameworks; and (6) systematically evaluate interventions instituted in the workplace to minimize stress. In this respect, it is also important to assess the cost implications and consequences of the interventions so that we can attempt to influence the decisions of senior management on future policies and health prevention programs for working women.

REFERENCES

Davidson, M. J., & Cooper, C. L. (1984). *Working women: An international survey*. Chichester, UK: Wiley.

Karasek, R. A. (1979). Job demands, job decision latitude and mental strain. *Administrative Science Quarterly, 24*, 285–308.

Lewis, S., & Cooper, C. L. (1989). *Career couples*. London: Unwin Hyman.

Index